2012

HENRY JAMES

HENRY JAMES

A Collection of Critical Essays

Edited by
Ruth Bernard Yeazell

Prentice Hall, Upper Saddle River, New Jersey 07458

Library of Congress Cataloging-in-Publication Data

Henry James : a collection of critical essays / edited by Ruth Bernard
    Yeazell.
        p.   cm.—(New century views)
    Includes bibliographical references.
    ISBN 0–13–380973–0
    1. James, Henry, 1843–1916—Criticism and interpretation.
    I. Yeazell, Ruth Bernard.   II. Series.
    PS2124.H435   1994
    813'.4—dc20   92–43861
                                                                        CIP

Acquisitions editor: Alison Reeves
Editorial assistant: Heidi Moore
Copy editor: Liz Pauw
Editorial/production supervision and
    interior design: Joan Powers
Cover design: Karen Salzbach
Prepress buyer: Herb Klein
Manufacturing buyer: Robert Anderson

© 1994 by Prentice-Hall, Inc.
A Pearson Education Company
Upper Saddle River, New Jersey 07458

Printed in the United States of America
10 9 8 7 6 5 4 3 2 1

ISBN 0-13-380973-0

Prentice-Hall International (UK) Limited, London
Prentice-Hall of Australia Pty. Limited, Sydney
Prentice-Hall Canada Inc., Toronto
Prentice-Hall Hispanoamericana, S.A., Mexico
Prentice-Hall of India Private Limited, New Delhi
Prentice-Hall of Japan, Inc., Tokyo
Pearson Education Asia Pte. Ltd., Singapore
Editoria Prentice-Hall do Brasil, Ltda., Rio De Janeiro

Contents

HENRY JAMES

Introduction

Ruth Bernard Yeazell

In 1873, at the age of thirty, Henry James published a short story about a painter and his model whose cheerful ironies at once testify to the writer's own youthful confidence and anticipate many of the subsequent turns of his fiction. "The Sweetheart of M. Briseux" begins with the visit of the English narrator to a provincial French museum, which has lately acquired a portrait of an anonymous Lady in a Yellow Shawl—an early work by a celebrated painter and native son. Indeed, "this was the very work that had made the painter famous," the narrator reports, and as he prolongs his own gaze at it, he confirms its status as a masterpiece. The painting speaks eloquently to him of the early genius of the artist, even as it speaks with equal force of the character of its subject. When the narrator inquires about the woman's identity, however, the concierge replies only with a bemused shrug and the predictable speculation of a Frenchman: "Mon Dieu! a sweetheart of M. Briseux!—*Ces artistes!*"[1] But as the remainder of the tale goes to show, the history behind this painting is not that of a love affair, at least not in any ordinary sense of the phrase. The young Henry James deliberately set out to write a very different romance of the artist.

The narrator returns after a brief interval to discover another visitor gazing intently at the painting, a woman "comely" but "no longer young," whom he readily identifies as the original of the portrait. Significantly, in light of the kind of story James is *not* telling, the anonymous lady proves "no French-woman" but a "modest" English spinster: though she has in effect given herself to art rather than to marriage, she was never the artist's mistress. In fact, she met M. Briseux for the first and last time on the day he painted her portrait. At the time of that climactic encounter, she explains, she was engaged to a conventionally desirable, if utterly vapid, young man who also aspired to be a painter, but he possessed neither talent nor imagination. Increasingly disillusioned with her suitor, and inclined to postpone the marriage, she had finally promised to name the day if he would paint her portrait.

---

[1]All quotations from "The Sweetheart of M. Briseux" are taken from *The Complete Tales of Henry James*, 12 vols., ed. Leon Edel (Philadelphia: J. B. Lippincott Company, 1962–64), 3:53–87, which reproduces the text originally published in the *Galaxy* of 1873. James did not reprint the story in book form.

When Briseux accidentally discovered her alone in the studio, his contemptuous dismissal of the work in progress—it's "ridiculously bad; impossibly bad!"—coupled with his extraordinary assurance of his own powers inspired her to act. She permitted him to redo the portrait, and when her fiancé returned, predictably outraged, she broke off the engagement. By the time that she left the studio at the end of the day, she felt sure that her choice was justified, and the subsequent acclaim of the critics has confirmed her judgment. Though thirty years have passed since her portrait was painted, she appears to have no other story to tell.

Like later, more familiar tales such as "The Real Thing" (1890), "The Sweetheart of M. Briseux" ironically insists on the psychological, indeed ontological, priority of art over "life," even as it works to undo that conventional opposition. The heroine reports that when she made her momentous decision, the feeling that possessed her "was so profound that often in memory it seems more real and poignant than the things of the present"; and the story implies that in acting on that feeling, she makes a better and paradoxically more vital commitment of herself than she would by marriage. As she explains, "Poor little Briseux, ugly, shabby, disreputable, seemed to me some appealing messenger from the mysterious immensity of life; and Harold, beside him, comely, elegant, imposing, justly indignant, seemed to me simply his narrow, personal, ineffectual self." Rather than suggest that art should somehow be preferred to life, in other words, James characteristically argues that "it is art that *makes* life, makes interest, makes importance" in the words of his late and often-quoted letter to H. G. Wells.[2] And rather than understand such words merely as a defense of the professional artist—though they are certainly that—James encourages us also to read in them a deep paradox about the vitality of human consciousness and imagination. The hero of *The Ambassadors* (1903), for example, is no artist, but he is "a man of imagination"[3]; and despite his belief that it is too late for him to "live," one of the great achievements of that novel is to convince us that there is more life in the imaginative experience of the aging Strether than in any worldly adventure of the handsome young Chad.

All of which is not to deny the cost such Jamesian triumphs exact, even in a minor comedy like "The Sweetheart of M. Briseux." The heroine of that tale, after all, is also not an artist, and one could argue that when James determines his plot, he in more than one sense manages to frame her—arranging for her not to choose art but merely to become its object. Briseux may accord her the immortality he promises, but she will achieve that status only as an anonymous Portrait of a Lady. Significantly, by the time she leaves the studio, the painter himself has all but forgotten her: "I had served his purpose and had

[2]To H. G. Wells, 10 July 1915, *Henry James: Letters*, 4 vols., ed. Leon Edel (Cambridge: Harvard University Press, 1974–84), 4:770.
[3]Henry James, Preface to *The Ambassadors* (1909; rpt. New York: Augustus M. Kelley, 1971), 1:viii.

already passed into that dusky limbo of unhonored victims, the experience—intellectual and other—of genius." Even a sympathetic reader might find the ease with which James imagines his heroine ready to sacrifice everything for a portrait a bit chilling, as if the artist in him were indulging himself at the expense of his model—of all the models which he, like his fictional painter, would knowingly exploit for his art. And though gentlemen as well as ladies have certainly been known to sit for their portraits, many late twentieth-century readers would be quick to note that the genders of artist and model in this tale are hardly accidental. Such readers might recall in this connection the terms on which the young James had consoled himself for the death of his beloved cousin Minny Temple a few years earlier: "the more I think of her," he wrote to his brother William three days after he learned of her death, "the more perfectly satisfied I am to have her translated from this changing realm of fact to the steady realm of thought."[4] And they might also look ahead to James's own great *Portrait of a Lady* (1880–81) of a decade later, a novel whose searching study of the temptation to aestheticize its heroine itself composes a beautifully wrought memorial to that same dead cousin. As in yet another tribute to Minny Temple, his late tragedy, *The Wings of the Dove* (1902), James at once anatomizes and exploits the desire to translate a living woman into "the steady realm of thought." That work also features a magnificent portrait of a lady, a portrait that resembles the self-sacrificing heroine above all by prefiguring the terms on which she will eventually inspire the imaginations of both hero and novelist: "And she was dead, dead, dead."[5]

But if James's art thus partly reproduces the destructive gaze his culture often turns upon women, it also typically grants the subject of the portrait her own subjectivity. Like many of James's later and more substantial works, "The Sweetheart of M. Briseux" offers what it calls "the picture of a mind"—and that mind is the heroine's. The tale may open with the Englishman's report of how it feels to gaze on her portrait, but his voice soon gives way to hers, and the story she tells derives its energy from her own relentless observation of the young man who has proposed himself as her husband. Having accepted him as a suitor, she reports, "the first use I made of my maturity—cruel as it may seem—was to turn round and look keenly at my lover and revise my judgment." Her devastating account of what she sees, or rather fails to see, in that "extremely ornamental" young man comprises virtually half her narrative; the other half recounts her meeting with M. Briseux, his painting of her portrait, and the breaking of her engagement. "The sore point" with her

---

[4]To William James, 29 March 1870, *Letters*, 1:226. In justice to the fullness of James's imagination, even in the comparative immediacy of correspondence, it should be noted that the letter contains its own self-critique on this score. "But I have scribbled enough," a later paragraph begins. "While I sit spinning my sentences she is *dead*: and I suppose it is partly to defend myself from too direct a sense of her death that I indulge in this fruitless attempt to transmute it from a hard fact into a soft idea" (227).

[5]Henry James, *The Wings of the Dove* (1909; rpt. New York: Augustus M. Kelley, 1971), 1:221.

former lover, she reports, "was not that he had lost me, but that I had ventured to judge him." As when Mrs. Osmond eventually turns her critical gaze on Mr. Osmond in *The Portrait of a Lady*—or, for that matter, when Maggie Verver begins to review the oppressive design of her life in *The Golden Bowl* (1904)—James reverses the direction of the look, and explores the narrative possibilities of the mind's awakening. In the climactic episode of *The Portrait of a Lady*, the fireside vigil at which the heroine reviews the history of her marriage, Isabel literally closes her eyes, but "her mind, assailed by visions, was in a state of extraordinary activity." And for the later James especially, such mental "activity" was the very stuff of narrative. In his Preface to the New York Edition nearly thirty years later, he singled out Isabel's fireside vigil as "obviously the best thing" in the book: "it is a representation simply of her motionlessly *seeing* and an attempt withal to make the mere still lucidity of her act as 'interesting' as the surprise of a caravan or the identification of a pirate."[6]

Though James's imaginative sympathies clearly have their limits—he makes no effort, for example, to supply the luckless suitor in "The Sweetheart of M. Briseux" with any consciousness of his own—the power of seeing and judging in his work is hardly confined to his fictional artists. The writer of that tale identifies as much with Briseux's model as he does with Briseux. But to the youthful author, the analogy between his own art and that of the painter carried particular force. For the visual artist, James seems to have believed, was understood to be primarily a maker of representations rather than a moralist or an entertainer; whether a painting succeeded or failed depended on the skill of the artist, and not on the extraneous criteria by which Protestant England in particular still judged the writer of fiction.

A century later, as several of the essays in this volume attest, we tend to be less confident that art of any kind can be so firmly distinguished from social and moral pressures. But for the young Henry James, to identify with the maker of pictures was to identify with the glory of art: and there is surely something of the beginning writer's own brashness in his affectionate portrait of the young and supremely self-confident Briseux—"the impudent little Bohemian" who "spoke with penetrating authority." Like the novelist, whose letters home in these years cheerfully confessed to his "ferocious ambition" and repeatedly predicted the eventual fulfillment of his "genius,"[7] Briseux assures the heroine that "the day will come when people will fight for the

[6]Henry James, *The Portrait of a Lady* (New York: Charles Scribner's Sons, 1908), 1:204, xxi.
[7]To Mrs. Henry James, Sr., 17 Feb. [1878], *Letters*, 2:156; 14 May [1879], 2:232. The second of these is worth quoting more fully: "I know too perfectly well what I intend, desire and attempt, and am capable of following it in absolute absence of perturbation. Never was a genius—if genius there is—more healthy, objective and (I honestly believe) less susceptible of superficial irritations and reactionary impulses. I know what I want—it stares one in the face, as big and round and bright as the full moon; I *can't* be diverted or deflected by the sense of judgments that are most of the time no judgments at all."

honor of having believed me" and proudly declares himself "a man of genius if there ever was one." Though the contest between the scruffy little painter and the handsome dilettante hardly constitutes an orthodox romantic triangle, Briseux's success with the "sweetheart" makes for an exuberant bit of Jamesian self-romanticizing. Indeed, the tale plots the artist's triumph not merely with his model but with the general public: at the close of her narrative, the heroine reports how she subsequently learned of the portrait's glorious reception at the Paris salon, when she received in the mail "an enclosure of half a dozen cuttings from newspapers, scrawled boldly across with the signature of Pierre Briseux. . . . The picture was an immense success, and M. Briseux was famous." There is no better sign that this tale shares in the "splendid vivacity and energy, and the almost boyish good faith" of its imaginary portrait than the bold scrawl of that signature across the page of newsprint.

James would produce many other tales of artists and writers, but few of them reveal anything like this confident identification of artistic genius and worldly success. Especially in the late 80s and 90s, his fictions of authorship register a growing sense of despair about his ability to reach a mass audience: the explosion of magazine fiction in these decades, much of it produced by women writers, the increasing dominance of the market by best-sellers, his own failed experiments in the theater, all testified for him to an "age of trash triumphant"[8]—an age, needless to say, in which his own work would be little read and poorly paid. But his response to this state of affairs was far from simple, and not only in the sense that he continued to court the popularity he simultaneously scorned, as recent studies have argued.[9] If tales like "The Author of Beltraffio" (1884), "The Death of the Lion" (1894), "The Next Time" (1895), "The Figure in the Carpet" (1896), and "The Birthplace" (1903) helped to invent the modernist gap between high culture and popular taste, they also subjected it to the play of magnificently Jamesian ironies, making subtle and often witty narratives out of the contradictions and double-binds that trapped writers and readers alike.

The last such tale James published is by no means his finest, but it reveals with a peculiar poignancy both the aging writer's continued anxiety about the meaning of literary success, and his deep ambivalence about the relations of art and "life." Strikingly, "The Velvet Glove" (1909) also marks the third and final appearance of the imaginary sculptor, Gloriani—a figure who seems to have crystallized for his creator both the glories and the dangers of an art that meets with worldly reward. Among the very few characters whom James

---

[8]Henry James, "The Next Time" (1895), *Complete Tales*, 9:187.
[9]See especially, Michael Anesko, *"Friction with the Market": Henry James and the Profession of Authorship* (New York: Oxford University Press, 1986); Jonathan Freedman, *Professions of Taste: Henry James, British Aestheticism, and Commodity Culture* (Stanford: Stanford University Press, 1990); and Marcia Jacobson, *Henry James and the Mass Market* (University, AL: University of Alabama Press, 1983).

carries over from one narrative to another, Gloriani has by far the longest fictive life: having initially made his appearance in an early chapter of *Roderick Hudson* (1875), where he is said to possess "a definite, practical scheme of art" and to produce statues at once "florid and meretricious," he resurfaces as "the great Gloriani" of *The Ambassadors* (1903), where his Parisian garden provides the setting for the critical scene of the novel. His "long career" now behind him, his works on display in the world's museums, the "distinguished" sculptor appears to Strether crowned "with the light, with the romance, of glory"; and it is partly in response to the artist's penetrating look ("the deepest intellectual sounding to which he had ever been exposed") and to "the terrible life" behind his "charming" smile that Strether delivers his famous exhortation to Little Bilham to "live." From the novel generally considered James's first to this late masterpiece, the great sculptor seems to have grown both far more distinguished and more terrifying: as "the glossy male tiger, magnificently marked," whose presence conveys to the envious Strether "a waft from the jungle," Gloriani figures a power at once erotic and violent. His is an art, presumably, born of a thoroughgoing experience of the world. When James's imagination returned to him a final time in "The Velvet Glove" six years later, it was only to name Gloriani as the host of a party once more: the sculptor himself never appears. But something of the ambivalent longing with which he is associated nonetheless suffuses the narrative.[10]

The immediate origin of "The Velvet Glove" can be traced to a potentially awkward incident in James's friendship with his fellow-novelist, Edith Wharton, when he was informed by a New York editor that she had requested an article from him, promoting her latest novel, *The Fruit of the Tree* (1907). Wharton insisted she had made no such request, and though James briefly contemplated writing the piece anyway, he reconsidered after reading her novel.[11] A number of circumstantial details link "The Velvet Glove" to Whar-

[10]Henry James, *Roderick Hudson* (Boston: James R. Osgood and Company, 1876), 97, 98; *The Ambassadors* (New York: Charles Scribner's Sons, 1908), 1:193, 196, 197, 218, 219. Though James's earliest novel, strictly speaking, was *Watch and Ward*, which appeared serially in the *Atlantic* in 1871, it was not published as a book until 1878, three years after *Roderick Hudson* and was omitted from the New York Edition of his collected works in 1907–1909. *Roderick Hudson* also inspired James's most notable act of literary "resuscitation," to use his term—that of Christina Light, who reappears, together with her husband, the Prince Casamassima, her companion, Madame Grandoni, and her maid, Assunta, in *The Princess Casamassima* of 1886. See the Preface to the latter novel (1908; rpt. New York: Charles Scribner's Sons, 1922), 1:xx.

[11]For the history of this affair, and the evidence that links it to the tale, see Leon Edel, *Henry James, the Master: 1901–1916* (Philadelphia: J. B. Lippincott Company, 1972), 352–59; and *Letters*, 4:xxviii, 461–63, 504–5, 521–22. In her autobiography, Wharton herself called the tale "perhaps the most beautiful of [James's] later short stories," and traced its origin to "the fact that a very beautiful young Englishwoman of great position, and unappeased literary ambitions, had once tried to beguile him into contributing an introduction to a novel she was writing—or else into reviewing the book; I forget which." That Wharton's memory may be self-serving here is not incompatible, of course, with the possibility that such a young Englishwoman really existed and also made her contribution to the story. See *A Backward Glance* (New York: D. Appleton-Century Company, 1934), 308–9. Cf. also R. W. B. Lewis, *Edith Wharton: A Biography* (New York: Harper & Row, Publishers, 1975), 254–55; and Roger Gard's notes to the story in his edition of *The Jolly Corner and Other Tales* (Harmondsworth: Penguin Books, 1990), 302–3.

ton, including its original title, "The Top of the Tree," and in a letter responding to her praise of the tale, its author paid her the somewhat ambiguous compliment of declaring that "the whole thing *reeks* with you."[12] But as with any Jamesian fiction, the "germ" that apparently inspired it has been much transmuted. Appearing in the same year as several volumes of the so-called New York Edition of James's collected works, the story concerns an English author named John Berridge, who has recently been "tast[ing] in their fullness the sweets of success" in the form of his hit play, *The Heart of Gold*. Performed and read all over Europe, the play is now enjoying a triumphant run in Paris with Berridge in attendance. The tale opens in the midst of a party at Gloriani's studio, as the "new literary star" is approached by a strikingly handsome and charming young man who wishes to meet him. While the "young Lord," as Berridge immediately entitles him, nervously inquires if the famous author "would mind just looking at a book by a friend of his," Berridge decides that he has somewhere seen this magnificent figure before—"had in fact imaginatively, intellectually, so to speak, quite yearned over him." Only upon the belated arrival of a woman who matches the Lord in elegance and beauty does Berridge remember how he previously encountered the pair on a train journey in Italy. From this brief and wordless meeting, without "a scrap of evidence," Berridge's imagination had immediately spun out a glorious romance, a vision of "admirable"—and distinctly nonmarital— "intimacy." The couple had seemed to him "preoccupied . . . with the affairs, and above all with the passions, of Olympus"; and it is as creatures of a superior race, divine "Olympians," that he now continues to think of them, elaborating his "romantic structure" with allusions to painting and drama, to "old-world legend," Greek mythology, and pastoral.[13]

The woman in question turns out to be a Princess, and Berridge's enchanted state prolongs itself when she turns away from "the greatest . . . of contemporary Dramatists," who happens also to be at the party, and addresses him instead, assuring him that she's read "everything, you know, and *The Heart of Gold* three times." Even when they are separated, her eyes continue to court him. Berridge, convinced that "she couldn't like him as much as *that* either for his acted clap-trap or for his printed verbiage," briefly entertains the fantasy that "she liked him, and to such a tune, just for himself," having chosen him like a goddess singling out "some prepossessing young shepherd." But his illusion begins to fade when he realizes that the Princess is also the literary friend the young Lord had previously mentioned—the author, among other works, of a dreadful novel called *The Top of the Tree*. Her pseudonym is Amy Evans, and she writes, as she cheerfully tells Berridge, in English, since it gives her "the biggest of publics": "I 'just love'—don't they say?—your American millions." Bewilderingly suspended between visions of Olympian

---

[12]To Edith Wharton, 9 May 1909, *Letters*, 4:521.
[13]All quotations from "The Velvet Glove" (1909) are taken from *Complete Tales*, 12:233–66, which reproduces the tale as it was reprinted in James's *The Finer Grain* of 1910.

romance and his disquieting impression of the bestselling author, Berridge readily obeys her summons to ride home with her in her car. But his pleasure in their idyllic drive through an April evening in Paris, her gloved hand resting on his, abruptly dissipates as he realizes that she has snatched him up only to ask him to write a Preface for her latest novel, *The Velvet Glove*—a "lovely, friendly, irresistible log-rolling Preface," as she puts it in her best American idiom. Despairing and humiliated, appalled at this "conceiver of twaddle both in herself and in him," yet still under the spell of the magnificent Princess, Berridge refuses—his final speech firmly distinguishing between the romance of the woman and the woman as romancer. "Princess," he tells her, "You *are* Romance"; and when she protests that she doesn't understand, he insists, "You don't need to understand. Don't attempt such base things. Leave those to us. Only live. Only be. *We'll* do the rest." The tale ends when he drives home his reiterated "You *are* Romance!" with an intensely aggressive kiss—"his lips, for a long moment, sealing it, with the fullest force of authority, on her own."

This too is a kind of Jamesian comedy, but a comedy considerably uneasier than that of "The Sweetheart of M. Briseux." Indeed, read in the light of literary history, especially as that history has been revised in the last few decades by feminists and critics of popular culture, "The Velvet Glove" seems to offer exemplary evidence of the anxieties that beset ambitious male writers at the turn of the century. The tale openly figures authorship as an arena of masculine emulation and struggle: introduced by his hostess to "the man in the world he most admired, the greatest then of contemporary Dramatists," Berridge feels compelled to recognize "that they had, for the few minutes, only stared and grimaced, like pitted boxers or wrestlers." While "the head of the profession" inspires awe, the female entrant into the ring merely arouses contempt. Berridge can only deem it perverse that "a creature so formed for living and breathing her Romance" should instead be engaged in "the dreadful amateurish dance of ungrammatically scribbling it, with editions and advertisements and reviews and royalties and every other futile item." Yet the very force of such contempt requires explanation: with her cheerful talk of her "biggest of publics," those "American millions" who love her, "Amy Evans" poses a different sort of challenge to Berridge's self-complacency as a writer, a challenge all the more irritating because he judges her efforts so undeserving of reward. In this context, his insistence that she live romance rather than write it seems less a tribute to her divine appeal than a conventional effort to keep her in her place. Or rather, the tale acknowledges these impulses as one, identifying the wish to make her a goddess with the wish effectively to deprive her of consciousness: "You don't need to understand. . . . Only *be*." Wherever Berridge stands in relation to "the great Dramatist," it seems, he knows where he stands as long as a woman's difference clearly marks his place. When he seals his final speech by kissing the Princess "with the fullest force of authority," the scarcely buried pun in "authority" testifies to this disquieting identification of writerly prowess and sexual power.

But where does Henry James stand in relation to the protagonist of this tale? It would be tempting to argue that John Berridge is deliberately intended as a fool, but the evidence does not make such a reading easy. For one thing, the tale gives us no reason to dispute his judgment of Amy Evans as an artist: indeed, by reproducing several florid sentences from one of her novels in his own text, James goes out of his way to confirm the vacuity of her writing. And by consistently focalizing the tale through its protagonist, James seems to collude in the wish to deny her any consciousness. Unlike "The Sweetheart of M. Briseux," not to mention many of James's greatest fictions, "The Velvet Glove" appears to suggest that a beautiful woman has no business claiming a subjectivity of her own. If she'll only just "be," as Berridge says, "*we'll* do the rest." Though Leon Edel has argued with some persuasiveness that the style of Amy Evans directly parodies that of Wharton,[14] we need not identify the imaginary writer too closely with any real one to recognize her as belonging to a series of such scribbling women in James's fiction, a series that consistently associates the sex with inferior, but distressingly popular, productions. By retitling his tale, James seems to have softened the original pointedness of the allusion to Wharton; but it is worth recalling that the proverbial velvet glove was said to cover an iron hand—a hand conventionally associated with the power of an emperor.[15] For all its light irony, in other words, the tale as a whole seems to betray something of its protagonist's uneasily aggressive impulses.

But more than literary rivalries are at stake in "The Velvet Glove," and more than authorial one-upmanship prompts its concluding embrace. The pathos of this late story has less to do with the aging writer's worries about the marketplace than with his questioning of the very value of art. Like so many Jamesian fictions before it, "The Velvet Glove" turns on the opposition of art and "life," but unlike most of its predecessors, it seems radically uncertain whether the imagination can provide an adequate substitute for the sheer experience of the senses. In "The Sweetheart of M. Briseux," the heroine apparently has no doubt that by choosing to sit for her portrait rather than marry she has paradoxically decided for "the mysterious immensity of life." Thirty years later, suffused with its hero's regrets for his lost youth, *The Ambassadors* poses a far more complicated case; yet the novel nonetheless manages to suggest that what Strether's imagination makes of Chad's affair is ultimately richer and fuller than anything that young man actually experiences. While Chad may be notably cleverer than the rejected suitor in the early tale, he shares in the failure to "see." But when the protagonist of "The Velvet Glove" meets up with still another of these handsome but imperceptive young men, he finds himself longing for the very "life in irreflective joy" that

---

[14]See *Henry James, the Master*, 357–59.

[15]Some accounts associate the phrase *une main de fer dans un gant de velours* (an iron hand in a velvet glove) with Emperor Charles V; in his *Latter-Day Pamphlets* (No. 2), however, Thomas Carlyle attributed it to James's much admired Napoleon.

this specimen represents: "What was the pale page of fiction compared with the intimately personal adventure that, in almost any direction, he would have been all so stupidly, all so gallantly, all so instinctively and, by every presumption, so prevailingly ready for? Berridge would have given six months' 'royalties' for even an hour of his looser dormant consciousness."

Despite the feminist reading offered earlier, we should note that it is not only the beautiful woman of this tale who has no need to think. As he converses with the young Lord, Berridge finds that his companion "delightfully, hadn't the least real idea of what any John Berridge was talking about, and the latter felt that if he had been less beautifully witless, and thereby less true to his right figure, it might scarce have been forgiven him." The deepest opposition here is not that between the sexes but between those who consciously observe life and those who unconsciously live it. As in other Jamesian fictions, handsome youth takes its pleasures "all so stupidly . . . so instinctively." But few of James's protagonists appear so ready to sacrifice the rewards of the mind as his last imaginary writer:

> He hadn't, for himself, waited till now to be sure of what he would do were *he* an Olympian; he would leave his own stuff snugly unread, to begin with. . . . He should have been as unable to write those works in short as to make anything else of them. . . . He should have consented to know but the grand personal adventure on the grand personal basis.

Though poor Berridge manages to end with nothing more than a kiss, that closing gesture amounts in this context to a last, futile claim to "personal adventure," a wordless declaration for life. The kiss pays tribute not so much to the desirability of the Princess as to the romance she represents—a romance whose eroticism is at once intensely felt and strikingly indeterminate. Indeed, a late twentieth-century reader might be tempted to conclude that this aggressive act is something of a cover-up, that the "real" desire circulating through the tale is the hero's original yearning for the glamorous young man. But it seems truer to say that Berridge responds to both partners in the affair with a mixture of desire, identification, and jealousy, and that the longing registered in the tale has less to do with particular persons of either sex than with the experience of intimacy itself. "The Velvet Glove" testifies as much to the artist's loneliness as to the complicated indirections of his sexuality.

If James's last imaginary writer seems poignantly eager to abandon art for life, however, there is a final irony in his appearing to forget that this is a life he has himself invented. More precisely, of course, it is a "Romance"—a vision of youth and erotic intimacy conjured up by his own literary sensibility. The young lovers are "like beautiful fabulous figures in some old-world legend," they are "Olympians," "figures of exquisite Arcadian stamp," at once inhabitants of *A Winter's Tale* and a "Claude Lorrain sea-strand." Indeed, Berridge's concluding insistence that the Princess *is* "Romance" seems directly controverted by an earlier passage in the tale, when his recollection of his first encounter with the pair prompts him to realize that "for the romantic structure he was immediately to raise, he had not had a scrap of evidence."

> If he had imputed to them conditions it was all his own doing: it came from his inveterate habit of abysmal imputation, the snatching of the ell wherever the inch peeped out, without which where would have been the tolerability of life?

The "tolerability of life," note, depends on the projections of an imaginative mind: without such "romantic structures" as Berridge raises, life itself would be unbearable. In this sense, "The Velvet Glove" is not so different from "The Sweetheart of M. Briseux," though the heroine of that tale readily sacrificed just such a handsome young man as Berridge yearns over. For both tales acknowledge that desire depends on imagination—that "art *makes* life," in the words of the letter to Wells. Yet if there are moments in "The Velvet Glove" when James seems half-inclined to forget this deeply held conviction, when he seems to share in his hero's longing for experience unmediated, it may be that another passage in the tale provides a clue to what has happened. "That was the disservice, in a manner, of one's having so much imagination," Berridge thinks:

> the mysterious values of other types kept looming larger before you than the doubtless often higher but comparatively familiar ones of your own, and if you had anything of the artist's real feeling for life the attraction and amusement of possibilities so projected were worth more to you, in nineteen moods out of twenty, than the sufficiency, the serenity, the felicity, whatever it might be, of your stale personal certitudes.

The trouble with having so much imagination, in other words, is that you keep finding yourself attracted by the very possibilities you imagine. It is not surprising that the aging writer should momentarily surrender to the illusion of youthful "life" he has created.

"The Velvet Glove" may have been James's last artist tale, but it was not his last portrait of the artist. That can rather be found in the several volumes of his autobiography—*A Small Boy and Others* (1913), *Notes of a Son and Brother* (1914), and *The Middle Years* (1917), the last of these uncompleted at the time of his death. Begun as a memorial to his brother William, and never reaching the period of the author's own creative maturity, these volumes still represent the future novelist by recalling him as the intensely curious and frequently bemused observer of others. The most personal of James's works, they seem untroubled by the "stale personal certitudes" affecting poor Berridge: perhaps because the novelist was looking back from such a distance on the world of his childhood, he felt free to imagine the small boy and others as Jamesian characters, to invest them with something of that "splendid vivacity and energy, and . . . almost boyish good faith" of M. Briseux's imaginary portrait. Best read partly as fiction, since they both reconstruct and rewrite the past, these late volumes nonetheless offer moving evidence of how, in the words of *A Small Boy*, "the house of life and the palace of art became so mixed and interchangeable."[16]

When James wrote "The Art of Fiction" in 1884, he still felt compelled to invoke the prestige of painting in order to defend the seriousness of his craft. The English might have outgrown "the old superstition about fiction being 'wicked,'" he observed, but they continued vaguely to distrust the whole business of story-telling. While painters' attempts to represent reality met with understanding, novelists were always expected to apologize for themselves, to confess that they were engaged in nothing but "make-believe." Hence James's well-known impatience with Trollope for seeming to do just that, and his own effort to claim for the art of the novelist all the respect accorded that of the painter: "Their cause is the same, and the honour of one is the honour of another."[17] Of course, James was hardly the first to defend fiction as art: he was writing "The Art of Fiction," after all, in response to a piece with the same title by Walter Besant, and literary historians have shown that a number of its arguments were already much in the air when James wrote.[18] But no one did more to assure that the novel would be taken seriously, and for subsequent generations of novelists and critics, he became the figure most closely identified with elevating the status of the art. Percy Lubbock's attempt to codify the Master's practice in *The Craft of Fiction* of 1921 marks one stage in this process; R. P. Blackmur's collection of James's Prefaces to the New York Edition, published as *The Art of the Novel* in 1934, marks another. Written exactly a half-century after "The Art of Fiction," Blackmur's introduction compared the Prefaces to Aristotle's *Poetics*, calling them "the most sustained . . . eloquent and original piece of literary criticism in existence."[19]

For the critics collected in this volume, then, there is no more question that the novel is "*discutable*," to adopt James's own borrowing from the French[20]: by the time that Lionel Trilling published the first of these essays in 1948, that issue had long since been resolved. So too, as Trilling saw it, there was no more question about James's reputation—a fact all the more striking because the work he was introducing, *The Princess Casamassima* (1886), had

16Henry James, *A Small Boy and Others* (1913; rpt. New York: Charles Scribner's Sons, 1941), 351.

17Henry James, "The Art of Fiction" (1884), rpt. in *Henry James: Essays on Literature, American Writers, English Writers*, ed. Leon Edel and Mark Wilson (New York: Library of America, 1984), 45, 46.

18See especially Richard Stang, *The Theory of the Novel in England, 1850–1870* (New York: Columbia University Press, 1959); Kenneth Graham, *English Criticism of the Novel, 1865–1900* (London: Oxford University Press, 1965); and the editors' very helpful commentary and notes on James's essay in *The Art of Criticism: Henry James on the Theory and the Practice of Fiction*, ed. William Veeder and Susan M. Griffin (Chicago: University of Chicago Press, 1986), 184–96.

19Henry James, *The Art of the Novel: Critical Prefaces*, ed. R. P. Blackmur (1934; rpt. New York: Charles Scribner's Sons, 1962), vii, viii.

20"The Art of Fiction," 44.

been notably unpopular when it was published. Recalling how the novelist consoled himself at the time by wryly predicting that "some day, all my buried prose will kick off its various tombstones at once," Trilling began his essay by announcing that the moment of "resurrection" had arrived. "On all sides James is being given the serious and joyous interest he longed for in his lifetime."

In the immediate aftermath of the Second World War, the darkly ironic vision of *The Princess Casamassima* seemed prescient, and Trilling was especially concerned to show how the elements of romance in its plotting were not incompatible with "moral realism." If in this regard his essay still constitutes something of a brief in the novelist's defense, it nonetheless anticipates much subsequent criticism by primarily focusing on the workings of his art. Indeed, it is one measure of how accurately Trilling had judged the temper of the time that so many studies appeared over the next few decades analyzing James's achievement. Often drawing on the novelist's own critical language and assumptions, especially in the Prefaces, such studies typically concerned themselves less with attacking or supporting him than with formal analysis and interpretation.[21] Though in recent decades the spirit of criticism has grown more skeptical, it has characteristically been inclined not so much to debate James's standing as an artist as to question the values on which his art is premised. While many critics continue to take the novelist's own theorizing as a guide to his narratives—and, for that matter, to narrative generally—recent commentators have also tended to approach the critical writings themselves as fictions to be analyzed. At a time when the authority of authors has been much in question, James's very mastery has sometimes placed him under suspicion.

These are, of course, large and necessarily loose generalizations, but something of this shift in critical sensibility can be gathered from the two sets of paired essays that appear in the center of this volume. I have deliberately juxtaposed Trilling's account of politics in *The Princess Casamassima* (an essay reprinted in *The Liberal Imagination* of 1950) with Mark Seltzer's Foucauldian reading of the same novel, and followed Ian Watt's explication of the first paragraph of *The Ambassadors* with Julie Rivkin's argument for how that novel enacts a Derridean "logic of the supplement," in order to call attention both to their differences and their continuities. While Trilling contends that the "imagination of disaster" in *The Princess Casamassima* coexists with an "imagination of love," Seltzer looks suspiciously at the novel's own relation to the exercise of power it represents. Trilling celebrates James's refusal to

[21]There were, of course, notable exceptions to this rule—most notoriously, Maxwell Geismer's wholesale attack on *Henry James and the Jacobites* (Boston: Houghton Mifflin Company, 1963), but also such more measured assessments as Charles Thomas Samuels, *The Ambiguity of Henry James* (Urbana: University of Illinois, 1971) and Philip M. Weinstein, *Henry James and the Requirements of the Imagination* (Cambridge: Harvard University Press, 1971). Significantly, however, Samuels opened his book by protesting the current absence of debate over James's value and the dominance of the field by interpretative studies.

condescend to his lower-class characters; Seltzer argues for his inevitable complicity in acts of "policing" and surveillance. Yet both insist on taking the politics of the novel seriously, deliberately setting themselves against a tradition of classifying James as unpolitical.

The essays by Watt and Rivkin, in contrast, approach the novelist with modes of reading that might best be called rhetorical. After lucidly sketching both the history and the potential limitations of "explication" as a method, Watt offers his reading of a single paragraph from *The Ambassadors* as an exercise in practical criticism. While Watt alludes to the work of I. A. Richards, Leo Spitzer, and Erich Auerbach, among others, Rivkin begins with Jacques Derrida; yet she invokes him not to "deconstruct" *The Ambassadors* but to show how it anticipates his critique of representation. Her reading of James's Preface as an ambassadorial "supplement" to the novel is also an exemplary instance of the recent tendency to take the critical writings as texts for criticism. Not surprisingly, perhaps—given Strether's own history in Paris—both accounts of the novel's language emphasize its modes of indirection and delay.

While such differences of critical method are instructive, they also have a salutary tendency to break down, especially when confronting so complicated a writer as James. I have chosen the essays here primarily for their power to illuminate the novelist and to ask compelling questions, not to serve as representative types of criticism. The sequence in which they appear roughly corresponds to a Jamesian chronology rather than to the order of the individual articles' publication, though the volume begins with a useful overview of the novelist's career in Peter Brooks's study of his lifelong impulses toward melodrama. Given the persistent association of James with matters of technique and form, it is worth noting, finally, how many of the commentators here seek to understand his novels by turning to history—not just the history of politics mentioned earlier, but of economic arrangements and value, assumptions about gender, and attitudes toward the very function of art. Though we sometimes speak as if the art of fiction could somehow be divorced from history, we should remember that James himself had no such illusion. "As the picture is reality," he wrote in "The Art of Fiction," "so the novel is history." When he famously announced in the same essay that "the only reason for the existence of a novel is that it does attempt to represent life,"[22] he understood representation as the work of artists as well as historians—and he took "life" to be a very capacious category indeed.

[22]"The Art of Fiction," 46.

The Melodrama of Consciousness

Peter Brooks

"For if he *were* innocent what then on earth was I?"

—*The Turn of the Screw*

The plunge of civilization into this abyss of blood and darkness by the wanton feat of those two infamous autocrats is a thing that so gives away the whole long age during which we have supposed the world to be, with whatever abatement, gradually bettering, that to have to take it all now for what the treacherous years were all the while really making for and *meaning* is too tragic for any words.

—Letter to Howard Sturgis, 4 August 1914

James's earliest fictional exercises have been described by Thomas Sergeant Perry as lurid stuff: "The heroes were for the most part villains, but they were white lambs by the side of the sophisticated heroines, who seemed to have read all Balzac in the cradle and to be positively dripping with lurid crimes. He began with these extravagant pictures of course in adoration of the great master whom he always so warmly admired."[1] That such overtly Gothic and melodramatic elements should have characterized James's juvenilia will not surprise anyone attentive to the plot, situation, and issues of such early novels as *Watch and Ward, Roderick Hudson,* and *The American*; or indeed, anyone who has reflected on the continuing dark strain in the Jamesian imagination, its unremitting concern with the menacing, the abysmal, the violent, and the unknown. "I have the imagination of disaster," he wrote in 1896, "and see life as ferocious and sinister."[2] If there is in his fiction an evolution away from some of the more obvious and external devices of melodramatic representation and rhetoric, the underlying melodramatic ambition remains, and indeed reasserts itself with the "major phase."

From Peter Brooks, *The Melodramatic Imagination: Balzac, Henry James, Melodrama and the Mode of Excess,* (New Haven: Yale University Press, 1976; rpt. New York: Columbia University Press, 1984), 153–79. Copyright © 1976 by Yale University. Copyright © 1984 by Peter Brooks. Reprinted by permission of the author. This selection is part of a longer chapter entitled "Henry James and the Melodrama of Consciousness."

[1]Quoted in Percy Lubbock, ed., *The Letters of Henry James* (New York: Scribners, 1920), 1:8.

[2]Henry James, *Letters to A. C. Benson and Auguste Monod,* ed. E. F. Benson (London: Elkin Matthews and Marrot, 1930), p. 35. The phrase returns in *The Spoils of Poynton*: in the last chapter, Fleda Vetch, setting out for the visit to a Poynton she will find consumed by fire, has "the sudden imagination of a disaster" ([New York: Scribners, 1908], p. 262).

The evolution of James's judgments of Balzac is significant in this respect. What we find is not a progressive turning away from Balzac's grandiose representations, his "lurid documents" and his "visions," but rather a greater acceptance of them. If the principal essay on Balzac in *French Poets and Novelists* (an essay first published in 1875) reveals a certain discomfort with the novelist's lapses from "realism," with his visionary and "romantic" side, in the essays of 1902 and 1905—"Honoré de Balzac" in *Notes on Novelists* and "The Lesson of Balzac"—he has come to terms with his unremitting admiration of his master. Balzac is imaged with a certain nostalgia as "the last of the novelists to do the thing handsomely," a prelapsarian giant whose lesson must be studied if the novel is to recover its "wasted heritage."[3] James unhesitatingly concedes that "Balzac's imagination alone did the business," that the observer and the visionary are inseparable, that Balzac's heightened mode of representation is the necessary vehicle of his subject.[4] The passage where James in the 1902 essay makes implicit reparation for his strictures of 1875 [quoted elsewhere in this study] follows a discussion of "the romantic" in Balzac that shows a relaxation and a broadening in James's attitude, a conscious acceptance of a mode beyond conventional realism. "He has," writes James, " 'gone in' for his subject, in the vulgar phrase, with an avidity that makes the attack of his most eminent rivals affect us as the intercourse between introduced indifferences at a dull evening party."[5] The phrase, in its implicit reference to the milieu exploited in much of James's own fiction, suggests awareness and acceptance of the necessary heightenings and extrapolations of the melodramatic mode.

Close to the time he was composing the late essays on Balzac, James undertook his celebrated discussion of "romance" in the preface to *The American*. Shortly before the much-quoted passage on "the balloon of experience," he worries about the definition of "the romantic" and its use, virtually from an epistemological perspective. "The romantic stands, on the other hand, for the things that, with all the facilities in the world, all the wealth and all the courage and all the wit and all the adventure, we never *can* directly know; the things that can reach us only through the beautiful circuit and subterfuge of our thought and our desire."[6] This striking characterization of "the romantic" as the realm of knowledge reached through desire recalls central themes in our description of melodrama, a form that facilitates the "circuit" of desire, permits its break through repression, brings its satisfaction

---

[3]Henry James, "The Lesson of Balzac" (1905), in *The Question of Our Speech*, reprinted in Henry James, *The Future of the Novel*, ed. Leon Edel (New York: Vintage, 1956), pp. 118, 102.

[4]Henry James, *Notes on Novelists* (New York: Scribners, 1914), p. 132.

[5]*Notes on Novelists*, p. 141.

[6]Henry James, *The American* (New York: Scribners, 1907), p. xvi. I shall as much as possible refer to James's novels in the New York Edition (1907–1909) and give page references in parentheses in the text. When quoting from works not included in the New York Edition, or from the original (unrevised) versions, I shall give the reference in a footnote.

in full expression. As he proceeds in his attempt to isolate and delineate the romantic element, James rejects any definition dependent on traditional accessories or characters ("as a matter indispensably of boats, or of caravans, or of tigers, or of 'historical characters,' or of ghosts, or of forgers, or of detectives, or of beautiful wicked women, or of pistols and knives") and on the number and magnitude of dangers. What he calls "the dream of an intenser experience" may be found in common occurrences "that 'look like nothing' and that can but inwardly and occultly be dealt with, which involve the sharpest hazards to life and honour." The phrase images clearly James's commitment to a mode that would render a sense of the inner melodrama played out in reaction to life and conferring intensity and value on life. The "intenser experience" is a matter of vision and of treatment: if Flaubert's Emma Bovary is herself of a romantic temper, "nothing less resembles a romance than the record of her adventures": a phrase that strikes close to the heart of James's lifelong critical reserve about Flaubert, his repeated preference for Balzac. The discussion terminates on a parenthetical note which suggests that, whatever the difficulties of finding the demarcation of the real and the romantic may be, "I am not sure an infallible sign of the latter is not this rank vegetation of the 'power' of bad people that good get into, or *vice versa*. It is so rarely, alas, into *our* power that any one gets!" (p. xx). Such is the force of personalized evil and, potentially, of its opposite.

The Jamesian definition of romance, then, encompasses many of the elements, and indeed the very terms, that we found basic to melodrama: the confronted power of evil and goodness, the sense of hazard and clash, the intensification and heightening of experience corresponding to dream and desire. If the discussion of romance is advanced partly in criticism of his early novel, there is clearly at the same time both a "discovery" of the romantic element in his work and an acceptance of its necessity. It is not simply that James in 1907 has recognized the romantic nature of his novel of 1877, but that he has recognized, and stated more clearly than previously, the romantic element inherent to all his work, and his need for it. The point needs making, because the inclusion of James in a discussion of the melodramatic imagination will to many readers initially appear perverse. James is of course reputed for his subtlety, his refinement, his art of nuance and shading; and his world is preëminently the highly civilized and mannered. What sense then does it make to conceive him as a melodramatist and to claim particular illumination of his work from this source?

The term *melodrama* when it is employed by critics of James usually points to more or less deplorable characteristics encountered in such early works as *Roderick Hudson* or *The American*, though not entirely eliminated from *The Portrait of a Lady*, *The Bostonians*, *The Princess Casamassima*. Jacques Barzun and Leo B. Levy are the main exceptions. Barzun proposes to use melodrama as an inclusive term for "those fictions that record man's horror in the face of evil" and notes James's representation of "panic, fear, the mystery of the horror."[7] Levy, whose study is focused on the relation of James's melodrama to his experience as a playwright, instances the "failure of communication between different moral states" in James's fiction; he refers us to literal melodrama with the statement that " 'outraged virtue' and depravity in open conflict is the essential Jamesian melodrama"; and he suggests the underlying reason for recourse to melodrama as the means to infuse "his most deeply felt moral concerns with a sense of peril and crisis."[8] These are useful perceptions; we can hope to extend them from a more thorough grounding in the nature of melodrama and the uses of the melodramatic mode. Though neither Barzun nor Levy discusses James's late fiction in any detail, they are both aware that the melodramatic persists in it. We must work toward this late and complex melodrama, a melodrama at the service of what James calls "the author's instinct everywhere for the *indirect* presentation of his main image," to say how in his transmutations of melodramatic materials and techniques James remains faithful to its premises.[9]

The American can stand for the use of melodrama in the early fiction. As we noted in the first chapter, Newman's experience in that novel brings into play a number of melodrama's specific devices, even its claptrap. James is not content to have American innocence baffled and betrayed by the manipulations of decadent French aristocrats in their fortress-like hôtel in the Faubourg Saint-Germain. He must further intensify the clash by creating a hidden crime in the Bellegarde heritage, the murder of the old marquis by his wife, who has denied him his medicine and transfixed him with her fully Balzacian glance: "You know my lady's eyes, I think, sir; it was with them that she killed him; it was with the terrible strong will that she put into them."[10] The deed is recounted by old Mrs. Bread, the English governess, as the dusk gathers on a bleak hillside by the ruined castle of Fleurières; and Newman is provided with documentary evidence in the form of the deathbed accusation scribbled by the old marquis. Underlying the social drama played out in Newman's courtship of Claire de Cintré is this bloodcurdling deed, rendered with all possible shades of horror, supported by sure signs to the determination of guilt. After his encounter with Mrs. Bread, Newman appears to be in a position to act as the providential hero of melodrama: he possesses the signs necessary to expose the villain and perhaps to free the innocent heroine from her claustration in the convent of the rue d'Enfer, to purge the poisoned air of the social order.

That Newman does not so rout the villains is a first sign of the typical Jamesian transmutation of melodrama, his primary interest in the melodrama

[7]Jacques Barzun, "Henry James, Melodramatist," in *The Question of Henry James*, ed. F. W. Dupee (New York: Holt, 1945), pp. 255–56.

[8]Leo B. Levy, *Versions of Melodrama: A Study of the Fiction and Drama of Henry James, 1865–1897* (Berkeley and Los Angeles: University of California Press, 1957), pp. 3, 30, 116.

[9]"Indirect presentation": see Preface to *The Wings of the Dove*, 1:xxii.

[10]*The American*, in the text of 1881 (reprint ed., New York: Signet Classics, 1963), p. 278.

of consciousness. The clash of good innocence and sophisticated villainy in this novel at the last works to an intensification of the terms of Newman's choice between revenge and renunciation, a choice that is the final test of his inner being, that must call upon his deepest moral inwardness for a difficult victory of generosity and natural nobility. Newman's renunciation of revenge should not be construed as James's renunciation of melodrama. It marks on the contrary a deep understanding of the fundamental concerns of melodrama and its possible uses. If melodrama as a form exists to permit the isolation and dramatization of integral ethical forces, to impose their evidence and a recognition of the force of the right, the mode and terms of Newman's choice stand squarely within the tradition. What differs is that the melodrama of external action—the suspenseful menace, pursuit, and combat—all are past by the time he resolves the ethical conflict.[11] External melodrama has been used to lead into the melodrama of ethical choice.

In later novels, the melodrama of external action will tend to be more and more superseded in favor of a stance, from the outset, within the melodrama of consciousness. Such for instance is the case with *The Portrait of a Lady*, where all of Isabel Archer's career is framed in terms of choices, and the terms of choice are themselves progressively polarized and intensified, so that Isabel's final decision to return to Gilbert Osmond in Rome is freighted with lurid connotations of sacrifice, torture, penance, claustration. Leo B. Levy argues that "the real subject of the novel has become the intensification of oppositions for its own sake."[12] It might be more accurate to say that oppositions are intensified for the sake of the choice between them, so that the adventure of consciousness can be fully melodramatic. James in his preface to the novel draws our attention to the crucial episode of the melodrama of consciousness, Isabel's "extraordinary meditative vigil," as an example of "what an 'exciting' inward life may do for the person leading it" (1:xx). Here the stuff of consciousness becomes explicitly dramatic and exciting: "Her mind, assailed by visions, was in a state of extraordinary activity . . ." (2:204). It is probable that the discomfort felt by many readers and critics faced with the ending of the novel derives from the absolute terms that James has staked on Isabel's choice, a feeling of moral assault or psychic scandal of the type that we found literal melodrama to produce.

The melodrama of consciousness that reaches its first maturity in *The Portrait of a Lady* will be pursued by James in his subsequent fiction, with the indirection provided by an increasing rigor of "point of view," and yet also with deepening intensity. The greater inwardness of the drama will be matched on the plane of external action by an effort to make those gestures or

---

[11]This has affinities with "drawing-room melodrama" as defined by Maurice Willson Disher: "It is the kind of melodrama on which the curtain does not rise until deeds of blood and violence are past." *Melodrama: Plots That Thrilled* (London: Rockcliff, 1954), p. 80.

[12]*Versions of Melodrama*, pp. 51–52.

acts that are executed and recorded fully paying, fully charged with meaning. Critical reserve has been voiced about such overtly melodramatic endings as that to *The Bostonians*, where Basil Ransom hurries Verena Tarrant out into the night while Olive Chancellor rushes onstage to offer herself to the well-bred furies of the disappointed Music Hall crowd, or that of *The Princess Casamassima*, where the German revolutionary Schinkel and the princess batter down the door to Hyacinth Robinson's room, to find him lying in gore, shot by his own hand with the bullet designated for the Duke. If James uses such strong and violent action in these endings—as later he will use the violent, exorbitant evocations of the last encounter between Strether and Mme de Vionnet in *The Ambassadors* and the storm-burst of evil at the Venetian climax of *The Wings of the Dove*—it is because such action best correlates to and delivers, over the footlights as it were, the intensity of his melodrama of consciousness. If in *The American* we feel to a degree the outer, manifest melodrama working to shape the dimensions of Newman's final inner choice, later in James's career we sense the inner melodrama reflecting upon and charging the outer action. External action tends more and more toward the revelatory, toward rendering of the critical moment and gesture that summarize and release the significant vision: Isabel's discovery of Gilbert Osmond and Madame Merle "unconsciously and familiarly associated" (2:205), Strether's discovery—"a sharp fantastic crisis that had popped up as if in a dream"—of Chad and Mme de Vionnet in the rowboat (2:257–58), Hyacinth Robinson's view of the princess and Paul Muniment standing at the door of her house—while Hyacinth feels "his heart beat insanely, ignobly"—then entering together (2:324). The exiguity and restraint of the external action is overborne by the weight of revelatory meaning that the novelist, through his preparations, juxtapositions, and use of a post of observation, has read into it.

The reasons for outward and inward melodrama in James are the same: his desire to make ethical conflict, imperative, and choice the substance of the novel, to make it the nexus of "character" and the motivation of plot. Yvor Winters approaches this question in terms similar to mine when, in his consideration of Jamesian "obscurity," he notes that James's virtues are closely related to his defects: "His defects arise from the effort on the part of the novelist and of his characters to understand ethical problems in a pure state, and to understand them absolutely. . . ."[13] The heightening of experience and the intensification of choice are motivated by the desire of the novelist, and those characters who act as his "centers of consciousness," to find, to see, to articulate and eventually to dramatize in their actions moral problems seized in their essence, as pure imperatives and commitments. This must not be construed to mean that characters are themselves integral, representative of pure moral conditions, black or white. Especially in James's mature work,

    [13]Yvor Winters, "Maule's Well, or Henry James and the Relation of Morals to Manners," in *Maule's Curse* (Norfolk, Conn.: New Directions, 1938), p. 210.

there is always a subtle mixture of motive and fine shadings of ethical coloration in his major characters, and most of all in his "villains." It is rather that characters, whatever their nuances, make reference to such absolutes, recognize, more or less clearly, their existence and force, and in their worldly actions gesture toward them. The movement of the typical Jamesian plot from complex and often obscure interrelationship to crisis imaged as revelation signals his need to disengage from the complications of reality a final confrontation, however nuanced, of moral integers. Good and evil do exist, and an inability to see and understand them, even when they are exquisitely alloyed, is to fail in the reading of reality, to oversimplify in the manner of a Flaubert, to misestimate what life is really about and art is really for.[14]

The conflict of good and evil—terms that we must further explore and refine—must hence be led to confrontation, articulation, acting out. As Balzac's novels regularly worked toward the scenic "showdown," the *scène à faire*, so James developed more and more consciously his conception of the novelistic "picture," which, as in the examples cited from *The Princess Casamassima* and *The Ambassadors*, can be a tableau of represented meaning, and the "scene," the dramatized significant moment. The scenic method is part of James's technique from the very beginning, yet evidently sharpened and made more conscious by his experience in the theatre, his struggle to write stage drama. When he wrote to himself in his Notebook, in 1896, "I realize—none too soon—that the *scenic* method is my absolute, my imperative, my *only* salvation," he was recording a final coming to consciousness of what he had as an artist known for a long time.[15] Theatrical conventions, enactment, theatricality itself were the semiotic preconditions for the novel as James understood it.

James was attracted to the theatre for other reasons similar to Balzac's: because it promised a sociable, institutional glory, and because it offered the possibility of popular and financial success. The latter motive has bothered some critics who wish to see James as confined to the rarified medium and emotion; yet there is abundant evidence that James throughout his career longed to succeed in popular forms, to meet a Balzac on his own terrain. And it is clear that he envisioned success in the theatre as a way to reëstablish contact with a glorious public tradition extending back to Romanticism. But he was forced to work in the wrong theatre, to write for the London, rather than the Paris, stage. His admiration for French acting and drama is fully evident in the articles he contributed as a young man to the New York *Tribune*, in the ideals he advances in his critiques of the London theatre, in numerous passages of the Notebooks. Of the Comédiens-Français he wrote, in

14See in particular James's principal essay on Flaubert, "Gustave Flaubert" (1902) in *Notes on Novelists*, pp. 65–108.

15*The Notebooks of Henry James*, ed. F. O. Matthiessen and Kenneth Murdock (New York: Oxford University Press, 1947), p. 263. See also *The Complete Plays of Henry James*, ed. Leon Edel (Philadelphia and New York: Lippincott, 1949).

a phrase that suggests his own continuing ideal in both theatre and novel, "they solve triumphantly the problem of being at once realistic to the eye and romantic to the imagination."[16] When he began work on his stage adaptation of *The American*—which was in fact to reduce the novel's complex melodrama to the most schematic and stagy melodrama—he invoked uniquely French masters: "À *moi*, Scribe; à *moi*, Sardou, à *moi*, Dennery!"[17]

The three playwrights mentioned delineate with fair accuracy James's conception of his theatrical tutors. Scribe and Sardou, to whom one should add Alexandre Dumas *fils*, so often discussed by James, represent the tradition of melodrama domesticated, melodrama become the "well-made play." We have mentioned earlier [in this study] the elements of this domestication, its preservation of the hyperbolic dramaturgy of melodrama together with its search for greater "realism" of detail and situation, and its falling off from the cosmic ambitions of earlier melodrama. Scribe, Sardou, and Dumas offered to James models of impeccable construction, plotting, suspense, and confrontation. Dennery, on the other hand, was a true melodramatist throughout his long career, and James's admiration for him is significant. We in fact find James responding with pleasure to the New York production of Dennery's *Les Deux Orphelines*, a melodrama of 1874 that is one of the latest representatives of the genre to preserve quite intact its conventions: it offers a compendium of melodramatic themes and devices, foundlings, poverty, blindness, disguised identities, culpable parents, incipient revolution, conversion, renunciation, and heroics.[18] We should recognize James's nostalgia for the grandiose possibilities of Romantic melodrama. As he wrote in tribute on the death of Frédérick Lemaître, in 1876, "The theatre of our own day, with its relish for small, realistic effects, produces no more actors of those heroic proportions." He closes that article with an evocatory flight: "But Frédéric Lemaître, as we see him in his *légende*, is like a huge, fantastic shadow, a moving silhouette, projected duskily against the wall from a glowing fire. The fire is the 'romantic' movement of 1830."[19] As Balzac represented the prelapsarian novelist to whom all was possible, the French Romantic stage suggested a prelapsarian theatre.

That James was actually obliged to work within conventions at once narrower and more vulgar, for an audience more socially segregated (such was the case in London) yet less conditioned to the possibilities of the dramatic art, was the assurance of failure, whether for *The American* or for the curiously late-Romantic *Guy Domville*. Only Ibsen, who can be said to have

16Henry James, "The Théâtre-Français," in *French Poets and Novelists* (Boston: Houghton Mifflin, 1878), p. 323.

17James, *Notebooks*, p. 100.

18See Henry James, "Notes on the Theatres: New York," in *The Scenic Art*, ed. Allan Wade (1948; reprint ed., New York: Hill and Wang, Dramabook, 1957), pp. 24–25.

19Henry James, *Parisian Sketches*, ed. Leon Edel and Ilse Dusoir Lind (New York: New York University Press, 1957), p. 82.

reinvested in the structure of the "well-made play" some of the intense ethical concern of melodrama—transmuted in his late plays into the melodrama of consciousness—offered a valid contemporary example, though one socially too foreign to James to be of immediate use. As Leon Edel has pointed out, it was to Ibsen that James looked in creating Rose Armiger in that curious melodrama, at once mannered and sensational, *The Other House*.[20] Rose Armiger drowns the small child Effie Bream in the hope of marrying Tony Bream, who has made his late wife a promise not to marry again during the life of the child—a promise extorted on her deathbed, at the close of act I, which dominates the play as a fully melodramatic absolute vow. *The Other House* was originally written as a play, then revised into a short novel for serialization in the *London Illustrated News*, the most "popular" medium for which James ever wrote, then once more reworked as a play for Elizabeth Robins, but never staged. It is lurid fare, and an interesting demonstration that James still in the 1890s was attracted to the possibility of doing something popular, and something that would give overt expression to the most melodramatic elements in his imagination.

Years later, in 1910, as he worked with the pieces of an outline for a new fiction, James wrote in his Notebook: "Oh, blest *Other House*, which gives me thus at every step a precedent, a support, a divine little light to walk by."[21] The "divine light" shed by his melodrama was that of a fully developed scenic and dramatic technique translated into novelistic form. The original transcription of *The Other House* from play to novel was the most telling demonstration for the author of how the lessons of his grim theatrical years could be put to use in fiction. Leon Edel and Leo B. Levy have well described the direct effect of the theatrical experience on James's novelistic technique from *The Spoils of Poynton* onward. Levy refers us to "the scenic intensities that are the primary literary experience of the reader of James," and while this is characteristic as well of the fiction before the theatrical years, the practice of the theatre confirmed and sharpened James's sense that to "dramatize" a subject—as he so often exhorted himself, and others, to do—meant to have almost literal recourse to the dramatist's tools, and especially to the direct verbal and physical encounters that the stage allows and needs.[22]

What James called "the little drama of my 'Spoils' " (p. vii) stands at the inception of the line of James's most theatrical fiction, and its climactic scenes convey a sense of drawing room melodrama at its best. Place is conceived as

---

[20]See Edel, Foreword to *The Other House* in *The Complete Plays of Henry James*, pp. 677–79.
[21]James, *Notebooks*, p. 348.
[22]Levy, *Versions of Melodrama*, p. 96. Levy's subtle and useful argument is possibly flawed by an excessively loose definition of stage melodrama, which seems to include Scribe, Sardou, Dumas *fils*, and other writers of "well-made plays." This leads to a lack of precision in discussing what James learned from the technique of such master craftsmen, and his adherence to the ethos and imagination of melodrama. Both are important in James, and they are interrelated, but they are not identical.

stage set, and within its confines a limited number of selected stage properties and gestures are made to bear the weight of an impassioned drama. At
the end of chapter 14, for instance, Owen Gereth, who has come to tea with
Fleda Vetch, breaks through his long muddlement and reserve to declare his
love for her, and his desire to break his engagement with Mona Brigstock. At
the moment of declaration, "as the door opened the smutty maid, edging in,
announced 'Mrs. Brigstock!'" (p. 168). With this inopportune arrival of
Mona's mother, a new scene begins—chapter 15—and with it our attention,
like Mrs. Brigstock's, is drawn to a trivial object that is given disproportionate
dimensions, made into a stage property that stands for a "real" object that in
turn acts as a sign of human action. Mrs. Brigstock's eyes attach themselves to
the barely nibbled biscuit that "in some precipitate movement" has been
brushed to the floor. It was, we are told, "doubtless a sign of the agitation that
possessed [Fleda]. For Mrs. Brigstock there was apparently more in it than
met the eye. Owen at any rate picked it up, and Fleda felt as if he were
removing the traces of some scene that the newspapers would have characterized as lively. Mrs. Brigstock clearly took in also the sprawling tea-things and
the marks as of a high tide in the full faces of her young friends" (p. 169). The
biscuit and then the tea-things (which can only metaphorically be "sprawling")
are, in the manner of stage properties, signs *for* signs: they are hyperbolic
conventional signs, magnified in order to release to scrutiny "more than meets
the eye."[23] The scene is an exemplary instance of James's capacity to invest his
confrontations with revelatory excitement without apparently violating decorum and the surface of manners, through imprinting on the objects and
gestures rendered the stamp of hyperbolic and theatrical meaning.

The scene develops from this encounter over the sign of the biscuit into a
vivid interchange which at the end explicitly reminds us of its "staginess,"
when Mrs. Brigstock announces that she came to see Fleda in order to
"plead" with her, and Fleda replies: "As if I were one of those bad women in a
play?" (p. 177). Here is a typically Jamesian procedure of ironizing dramatic
conventions all the while suggesting their imaginative appropriateness: a way
of having one's melodrama while denying it. If Fleda may be cast in this stock
role (a role, no doubt, from Dumas *fils*) by Mrs. Brigstock, she in no wise fills
it in the reader's mind. Yet James's evocation of the possibility allows us to
respond to her situation *as if* she were so theatrical a character. As in his
metaphors, another context is brought to bear on the literal context. Fleda's
own self-consciousness about her role frees her to act with a higher awareness
of the significances that may be read in her enactment: she is aware of the
signs that her actions generate, of her embodiment of meanings. Hence in her
subsequent climactic encounter with Owen, in chapter 16, she plays in full
consciousness of her words and gestures as heightened and interpretable

23On the theatre as the realm of signs for signs, see Petr Bogatyrev, "Les Signes du théâtre,"
Poétique 8 (1971), pp. 517–30.

signs. The scene unfolds in her sister's shabby living room, and we are repeatedly made aware of the characters' movements within a space conceived as a stage. Its most important property is the staircase, ever ready for Fleda's flight from Owen—her renunciation of him unless he first obtains his grant of freedom from Mona—up which she at the last will scramble. By making his readers live so consistently in a theatrical medium, and respond to the performances of his characters as if on the stage, James prepares and legitimates his "strong" ending, the burning of Poynton. This final scene reproduces the physical cataclysms typical of melodramatic third acts, strikes the set in a fully realized symbolic enactment.

Even more totally theatrical and scenic in their presentation are *What Maisie Knew* and *The Awkward Age*. The latter James recognized as his most finished play-as-novel, patterned on the practice of the French writer Gyp, and bringing to culmination all his studies in the dramatic form. The climactic scene of *The Awkward Age* is one of the most accomplished pieces of confrontation and cataclysm that James ever wrought. It is, again, realized without rending the fabric of "manners"—though it sends tremors through the social order—while yet opening up depths of violence, hostility, and conflict. The scene turns on an unidentified "French novel," the nexus of moral "horrors,"[24] which, it will be revealed, Nanda has borrowed from Vanderbank, has read, and then has recommended to Tishy Grendon. The book is another stage property, passed from hand to hand and commented upon by the characters. Aggie wants it, but Lord Petherton (who, we gather, from being the Duchess's lover has become Aggie's, now that she has "come out") keeps it from her, only to have it snatched by Harold Brookenham, who reads Vanderbank's name inscribed on the cover, whereupon it is grabbed by Mrs. Brookenham, who announces that the handwriting isn't Van's and passes it on to Mr. Longdon for confirmation; then Nanda confesses that she wrote Van's name, intending that the novel be returned to him. Mrs. Brook, recovering the volume, presses Nanda for a public declaration of whether or not she has read it. Mr. Cashmore takes possession of the book as Mrs. Brook continues to insist to Nanda:

> "Have you read this work, Nanda?"
> "Yes mamma."
> "Oh I say!" cried Mr. Cashmore, hilarious and turning the leaves.
> Mr. Longdon had by this time ceremoniously approached Tishy. "Good night."
> [p. 434]

End of scene, and end of act. The unspeakable horrors of the unspecified French novel have moved through the group like a tracer dye, revealing relations, making clear positions and motives that have thus far been uncer-

---

[24]James refers to what Nanda learns by the end of *The Awkward Age* as "horrors": *Notebooks*, p. 192.

tain. The terrifying role is Mrs. Brook's, for her insistence upon a public avowal from Nanda is a conscious effort to show her daughter up before the assembled set—and particularly before Van, the man who should be Nanda's suitor, whom Mrs. Brook desires for herself, and Mr. Longdon, the man who in compensation will offer her a retreat from the world—as corrupted and hence as unsaleable goods on the London marriage market. To the alert reader, the scene has all the shock of villainy unleashed. Mrs. Brook has created what Van will later call a "smash." His image for the scene is accurate: "It was a wonderful performance. You pulled us down—just closing with each of the great columns in its turn—as Samson pulled down the temple" (p. 439). The *scène à faire* of the novel has been Mrs. Brook's to do, and the narrowness of the stage, the conventionality of the characters and props involved, cannot blind us to its thunderous effect.

The technique of such revelatory dramatic confrontations, bathed in the "divine little light" shed by the composition of *The Other House*, is particularly appropriate to the kinds of situations repeatedly dramatized in James's fiction, especially at this period. Nanda Brookenham's dilemma, her showing up, and her defeat at the hands of the society orchestrated by her mother constitute one of the many versions of the Jamesian obsession with sophisticated versions of innocence and corruption. Nanda's story is one of the most subtle and pessimistic of these because it becomes evident that innocence as "purity" and as ignorance cannot survive in so treacherous a world (and Aggie, brought up in ignorance of good and evil by the Duchess, becomes the most inconsequential of strumpets upon her marriage); at the same time, the world insists on maintaining the hypocrisy of innocence. What supplants innocence as purity is necessarily consciousness, at root the knowledge of good and evil. This Nanda gains, but at the price of losing worldly rewards, losing in particular Van. It is on Van that the novel suggests the sharpest moral judgment: worldly, himself one of the corrupt and the conscious, he is unwilling to accept consciousness in Nanda. He draws back from her knowledge of good and evil, he fears consciousness as inseparable from corruption. The ironic result is to drive him once more, at the end, back to the solace of the fully conscious and corrupt Mrs. Brook. It remains for the gallant and betrayed Mitchy, and Mr. Longdon—the *vieillard généreux* of melodrama, the representative of an earlier and nobler generation—to recognize (but not to reward) the quality of Nanda's virtue within corruption.

The clash of untenable innocence with sophisticated corruption and evil also provides the theme and structure of *What Maisie Knew*. As in *The Awkward Age*, in this novel innocence cannot long maintain the state of purity if it is to survive. The point so often missed in discussion of *What Maisie Knew*, it seems to me, is that if the novel is about the limitations of the child's vision, it is also about its precocious sophistication, Maisie's premature but necessary education in "handling" people whose motives and intentions she may not understand, but whose relations to herself, whose greater or lesser utility to herself, she most uncannily masters and by the end manipulates. The final scene of the novel, where she turns the tables of the agonizing choice presented to her against her would-be protectors—demanding that Sir Claude give up Mrs. Beale if he wishes to keep her, Maisie, then choosing Mrs. Wix when it becomes apparent that Sir Claude can't and won't give up Mrs. Beale—registers her arrival at a sophisticated and usable practical knowledge of what is in her best interests. What is never seen—and is queried in the last line of the novel as in its title—is the extent to which Maisie knows what lies *behind* the behavior of the different adults, and combinations of adults, in her regard. If she has become an expert in human relationships as they affect her destiny, she is, we estimate, still largely ignorant of their overriding motivation—which here, as in *The Awkward Age*, is essentially sexual. So that her position in regard to the various sets of "parents" in the book is much like our position in regard to the "French novel" of *The Awkward Age*: like Maisie, we know the effects but not the content; we know the "horrors" only through their effect. Such knowledge through effect rather than cause and substance is indeed one of the voluntary constraints of the purely scenic form, "the imposed absence of . . . 'going behind,' " as James states it in the preface to *The Awkward Age* (p. xvii). This constraint means that the melodrama of consciousness can here be known only insofar as it suffuses outward action, speech, and gesture.

More generally, such an evacuation of the content is typical of the "horrors" at issue in the clash of innocence and evil in James's fiction at this period and in most of the later novels as well. If *The American* enters upon a full specification of the Bellegardes' black deed (though not in fact on specification of the reasons for Claire de Cintré's renunciation of the struggle), the fiction of the 1890s tends to exploit an evil all the more oppressive in that it is unnamed, undesignated, detectable only in its effects. Evil is a kind of blankness into which we read the content that we need, as with the misdeeds that cause little Miles, in *The Turn of the Screw*, to be sent home from school: misdeeds persistently guessed at by the Governess, posited, shaped, figured, invented. That such "ambiguity" was James's intent is sufficiently clear from the preface to *The Turn of the Screw*: "Only make the reader's general vision of evil intense enough, I said to myself . . . and his own experience, his own imagination, his own sympathy (with the children) and horror (of their false friends) will supply him quite sufficiently with all the particulars. Make him *think* the evil, make him think it for himself, and you are released from weak specifications" (pp. xxi–xxii).

The Turn of the Screw is exemplary of the tendency in all James's later fiction to intensify the manichaeistic struggle of good and evil, light and darkness, through a reflection of effect that does not designate cause, yet in not doing so creates a large and portentous menace that evokes a tremendous cause. It is as if James had discovered that to maintain the melodramatic terms of his vision and his presentation, in particular to maintain the conflict

of polarized moral conditions, while at the same time escaping the limitations
of overt, explicit melodrama (of the type of *The American*), he must make his
confronted terms rich in perceived and felt possibilities, emanations, effects,
while elaborately refusing designation of their ontology. *The Turn of the
Screw* shows the consequences of this decision to a high degree. The ontology
of the evil whose undoubted effects are chronicled in the story is so uncertain
that some readers, led by Edmund Wilson, have been led to see it as a study
in pure, and pathological, subjectivity.[25] The logic of the Wilsonian position is
clear: if there is no objective evidence of the presence of evil at Bly and of the
corruption of the children, then we should look in the very consciousness that
is perceiving such evil, to see if it may not be a projection of that consciousness; and here he finds hints enough to establish a plausible, if extrapolated,
case. The Wilsonian emphasis is a necessary corrective to the excessively
theological view of Dorothea Krook, for whom the story is a Faustian struggle
of corruption and attempted salvation, for she tends to ignore the epistemological complication.[26] Both views are in fact too limited in their exclusive
form. It is important to recognize that both the perceiving eye and the field of
perception are shifting and unreliable; or rather, that there is a perfect
relativity of movement, since one can never say at any given moment which
has shifted. The result is never a clear decision about the nature of the
horror, but rather a kind of moral ratio that is stated by the Governess in a
rare flash of self-doubt just before the end of the tale, as she presses Miles for
a designation of the horrors for which he has been expelled from school: "It
was for the instant confounding and bottomless, for if he *were* innocent what
then on earth was I?" (p. 307). The statement is hypothetical, and to try to
give it a clear answer assigning guilt and innocence is the wrong approach.
What is most important is the formula of the ratio itself, the either/or in the
struggle of darkness and light. The either/or assumes its melodramatic form as
the all-or-nothing; there can be no compromise in moral terms: if Miles is
innocent, the Governess is the agent of damnation. The logic here is that of
the excluded middle, which we encountered repeatedly in melodrama. It
once again images a world of cosmic forces in clash where choices of courses of
action and ways of being are absolute. What has changed from the world of
primary melodrama is that we no longer know how to choose because of our
epistemological doubt: we no longer can or need to identify persons as
innocence or evil; we must respond instead to the ratios of choice themselves.
    It is necessary to address a closer scrutiny to the terms corresponding to
"good" and "evil" in the Jamesian melodrama. The Jamesian "theology"
evidently gives a large part to the forces of blackness. "If ever a man's

    [25]Edmund Wilson, "The Ambiguity of Henry James," in *The Triple Thinkers* (New York:
Harcourt, 1938), pp. 122–64.
    [26]See Dorothea Krook, *The Ordeal of Consciousness in Henry James* (Cambridge: Cambridge
University Press, 1962), pp. 106–34.

imagination was clouded by the Pit," writes Graham Greene, "it was James's." Greene goes on to suggest that experience taught James "to believe in supernatural evil, but not in supernatural good."[27] James's sense of evil and what he called his "imagination of disaster" is remarkably intense. It has led critics to a comparison with Hawthorne and the American puritan tradition, the haunted sense of original sin and the intellectual preoccupation with "the unpardonable sin." Yet the manifestations of blackness in James often remind one less of Hawthorne than of Poe; or, since Poe was an author for whom James had little use, Balzac. They have a flamboyant and Gothic sense of the *tremendum* rather than the quiet anxiety of puritanism. As the "ghostly tales" most evidently demonstrate, James can be very close to the conventions and spirit of Gothic romance, its settings, characters, and oppressive atmosphere; the Governess's logic of the excluded middle looks directly back to Matilda's in *The Monk*: choices of allegiance to blackness or whiteness are absolute and irremissible. When, at the end of *The Turn of the Screw*, Miles's heart is "dispossessed," it can only stop. Nor is the Gothic feeling of tremendum confined to the ghostly tales; the "horrors" are present within the most polished and mannered social frameworks, and when they manifest themselves, it can be with thunderous force. James's prose makes recurrent use of terms that image the menace of evil: "sinister," "appalling," "portentous," "lurid," "chilling," "abysmal" return to invest superficially quiet crises with a sense of metaphysical darkness. We can often detect in James's prose the effort to give adequate representation to what he feels to be the latent sinister implications of an event, to shadow forth the inner horror. An example among many would be the series of letters that he wrote in August 1914 in reaction to the outbreak of the World War. We find a concern to make his prose adequate to the occasion, to make his statement live up to what he conceives as a monstrous betrayal of all the "civilization" that he, his friends, his class, his characters had believed in. The war is an "abyss of blood and darkness" that "gives away" civilization and progress, transforming the years of his maturity—and of Victorian and Edwardian glory—into "the treacherous years," whose meaning must now be read as totally other, on the far side of the excluded middle. Or, as he puts it to another correspondent, the war "seems to me to *undo* everything, everything that was ours, in the most horrible retroactive way."[28] The possession of an imagination of disaster includes the capacity to respond fully to disaster, to reflect its lurid colorings in one's life and art.

The theme of betrayal is central to James's fictions, he is fascinated by what Graham Greene calls "the judas-complex"; or, as J. A. Ward states it, the

---

[27]Graham Greene, *The Lost Childhood and Other Essays* (London: Eyre and Spottiswoode, 1951), pp. 26, 38.

[28]The letters are to Howard Sturgis (2 and 5 August 1914) and Rhoda Broughton (10 August 1914). See James, *Letters*, 2:384, 389.

problem of "improper intervention in the life of another."[29] The villain of
classic French melodrama was commonly called *le traître*, no doubt because
his villainy included a full measure of dissimulation and dupery. James's
usage, for all its subtlety, shows a certain fidelity to this tradition. Evil is
treacherous in that its darkest intent is dissimulated under layers of good
manners or even beneath the threshold of consciousness in the evildoer
himself; and evil is treachery in that it means denying to someone the means
to free realization of his (or so much more often in James, her) full potential as
a moral being. What opposes such treachery is not simply innocence, but
more forcefully loyalty, what might best be characterized in James's own
terms as "kindness": the refusal to do hurt, the refusal to betray, a full
awareness of the independence of other beings.

If the "tremendousness" of evil in James may make us concur with Greene's
judgment that he believed in supernatural evil—at least supernatural psychic
evil—it is not quite accurate to suggest that the good opposed to it hasn't the
same absolute value. In the face of evil, good appears in James's fiction
increasingly tenuous, privatized, interior, and complex. Good is not innocence
and certainly not purity, for a failure to incorporate the consciousness of evil is
simply to be a victim and a fool. Nanda Brookenham's story is again exemplary here, for it is both her superiority and her worldly tragedy that she
encompasses knowledge of evil within her virtue. This is necessary if goodness
is to assert its autonomy, its resistance to the manipulative demands of evil, its
interpretation of life. Nanda is potentially both Milly Theale and Kate Croy.
She looks back to Isabel Archer, for whom the mature consciousness of good
and evil is both a chastening lesson in how to be, in how to carry on the
struggle of existence, and its own reward. And she looks forward to Maggie
Verver in *The Golden Bowl*, who almost alone among Jamesian heroines can
use the knowledge of good and evil to restore the reign of good, a postlapsar-
ian good tempered by terrible wisdom.

It is remarkably difficult to talk about "goodness" in James because it is so
tenuous, so private and interior, based so exclusively on an individual commitment to a subjective perception of ethical imperatives that may have no
shared or community value. The moral sense for James and his characters, as
Yvor Winters states it, "was a fine, but a very delicate perception, unsupported by any clear set of ideas."[30] At its least persuasive, such an ungrounded
subjective moral sense can produce Strether's decision, at the end of *The
Ambassadors*, to return to Woollett, a decision based on his desire "to be
right," on his "only logic," which he states as "Not, out of the whole affair, to
have got anything for myself" (2:326). This renunciation smacks too much of a
narrowing puritanism—exactly what one thought Strether's adventure of

[29]Greene, *The Lost Childhood*, p. 44; J. A. Ward, *The Imagination of Disaster* (Lincoln:
University of Nebraska Press, 1961), p. 13.
[30]Winters, *Maule's Curse*, p. 175.

consciousness had led him beyond—to be entirely satisfactory. It is danger-ously close to renunciation for its own sake: like Olive Chancellor's favorite line from *Faust*, "*Entsagen sollst du, sollst entsagen!*" (which she repeats in Bayard Taylor's translation: "Thou shalt renounce, refrain, abstain!"), an atti-tude which James clearly recognizes in its unsupported state to be perverse and unbalanced.[31] On other occasions we are persuaded by the individual sacrifice to an ideal which the individual alone may barely perceive, and which he may not be able entirely to model his actions on, but which nonetheless achieves the status of a moral imperative. Such, I think, is Isabel Archer's return to Osmond—if one is willing to accept the idea of marriage as a sacrament, at least a human sacrament, and the principle of responsibility for one's acts—or Merton Densher's refusal to take Milly's legacy.

There is nonetheless throughout James's fiction an apparent discrepancy between motive and action, cause and effect, in the moral decisions that determine plot and character. As Yvor Winters again states the case, "There is a marked tendency . . . on the part of James and of his characters alike to read into situations more than can be justified by the facts as given, to build up intense states of feeling, on the basis of such reading, and to judge or act as a result of that feeling."[32] This judgment corresponds to our characterization of melodrama, particularly as put to the ambitious use of a Romantic dramatist such as Hugo or such a novelist as Balzac. In both cases, we noted, the emotion and signification found in the gestures of reality, extrapolated from them and postulated on them, is in excess of the representation itself, in excess of the "objective correlative," or more simply the vehicle, presented as embodying it. The need for melodrama, on this basis, is the need for a form of statement and dramatization that will make the plane of representation yield the content of the plane of signification. This means in practice a pressure on the surface—the surface of social forms, manners; and the surface of literary forms, style—in order to make surface release the vision of the behind: as Strether's pressure of imagination applied to Mme de Vionnet's hôtel conjures forth "the smell of revolution, the smell of the public temper—or perhaps simply the smell of blood" (2:274). The technique is expressionistic in that surface forms are treated, not for themselves, in their interrelation and as ultimate integers, but as signs of what lies behind them and charges them. Laurence Bedwell Holland has employed the term *expressionism* in a related sense to characterize James's use of form; citing Herbert Read, he talks of an expressionism whose "distinguishing feature is *pressure* and which is founded on the 'desire to exceed the inherent qualities of the medium.' "[33]

---

[31]Henry James, *The Bostonians* (1886; reprint ed., Harmondsworth, Middlesex, England: Penguin, 1966), pp. 75–76.

[32]Winters, *Maule's Curse*, p. 203.

[33]Laurence Bedwell Holland, *The Expense of Vision* (Princeton: Princeton University Press, 1964), p. 76. Holland has in mind the mannerist distortion of forms in James, a distortion that results from expressionism.

One of the media whose "inherent qualities" are exceeded in James's expressionism is social manners, the order of human interchange within an established social code, complete with its register of coherent, because conventional, signs. As F. R. Leavis has written, "It is doubtful whether at any time in any place he could have found what would have satisfied his implicit demand: the actual fine art of civilized social intercourse that would have justified the flattering intensity of expectation he brought to it in the form of his curiously transposed and subtilized ethical sensibility."[34] The fictional answer to this demand was the invention of a medium of social intercourse and manners that would allow the observer to read into it, to extrapolate out of it, the significances he needed, and to do so largely through the pressure of an insistence that distorts the literal forms. Thus indicators or tokens such as Eugenio's "slight, too slight smile," in the passage from *The Wings of the Dove* [discussed earlier] in chapter 1, or the nibbled teabiscuit confronting Mrs. Brigstock on the floor, in *The Spoils of Poynton*, achieve a charge of hallucinated meaning. At its most elaborated, this technique of pressure and metaphorical extrapolation can give passages that on any literalistic level must be considered grotesque, and which work at all only because the context of consistent expressionism legitimates them. To confine ourselves to a relatively brief example, there is this passage between Maggie and the Prince, in *The Golden Bowl*, following the breaking of the bowl:

> She had done for him, that is, what her instinct enjoined: had laid a basis not merely momentary on which he could meet her. When by the turn of his head he did finally meet her this was the last thing that glimmered out of his look; but it none the less came into sight as a betrayal of his distress and almost as a question of his eyes; so that, for still another minute before he committed himself there occurred between them a kind of unprecedented moral exchange over which her superior lucidity presided. It was not however that when he did commit himself the show was promptly portentous. [2:189]

So much has never ridden on the turn of a head, so much has never "glimmered out" of a look, so grandiose a moral exchange has never been wrested from so little. The text of muteness is elaborate, fully charged and fully significant. Yet the whole mode of the late fiction, as we shall see in more detail, its tone, language, image, its refusal of literalness and its insistently metaphorical evocation of melodramatic states of consciousness, so operates that such a passage becomes both legible and effective.

It is certain that the discrepancy between motive and result, between indication and what is postulated on it, contributes to what Winters calls "obscurity," Wilson "ambiguity," Leavis simply "unsatisfactoriness." Yet we must also see that this very discrepancy attracted the novelist's own attention, and that it is very much a subject, sometimes the central subject, of much of

[34]F. R. Leavis, *The Great Tradition* (1948; reprint ed., New York: New York University Press, 1963), p. 11.

the late fiction. The apparent blankness of referential meaning repeatedly becomes a central issue in the drama, the unspecifiable source of its most potent extrapolated and metaphorical meanings. James comes closest to a justification of the procedure in the preface to *The Princess Casamassima*, where he considers that he may from lack of knowledge not properly have rendered Hyacinth Robinson's "subterraneous politics and occult affiliations." The justification takes the form of saying that he need not have dealt with the thing itself so much as with the obscure appearances that it put forth, for "the value I wished most to render and the effect I wished most to produce were precisely those of our not knowing, of society's not knowing, but only guessing and suspecting and trying to ignore, what 'goes on' irreconcileably, subversively, beneath the vast smug surface" (p. xxii). He must deal rather with the "gust of the hot breath" emerging from the depths. "What it all came back to was, no doubt, something like *this* wisdom—that if you haven't, for fiction, the root of the matter in you, haven't the sense of life and the penetrating imagination, you are a fool in the very presence of the revealed and assured; but that if you *are* so armed you are not really helpless, not without your resource, even before mysteries abysmal" (p. xxiii). The terms here image a process similar to that we found at work in Balzac's novels, a penetration beneath and behind the surface of things to what is "subterraneous," "occult," to "mysteries abysmal." What lies behind surface and facade in this novel is notably Balzacian: secret societies comparable to "Les Treize," the mysterious superman Hoffendahl, a shadowy struggle in the depths. James's decision not to treat the content of the depths directly, to present it only through the charge it gives to the surface, the way it is reflected in the individual consciousness, determines the metaphorical quality of the novel's melodrama. Hyacinth, the princess, Paul Muniment, even Mr. Vetch, do not live out their lives simply on the plane of interpersonal relations. The motor of their acts and their imaginings lies in the depths; they are driven by something occult, mostly hidden even to themselves. When the content of the abyss surfaces, it is in the form of the letter from Hoffendahl to Hyacinth, taken from its first envelope and delivered, unopened, by Schinkel, who has himself received it from an unnamed intermediary. The letter is a blank, we can never know its content directly but must piece it together from Paul Muniment's and Schinkel's deductions and from its deflected result, Hyacinth's suicide.

"Abyss" is a word that recurs with insistent frequency in James's writing and holds a particularly significant place, as we shall see, in *The Wings of the Dove*. It may be taken to stand for all the evacuated centers of meaning in his fiction that nonetheless animate lives, determine quests for meaning, and which confer on life, particularly on consciousness, the urgency and dramatics of melodrama. There are parabolic instances of these pregnant voids in some of the late tales and novellas, *The Figure in the Carpet*, for instance, and *The Jolly Corner*, perhaps most notably *The Beast in the Jungle*. John Marcher's life is determined by his feeling of a looming menace, of something appalling and grandiose that is to befall him, of a beast lurking in the jungle in wait to spring at him. The lack of specificity of the image is total: all Marcher "knows" is that it is nothing he is to do, but rather something that is to happen to him. The very indeterminacy of the thing, the beast, confers its force, gives the result that Marcher's existence is completely determined by his "waiting." His wait is joined by May Bartram, and together they warily probe the central darkness, "sound the depths": "These depths, constantly bridged over by a structure firm enough in spite of its lightness and of its occasional oscillation in the somewhat vertiginous air, invited on occasion, in the interest of their nerves, a dropping of the plummet and a measurement of the abyss" (p. 92). The "abyss" here is many layered: it is the abyss of Marcher's unspecified menace and also the abyss of the unspoken between him and May Bartram, who has begun to see that his menace is to be precisely nothingness, the sterility of his solitary egotism. The abyss is hence also the void of their relationship, the depths of which she alone has partially sounded. The sentence figures as well the very composition of the tale itself, built as a bridgelike structure over its central void, gaining meaning precisely as the fragile structure of articulation over an abyss of the unspeakable that charges language with the meanings that the characters cannot consciously read out of the void. By the end of the tale, Marcher, revisiting May Bartram's grave and perceiving in the "deeply stricken" face of a mourner at another tomb what passion could mean, at last comes to the realization that his menace, his beast, is simply nothingness itself. He has missed the possibility of passion, of May Bartram's love; "he had been the man of his time, *the* man, to whom nothing on earth was to have happened" (p. 125). This lack of event—of passion, of relationship—makes of his whole life now, not a pregnant abyss, but an empty one: "what he presently stood there gazing at was the sounded void of his life" (p. 125). It is significant that with Marcher's recognition of the void comes, not a quiet falling-away, but one of the most highly wrought melodramatic endings in all James's fiction. "He saw the Jungle of his life and saw the lurking Beast; then, while he looked, perceived it, as by a stir of the air, rise, huge and hideous, for the leap that was to settle him. His eyes darkened—it was close; and, instinctively turning, in his hallucination, to avoid it, he flung himself, face down, on the tomb" (pp. 126–27).

What elicits this lurid and impressive ending is the very void over which the story has been constructed, the final emergence into the light of what Marcher has referred to as "the lost stuff of consciousness" (p. 117). As in *The Princess Casamassima*, the abyss, fully in the manner of the Freudian unconscious, throws up its flotsam, the indices of what has been lost to consciousness, repressed, become unusable. Marcher's void figures perfectly one aspect of the moral occult, the realm from which we are cut off in quotidian existence, but which we must sound and explore to discover the animating imperatives of our ethical life. That the moral occult remains a void for Marcher suggests his illegitimate exploitation of May Bartram and his incapacity to "live" in the only sense that mattered to James, as a full "vessel of consciousness." That Marcher's void and menace are imaged as a Beast in the Jungle of course makes the relation of the moral occult to the unconscious compelling. And when there is, as here at the end, a piercing of repression—a return of the repressed—the result is the melodrama of hysteria and hallucination.

The Beast in the Jungle is one of the best examples of James's virtually epistemological explorations of the abyss, and of the relation of melodrama to this exploration. Epistemological because Marcher's efforts, misguidedly, and May Bartram's, more pertinently, are all directed toward scrutinizing a blank at the center of existence that evidently contains the key to existence if one only knew how to read its message. The tale is that fragile, threatened structure over the abyss, and the reader must drop the plummet into a central meaning which is unarticulated and which finally signifies as the very absence of meaning. *The Beast in the Jungle* in this manner demonstrates how James transcends the problem of discrepancy between motive and result, the excess of emotion in respect to its vehicle, through a thematization of the problem itself, through a metaphorical construction where the vehicle evokes a tenor that is both "meaninglessness" and the core meaning of life. The tale is analogous in structure to such works as Melville's *Moby-Dick*, Conrad's *Heart of Darkness*, Faulkner's *Absalom, Absalom!* as they have been described by James Guetti in *The Limits of Metaphor*: works which, he maintains, demonstrate ever more audacious and desperate attempts to understand and to speak of a central "darkness" that is finally inexpressible, that can only be alluded to, can never be the achieved goal or objective of the teller's tale that it claims to be.[35] Like Marlow's discovery in the heart of darkness, it is "unspeakable," and the whole narrative construction is a metaphor whose tenor is ineffable, a tenuous "as-if" structure that can never say its meaning and its goal. If Marcher, like Marlow, does at the last penetrate to the heart of darkness, he is blinded and struck dumb by "the horrors"—we are reminded of Kurtz's dying line: "The horror! The horror!"—which then are figured, as in *The Turn of the Screw*, through the overt but deflected melodrama of the story's close.

The supreme example in James's work of a similar metaphorical construction over the void that refuses any sort of conclusion is *The Sacred Fount*, a fiction so baffling that some critics have judged it a self-parody and some have simply dismissed it as trivial. Though the book is indeed impervious to

---

[35]See James Guetti, *The Limits of Metaphor* (Ithaca: Cornell University Press, 1967). See also Tzvetan Todorov's interesting treatment of the void of meaning as structuring principle in many of James's stories, in "Le Secret du récit," in *Poétique de la prose* (Paris: Seuil, 1971), pp. 151–85. The image of the abyss has also been discussed by Jean Kimball, "The Abyss and *The Wings of the Dove*," *Nineteenth-Century Fiction* 10 (March 1956), pp. 281–300, but with little attention to its nature or its status in the narrative.

explication, its mode makes perfect sense in our context. It is the most developed case of the melodrama of interpretive consciousness. As in *The Turn of the Screw*, both the perceiver and the perceptual field on which he operates are shifting and unreliable. What is evident is that the unnamed narrator must make sense of that field with the means that come to hand. He resembles the perfect *bricoleur* in the sense defined by Claude Lévi-Strauss: he does not seek beyond the boundaries of the closed system—the party at Newmarch—and the given cast of characters and properties for his explanatory arrangements.[36] He rather establishes a set of ratios based on the observable phenomena—those people who have bloomed and those who have shriveled—and seeks an overall hermeneutic principle: that of drinking at "the sacred fount," an image that is never precisely defined but has evident connotations (since what he is describing is a set of liaisons) of libidinal energy. Whether his structure and his principle are sound or not can never be discovered. When Mrs. Briss at the end tells him he is simply crazy, we, and even he, must accept this as a reasonable hypothesis. But it is no more provable than it is provable that a game of chess is crazy. The point is what can be done within the perfect closure and the rules of the game. The artist Ford Obert defines for the narrator the "honor" of playing the game right: "Resting on the *kind* of signs that the game takes account of when fairly played—resting on psychologic signs alone, it's a high application of intelligence. What's ignoble is the detective and the keyhole."[37] The narrator, we might say, has found or created the Jamesian ideal of a society that meets the high expectations of the investigatory consciousness, where signs are fully significant to the hypersensitive observer, where they speak of relations and mysteries abysmal. The melodrama of *The Sacred Fount* can hence never be overt, can never reach the plane of outer representation as it does at the end of *The Turn of the Screw* and *The Beast in the Jungle*. It is perfectly and purely the melodrama of a heightened and excited consciousness that must find the stuff of an impassioned drama in the field of observation set before it. In this case, the "lurid document" and the "baseless fabric of vision" have truly become indistinguishable; we, and perhaps even the narrator himself, have no means for discriminating between them. The high coloring of his report seems indeed to be a function of the lack of provability of his vision: the higher the melodramatic consciousness soars in flight, the more ineffable becomes its tenor, the more its vehicle must be charged, strained, portentous.

The narrator is at the end, and the reader too, left alone with what he calls a "private and splendid . . . revel—that of the exclusive king with his Wagner opera" (p. 296). While Mrs. Briss's attack on his structure unnerves him, "I could only say to myself that this was the price—the price of the secret success, the lonely liberty and the intellectual joy" (p. 296). The terms used

[36]See Claude Lévi-Strauss, *La Pensée sauvage* (Paris: Plon, 1962), p. 26 ff.
[37]Henry James, *The Sacred Fount* (1901; reprint ed., New York: Grove Press, 1953), p. 66.

figure the sheer intellectual exaltation, excitement, drama that provide a reader's pleasure in *The Sacred Fount*. It is arguable that the story "fails" because its vehicles have been so overcharged and its tenor has become so hidden and absent that the reader feels duped. Yet if he is willing to play a game of unverifiable interpretations resting on uncertain epistemological foundations, he may find an inner melodrama of disturbing implications.

These explorations in the most ambiguous and baffling of James's fictions should make us aware of the extent to which the problem of the excess of feeling in respect to situation, the discrepancy between symbol and moral sentiment, the use of melodrama, and the problem of epistemology are all related. James from the very beginning was involved in an endeavor—presenting a dramatic account of the dilemmas of moral consciousness—that forced him to work with meanings that could not be grounded and justified, either in any known system of manners or in any visible and universally accepted code of moral imperatives. Hence he had on the one hand to work with concepts, states of being, decisions that could never be wholly justified by his representations, that were ever in excess of them, and on the other hand to heighten those representations so that they might deliver the terms of his higher, occult drama. If this meant at first, in such a novel as *The American*, using the literal devices of melodrama, he evolved toward a melodrama that was more and more in and of consciousness itself: where the perceptions and reactions of consciousness charge the terms of the ordinary with a higher drama. His theatrical experience helped him to sharpen the relation between the surface tokens of his drama and the tenor they were to convey. And, as if aware of the tenuousness of his constructions, the lack of clear reference of his terms—especially the polar concepts corresponding to "good" and "evil"—he undertook, mainly in the period of the 1890s and early 1900s, to write fiction that turns around the problem of the pregnant void or abyss, sounding its depths in the effort to know what is unknowable but which nonetheless confers upon the knowable its charge of meaning and affect.

The "abyss of meaning" may stand as the most elaborated version of James's preoccupation with the content of the moral occult, which, through its very unspeakability, determines the quest for ethical meaning and the gesture in enactment of meanings perceived or postulated. The existence of the abyss shows clearly why the Jamesian mode must be metaphorical, an approach from known to unknown, and why there must be an expressionistic heightening of the vehicle in order to approach and deliver the tenor. What James refers to in his prefaces as "going behind"—"behind the face of the subject"—is a technique itself largely metaphorical, an extrapolation of the depths of motive and causes from seized and identified appearances.[38] To the extent that "going behind" is psychological, the abyss is fully analogical to unconscious

---

[38]"Going behind": Preface to *The Awkward Age*, p. xvii; "behind the face of the subject": Preface to *The Wings of the Dove*, 1:xi.

mind; and especially in the late novels, the metaphorical texture of the prose will constantly suggest surfacing of matter from the unconscious. To the extent that this "matter" is essentially ethical in its eventual reference, the abyss is correctly a moral occult. It is merely logical that the most "abysmal" meanings are figured through the trope of muteness—Eugenio's slight smile, Maggie's silent exchange with the Prince—for this provides the ultimate approach to recognitions that are so delicate, obscure, submerged that they cannot be embodied in direct statement but only gestured toward. Gesture indicates the locus and shapes the contours of the abyss. The very rhythm and punctuation of late Jamesian conversations—"he hung fire," "this fairly gave him an arrest," "she took it in," "she stared"—suggest the need to postulate meanings in the margins between words, a desire to make the reader strain toward making darkness visible.

Gender and Value in *The American*

Carolyn Porter

1

Readers of *The American* have always found fault with a plot resolution that leaves Christopher Newman unmarried and Claire de Cintré in a convent. Of course, readers of Henry James have always had to accommodate themselves to endings marked by renunciation. As a colleague of mine once put it, "I have never read a James novel that I did not want to hurl across the room when I finished." But *The American* presents a different case from that of, say, *The Portrait of a Lady* or *The Ambassadors*, where the reader's frustration and disappointment are, so to speak, fully earned. For as James himself conceded, in the preface he wrote for the heavily revised New York Edition of 1907, the plot of *The American* is genuinely flawed.

Whereas in 1877 James had defended *The American*'s realism, roundly denouncing those who demanded a "prettier ending" as people "who don't really know the world and who don't measure the merit of a novel by its correspondence to the same,"[1] in 1907 he frankly confesses that the novel's plot is an "affront to verisimilitude."[2] The Bellegardes "would positively have jumped," he remarks, at the opportunity to "haul" Newman and "his fortune into their boat" (*AN*, 36). Since the novel cannot be defended as realistic, James proceeds to treat it as a romance. He thus seizes the opportunity of having erred as a young realist to deliver a definition of the romance that has become a critical chestnut. "The balloon of experience is in fact of course tied to the earth," James says, and "the art of the romancer is, 'for the fun of it,' insidiously to cut the cable, to cut it without our detecting him" (*AN*, 33–4). James's strategy in the preface to *The American* turns out to be an instance of the romancer's art it serves to define, for by shifting his ground from the question of why he so seriously misprised the behavior of the Parisian

From *New Essays on "The American"*, ed. Martha Banta (Cambridge University Press, 1987), 99–125. Copyright © 1987 by Cambridge University Press. Reprinted by permission of the author and Cambridge University Press. This selection includes the first four parts of a five-part essay.

[1]"To William Dean Howells," March 30, 1877, in *Henry James: Letters*, ed. Leon Edel (Cambridge, Mass.: Harvard University Press, 1975), Vol. II, p. 105.

[2]R. P. Blackmur, ed., *The Art of the Novel* (New York: Scribners, 1934), p. 37. Further references are given in the text in parentheses as (*AN*).

artistocracy to the question of his faulty "invention" as a romancer, James
succeeds in cutting the cable between the given case—the novel's flawed
realism—and the case he transforms it into—an imperfectly executed romance.

Here, as throughout the prefaces, James treats the novel before him as a
stimulus to critical meditation, and the cumulative effect of this technique is
so powerful that, ever since R. P. Blackmur placed the prefaces in one
volume, entitled *The Art of the Novel*, their local relevance as prefaces has
justifiably taken second place to their manifold richness as a compendium of
Jamesian critical theory. Yet the preface to *The American* is worth our
attention *as* a preface because of the extent to which it both represses and
reveals the actual sources of the novel's unsatisfactory resolution.

It is not, as James makes clear, merely a question of his having failed to
"really know the world." That he had seriously misrepresented the "real note
of policy in forlorn aristocracies" he openly and repeatedly admits (*AN*, 36).
The more pressing question is why he had allowed himself to be so misled. In
identifying the culprit as his infatuation with his "idea," James does not for a
moment abandon that idea as itself worthwhile. Rather, he enables himself to
defend it as the seed of a romance.

The "idea" of which he was "more than commonly enamoured" was that
Christopher Newman, as representative American, should be "beguiled and
betrayed," and in particular, "that he should suffer at the hands of persons
pretending to represent the highest possible civilization" (*AN*, 21, 22). What
gives this idea its attraction is that Newman, once "cruelly wronged," should
rise above the revenge he has it in his power to inflict (*AN*, 22). This "point
was of the essence," James notes, for by proving his "magnanimity," Newman
would prove to be the moral superior of the Bellegardes, exposing as false
their pretension "to represent the highest civilization" (*AN*, 22). In short, the
charm of James's idea lies in its constitutive irony—that it is finally the
Bellegardes, not Newman, who will prove commercial.

James's ardent devotion to this idea in the preface is not, like a good deal
else we find there, a retrospective enthusiasm. In a letter he wrote to William
Dean Howells in 1876, James describes the idea in the same terms: "My
subject was: an American letting the insolent foreigner go, out of his good
nature, after the insolent foreigner had wronged him and he had held him in
his power. To show the good nature I must show the wrong and the wrong of
course is that the American is cheated out of Mme de Cintré."[3] In the preface,
James not only remains faithful to the subject's inherent charm but waxes
lyrical over his "sad envy at the free play of so much unchallenged instinct,"
the "ecstasy of . . . ignorance" that had allowed him to imagine that he was
"acutely observing—and with a blest absence of wonder at its being so easy"
(*AN*, 25, 26).

---

[3]"To William Dean Howells," October 24, 1876, in Edel, ed., *Henry James: Letters*, Vol. II, p.
70.

Thus is the cable to the question of realism cut and the question of romance set afloat. The young author of 1876 had erred in his social observation but was, after all, "lucky to have sacrificed on this particular altar," since without his ignorance, he asks himself how he "could have written *The American*" at all (*AN*, 26). For what led him astray was his devotion to his idea, which is precisely what he now alleges made the novel a romance. He had "buried [his] head in the sand and there found beatitude" (*AN*, 21).

Yet defending *The American* as a romance proves difficult, especially given the exacting demands with which James invests that genre. Nowhere is this clearer than when he resorts to arguing that Christopher Newman was conceived as a center of consciousness. Seized by this "beautiful infatuation," James insists that it is Newman's "vision, *his* conception, *his* interpretation" that provides the novel with its coherence (*AN*, 37). Having diagnosed *The American's* flawed realism as the result of one infatuation, with his idea, James now defends it as romance by appealing to another. But James knows better than this. As a center of consciousness, Christopher Newman is a child compared to the Isabel Archer of *The Portrait of a Lady*. Compared to Lambert Strether in *The Ambassadors*, Newman is a neonate. James grudgingly admits that he was "perhaps wrong" in thinking Newman up to the task, but finally rests his case on Newman's "more or less convincing image" (*AN*, 39). The palpable insecurity of this conclusion is reflected in the image that James leaves us of himself "clinging to [his] hero as to a tall, protective, good-natured elder brother in a rough place" (*AN*, 39).

In fact, James remains as unsatisfied with his defense of *The American* as the reader is with the novel's resolution. He confesses to being "stupefied" still, since if Newman is the "lighted figure," the center of consciousness, why should he be left "severely alone" during the interval following Claire de Cintré's acceptance (*AN*, 38, 37, 38)? James's answer to this question is telling. What should have filled this interval was a picture of Newman and his "intended" "beautifully together," but James could not provide this picture, given the "crushing complication" he confronted: "since Madame de Cintré was after all to 'back out' every touch in the picture of her apparent loyalty would add to her eventual shame" (*AN*, 38). If Newman is to be "cruelly wronged"—and this is what provides the very opportunity for his demonstration of moral worth—the efficient agent of this cruelty must perforce be Claire de Cintré (*AN*, 22). Yet she must remain a morally beatific creature if Newman's final loss of her is to have moral weight. Little wonder that she recedes from view at the crucial moment. The fact is, she has never been very fully on view. Thus, when James adds that "with this lady, altogether, I recognize a light plank, too light a plank, is laid for the reader over a dark 'psychological' abyss," it is hard to resist the conclusion that he is doing the same thing again, laying a "light plank" at the end of the preface over a far deeper abyss in the novel than he can afford to acknowledge (*AN*, 39).

Claire de Cintré's mystification as a character is so blatant a cover-up that it compels us to press further the question of what lies behind the veil. For if there is a gap in the novel's representation of Claire de Cintré, a failure, as James puts it, to deliver the "delicate clue" to her "conduct," it is not because of a "psychological" abyss in her character (*AN*, 39). After all, her character has hardly achieved sufficient development to harbor an abyss. Rather, it is because of the role she is assigned by both James and Newman, as the embodied form of pure, transcendent value. Her emblematic status must be protected so feverishly precisely because the order of value she represents in the novel's thematic structure has threatened to disappear altogether. She is reified as a symbol in proportion to the erosion of what she symbolizes—a noncommercial, uncontaminated, and incorruptible value.

The female object of desire had figured centrally in the English novel from Richardson's day to James's without generating this particular problem. Why, then, does it erupt here? We can begin to answer this question by focusing on James's idea, whose development requires that Claire de Cintré remain beyond Newman's reach. Claire de Cintré's underdeveloped status as a character serves as a light plank over an abyss that is inevitable, given James's germinal idea, that idea to whose charm he has remained so devoted, first and last.

To understand why this is true, we need to note an odd lapse in James's accounts of *The American*, both early and late. The *proof* of Christopher Newman's moral superiority depends upon his being "wronged," as James insists in both 1876 and 1907, but what he fails to acknowledge is that Newman's *claim* to a moral destiny originates with his repudiation of money getting, the event that initiates his entire adventure. The novel is quite clear on this analogy, even if its author seems to have ignored its implications. The disgust with which Newman throws over his desire to get revenge on Wall Street at the novel's outset is loudly echoed in the disgust with which he lets the Bellegardes go at the end. This early and initiating claim to a noncommercial set of aspirations on Newman's part is significant, since it points up the fact that Newman's desire to marry Claire de Cintré is founded on his wish to enter a realm of value that transcends the one he has so dramatically exited.

As he explains to Claire, "You think of me as a fellow who has had no idea in life but to make money and drive sharp bargains. That's a fair description of me, but it's not the whole story. A man ought to care for something else, though I don't know exactly what."[4] The humor of Newman's self-confessed ignorance as to what that "something else" should be is underwritten by a certain pathos that gives his plea force. Newman's fundamental claim to our sympathy lies in his genuine desire to spring free of his commercial history, to care for "something else" (218). But of course he does not always, or even often, speak in these terms. When he discusses the wife he desires with Mrs. Tristram, he describes his ideal as "the best article in the market" (44). Newman's abandoned career as money maker, in short, has only given way to

---

[4] Henry James, *The American*, ed. James W. Tuttleton (New York: Norton, 1978), p. 160. Further references are given in the text in parentheses.

a second, as money spender, and his quest for a wife is necessarily fueled by his millions.

Consequently, his desire is unfulfillable. For the transcendent value he seeks to possess is by definition untranslatable into money. In seeking to marry Claire de Cintré, Newman wishes to acquire the unacquirable. If he were to succeed, she would have become acquirable. She would be translated into a money value, and thus would no longer possess transcendent value. Further, if this happened, the postulated basis for Newman's moral superiority—his aspiration to care for "something else"—would have vanished.

The reason for the novel's palpably forced ending, then, is that James was more devoted to sustaining a moral order of value than to anything else. His investment in his idea depended upon its adumbration of such value, and, willy-nilly, he forced his plot to confirm that value's existence. If the ending he refused would have exposed a world in which all value has been reduced to exchange value, the ending he imposed proves Newman's moral stature by enabling him to reenact that same refusal. For if Newman exposed the Bellegardes' secret to the world, he would in effect be blurting out the very discovery his dream of value forces him to repress—that there is no value except cash value, even at the heart of the "highest civilization."

A similar economy informs the preface, where James takes such pains to redeem the concept of value originally invested in his idea. By defining that idea as essentially, "charmingly—romantic," James's preface struggles to force *The American* into the mold of the romance, and thereby reenacts the struggle conducted in the novel, where James had to force social reality into the mold of his idea (*AN*, 25). His resort to treating Christopher Newman as a center of consciousness in the preface is not unlike his resort to gothic melodrama at the end of the novel; both resolutions are highly improbable and both serve the same purpose—the preservation of what James will call in a later preface "hard latent *value*" (*AN*, 120). The James of the prefaces has come to regard such value as dependent upon the imagination, the "beautiful circuit and subterfuge of our thought and our desire" to whose representation he commits the romance as a genre (*AN*, 32). But what had driven James finally to ground moral value in the artist's imagination is already apparent in *The American*, where the social ground of such value threatens to disappear.

That threat arises, ironically, because of the extent to which social reality *is* represented perceptively in *The American*. Madame de Bellegarde's commercial "audacity" is fully documented, only to be covered up by the claim, as Mrs. Tristram puts it, that the Bellegardes are "really aristocratic" and have "given [Newman] up for an idea" (152, 221). In 1876, James had believed that moral value of some sort inhered in the class distinctions of European aristocracy. As he told Howells at the time, "We are each the product of circumstances and there are stone walls which fatally divide us. I have written my story from Newman's side of the wall, and I understand so well how Mme de Cintré couldn't scramble over from her side!" This sums up the case being made by the young realist, who has argued "very materially" that if they married, Newman and Claire would have had no place to live. She couldn't have lived in New York, James insists, and once married to Newman, she couldn't have remained in France, so déclassé would her marriage make her.[5] James's insistence upon the "stone walls" dividing Claire and Newman is perfectly sincere, but the novel itself portrays a society in which the walls are crumbling, eroded by the force of money.

In short, James was more of a realist than he credits himself with being in the preface, and that was the problem. For he had to thwart, throughout the novel, the force of a social observation whose representation reveals cash value swallowing moral value at every step. James's idea committed him to maintaining difference, but the novel keeps undermining it because money dissolves difference. We can now see more clearly why Claire de Cintré is mystified as a character, for the central difference to be preserved in *The American* is not only that between America and Europe but also that between two kinds of women.

2

In "The Metropolis and Mental Life" (1903), Georg Simmel, the early-twentieth-century German sociologist, remarks, "Money is concerned only with what is common to all: it asks for the exchange value, it reduces all quality and individuality to the question: How much?"[6] Notoriously, the first word spoken by Christopher Newman in *The American*, and "the single word which constituted the strength of his French vocabulary" is "Combien?" (19). Simmel's perspective on the implications of this question acquires more pertinence when we recall the situation that provokes it. In the novel's opening scene, Newman is negotiating the purchase of a picture in the Louvre.

Much as the young James had described himself in one of his letters to the *New York Tribune*, "lounging upon an ottoman" at the exhibition of two art collections about to be sold in the Parisian "art market," Christopher Newman is introduced to us as "reclining at his ease" on a "commodious ottoman" in the Louvre, contemplating the purchase of a painting. In his *Tribune* letter, James calls attention to the difference between buying and looking when he expresses his envy at the "meditative rattle of coin in the side-pockets of amateurs not compelled, like most newspaper correspondents, to be purely platonic."[7] But his representation of Newman buying a picture in the Louvre

[5]"To William Dean Howells," March 30, 1877, in Edel, ed., *Henry James: Letters*, Vol. II, p. 105.
[6]*The Sociology of Georg Simmel*, ed. Kurt H. Wolff (Glencoe, Ill: Free Press, 1950), p. 411.
[7]*Henry James: Parisian Sketches*, ed. Leon Edel and Ilse Dusoir Lind (New York: Collier, 1961), p. 93.

blurs that distinction. The difference between looking and purchasing will be invoked humorously in the next chapter, where Tristram responds to Newman's announcement that he has "bought a picture" with the question, "Do they sell them?" (27). Yet the difference between the originals and the "copies that were going forward around them" is no sooner invoked than it is questioned (17). When Tristram remarks, "these, I suppose are originals," Newman replies, "I hope so . . . I don't want a copy of a copy" (27).

Newman's response invokes two contradictory sources of value. On the one hand, the copy derives its value from the skill with which it approximates the original, but this aesthetic order of value is internally unstable, as the history of art forgery amply demonstrates. A copy that imitates the original so successfully as to displace it on the market threatens to dilute its value *as* the original. If the original is to retain its inherent primary value, the distinction between it and all copies must be preserved. It is this threat, of a bad infinite regress, to which Newman playfully alludes when he says that he does not want a "copy of a copy." But he can afford to be playful about this threat because he harbors no genuine doubt about the originals on display. When it is a question of buying paintings, at least, Newman is content with copies. Indeed, we are told that he "often admired the copy much more than the original" (17).

When we inquire into the basis for his confidence in the originals, however, the economic order of value comes forcefully into view. For on what basis is the original's authenticity to be established, especially in the eyes of a naive American collector, save that it hangs where it does, in a museum, whose functional significance is to designate the paintings on display there as *not* for sale? In short, the painting's transcendent value as an aesthetic object depends upon its being priceless, upon its being removed from circulation in the art market and placed beyond the reach of money. The difference between an original and a copy, then, may putatively depend upon aesthetic criteria and operate within an aesthetic order of value, but this order itself, with its claim to an essential value, depends upon its distinction from an economic order of value. In short, the aesthetic value of an object is designated by the sign "not for sale."

It may be easy to tell the difference between Noémie's copy and Murillo's original, especially given how bad that copy is, but the more fundamental issue raised in James's presentation of the Louvre as the scene of a commercial transaction is that which is also suggested by the obvious envy of the "newspaper correspondent" at the Parisian art auction—the issue of whether there *is* a realm of value beyond the reach of Newman's millions, a realm that resists the power of money to erase the difference between original and copy, and thus to eradicate any order of value that is not, finally, commercial. This issue becomes the more pressing when the original and the copy in question are not paintings, but women.

Although he is at first comically obtuse to just what is being offered for sale by Noémie Nioche, Christopher Newman himself shifts the focus from paintings to women when he shifts his attention not merely from pictures to copies but from copy to copyist. Again, Simmel provides the keynote for understanding what renders difficult James's effort to mark the difference between a transcendent value and a commercial one. In *The Philosophy of Money*, Simmel remarks that "the abhorrence that modern 'good' society entertains towards the prostitute . . . declines with the increase in the price for her services," because an "exhorbitant price saves the object for sale from the degradation that would otherwise be part of the fact of being offered for sale."[8] Noémie Nioche displays in this scene a thorough understanding of the inflationary principle Simmel describes, the principle by which sufficient money can decontaminate and finally mystify prostitution. Noémie responds to Newman's "Combien?" with a price she herself regards as exorbitant. When he asks, "for a copy, isn't that a good deal?" Newman is already revealing the desire for an original that will take the form of his pursuit of Claire de Cintré, as well as his acumen as a man of business who knows what a copy should cost as compared to the original. But Noémie is also acute, insisting that her "copy has remarkable qualities; it is worth nothing less" (20).

It is symptomatic of Noémie's relatively impoverished state that even the most preposterous sum she can bring herself to name cannot inflate the value of her painting sufficiently to impress Newman. Nor is he altogether deceived. He realizes that she "had asked too much" but "bore her no grudge for doing so," since he initially thinks her honest in her high estimate of the copy's merits and since he understands her attitude as that of a good businesswoman, bargaining for the highest price possible (26). What Newman has not yet perceived, of course, is that Noémie is actually interested in selling herself rather than her picture. Indeed, the comedy of the scene as a whole is produced by the ironic gap between Noémie's blatant flirtation and Newman's remarkable misreading of it. When Noémie deposits "a rosy blotch in the middle of the Madonna's cheek" to demonstrate her capacity to finish the painting "in perfection," Newman's exclamation, "too red, too red . . . her complexion is more delicate," reveals the extent to which James is willing to broaden the joke on his hero (20). For us, in short, there is never a question about Noémie's intentions, so that the inflationary principle invoked in her sale of the copy carries over automatically to her implicit effort to sell herself. Given her own "remarkable qualities," she will not be cheap, and she makes this even clearer when she imitates a young lady of breeding in her response to Newman's request for her card. "My father will wait upon you," she says, but as her coy imitation is lost upon Newman, she has to drive it home: "Happily for you, you are an American. It's the first time I ever gave my card to a gentleman" (21).

Noémie's entire performance in this scene signals her high ambition to join

---

[8]*The Philosophy of Money* (London, 1978), p. 383.

the ranks of those courtesans whose talent for copying the habits and fashions of the upper classes provoked complaints such as the following from a contemporary Parisian journalist: "Everything brings together the demi-monde and the monde entier: everything allows us to confuse things which should not even be aware of one another's existence. . . . The nobleman's wife from the Faubourg St. Germain passes, on the staircase at Worth's, the elegant female from the Quartier Breda."[9]

If Noémie is a copy of the upper-class women whose ranks she aspires to join, Claire de Cintré is the original *par excellence.* The scene in which Newman appears before Madame de Bellegarde to offer his suit for Claire echoes the opening scene, although now the commercial offer is made in the sanctified space not of the Louvre, but of the Faubourg. Newman appeared to Noémie as a potential client, a man who might provide financial support for her rise into society in exchange for her sexual services. Now he appears to Madame de Bellegarde as a potential financial resource, one whose fortune might be large enough to buy her daughter's hand in marriage. Her response, "How rich?" echoes his opening "Combien?" Like Newman at the Louvre, Madame de Bellegarde is in the position of power here, despite the fact that, like Noémie, she is the seller, not the buyer. But then hers is a seller's market. Unlike Noémie or her copy, what Madame de Bellegarde has to sell is theoretically of inordinate value. Claire de Cintré is an original, so that the only question here is whether Newman has sufficient millions to buy the social equivalent of the "Mona Lisa."

Despite the apparent contrast between Noémie and Claire, the copy and the original, what is to keep us from seeing in Madame de Bellegarde's performance the same inflationary principle we saw at work in Noémie's bargaining with Newman? That is, is not Madame de Bellegarde exacting an exorbitant price in order to mystify and thereby deny Claire's degradation as an object for sale? There is, after all, no question that Madame de Bellegarde wishes to sell her daughter in marriage. She has already done it once, and been cheated of the fortune she expected in return. Given the lengths to which she has gone the first time, it is hardly surprising that she is even more wary and calculating than before. In allowing Newman's suit to go forward while not approving of him, she presumably intends to keep other options in view. What she does not, however, apparently bargain for is that her precious possession will retreat to a convent and thus preserve her status as undegradable, as without a price.

Madame de Bellegarde has already, however, proven a faulty judge of her daughter. From the moment Newman arrives on the scene, Claire's behavior begins to startle her. When Claire appears dressed for a ball on the same

9A. de Pontmartin, "Semaines litteraires," *La Gazette de France,* June 11, 1865, quoted in T. J. Clark, *The Painting of Modern Life: Paris in the Art of Manet and His Followers* (New York: Knopf, 1985), p. 111.

evening that Newman has come to meet her mother, the latter declares her
daughter "strange" and "audacious," and wonders aloud "what has taken
possession of my daughter?" (126–7). In deciding to marry Newman, Claire
again amazes her mother, who doubtless has assumed that her daughter's fine
breeding would preclude his success. But Claire apparently sees in Newman
the possibility of eluding the marketplace in which her mother wants to place
her. Although the clues to Claire's conduct are indeed delicate, they do
suggest that her attraction to Newman begins at the moment he claims that
"you ought to be perfectly free, and marriage will make you so" (115). In
response to this promise, Claire moves "toward . . . Newman" with "the air of
a woman who had stepped across the frontier of friendship and, looking round
her, finds the regions vast" (115). If Newman's proposal appears to Claire a
means of escaping her marketable status, her mother's blocking of that escape
leaves her little choice. In finally defying her mother, that is, Claire refuses to
be "sold again," as Mrs. Tristram puts it, but the extreme to which Claire is
driven in the effort to escape the marketplace reveals the extent to which the
assertion of transcendent value is threatened by the commercial values that
dominate Parisian society (79).

Further, it marks the extreme to which James himself was driven in his
effort to forge and sustain the distinction between commercial and transcendent values. Like the originals in the Louvre, to remain not for sale Claire
must be entombed behind the convent's high walls and iron railings. The
price of being priceless is a living death, a state in which Claire is hardly in a
position to embody anything. For what differentiates the museum from the
convent as the last refuge of undegradable and transcendent value is that the
museum at least displays its treasures, whereas the convent hides its members from view. Perhaps this is necessary, since after all the museum has
proven vulnerable, in the opening scene, to the invasion of commerce. Since
all evidence of the Carmelites' physical existence is reduced to the mere
sound of their voices, they are presumably safe.

The gothic extremity of this plot resolution testifies to the improbable
lengths to which James was driven in *The American* by the need to affirm a
locus of value untainted by money. Further, it sets in relief the question that
plot resolution serves to beg. Put most directly, that question is, on what
ground can we distinguish two women who are for sale, except by the
difference in their price?

On the one hand, plot and counterplot are designed to establish and
develop the difference between commercial and transcendent value on the
conventional basis of that between bad and good women. On the other hand,
the two plots threaten to converge. Indeed, had James suffered the marriage
between Newman and Claire to take place, that threat would come close to
being realized, on precisely the ground he takes, and inflicts such narrative
pains to avoid—that of a common, commercially determined value. For not
only would this marriage signify that Claire *had* a price, specifically the

unreported sum that Newman names to Madame de Bellegarde, but further, it would be curiously mirrored in the final alliance between Noémie and Lord Deepmere. If both women were sold, that is, the only difference between them would be their price, and even that distinction would have begun to fade, since Noémie approaches Claire's social height by raising her price to a level commensurate with that at which Claire's mother has been willing to sell her daughter.

As it is, Noémie's social rise follows from and depends upon her moral fall, but the former is so spectacular that the latter hardly matters. As Lord Deepmere explains to Newman in Hyde Park, as regards Noémie's role in Valentin's demise, "she couldn't help it, you know, and Bellegarde was only my twentieth cousin," and anyway, "she isn't known yet, and she's in such very good form" (300). Noémie does not, of course, actually rise to join the ranks of the nobility; we do not expect Lord Deepmere to marry her. But she does rise to float above class distinctions, and thereby to blur them, a dénouement that is far more disturbing than her marriage to Lord Deepmere would be. For as the Parisian journalist previously quoted reveals, it is the confusion of "things which should not even be aware of one another's existence" that produces anxiety. Noémie Nioche proves far better at copying the nobility's style and manner than she is at copying Murillo.

If, at the novel's end, she has joined Lord Deepmere and thus blurred class lines on the surface of the plot, her role in bringing about Valentin's death has blurred them at a deeper level. Noémie has not, of course, actually murdered Valentin, but then he would certainly be alive had he not become interested in her. By the same token, Madame de Bellegarde has not exactly murdered her husband, but then it is clear that had she not intervened in his medical care, he would have survived his illness. In short, if not murder, then, say, manslaughter lies behind both Noémie's rise in value on the market and Madame de Bellegarde's first sale of her daughter.

The two stories do not converge, thanks to James's strenuous efforts, but the class lines dividing the two women are obscured. Further, the major moral distinction between them—that Claire refuses to be "sold again," whereas Noémie sells herself again and again—itself begins to fade in the light of the common social condition that the novel suggests has led to both women's commodification—the decay of a patriarchal authority and protection.

3

The paternal authority of both M. Nioche and the murdered marquis has been overturned by their wives. Their daughters are thus left to fend for themselves in a social world where their fate as individuals depends upon the exchange value they can command. In Noémie's case, the lack of paternal authority is foregrounded; in Claire's, it is the lack of paternal protection. But authority and protection are fundamentally related by their dependence upon a paternal power that is absent in both cases.

When Newman asks M. Nioche whether his daughter obeys him, the latter retorts, "She can't obey, monsieur, since I don't command" (57). Married to a "bad woman" now "gone to her account," M. Nioche has undergone financial reverses that have left him a "reduced capitalist" (55). In his memory, the occasion on which he "found" his wife "out" coincides with the beginning of his financial decline (24). His "miseries" arrived in the dual form of his "dark days" and his "explosion with Madame Nioche" (57). It is therefore unclear to what extent M. Nioche's paternal impotence results from being cuckolded and to what extent from losing his money. But that he is powerless to control his daughter is clear. As he abjectly confesses, "she is stronger than I" (57). In Newman's eyes, at least, it is M. Nioche's impotence that enables Noémie to become a "little adventuress," placing herself on the market, where she proves, as Valentin recognizes, "a great one" (134).

One proof of Noémie's genius is that she turns her relationship with her father into a parody of paternal protection. He comes to fetch her each day from the Louvre and acts his own "high-toned" part in the play, but she is directing it, as Valentin sees instantly. But then he is interested in Noémie. Newman's "interest," in contrast, lies in her father (64). When Valentin bets him that M. Nioche will not prove a Virginius, Newman takes the bet, saying, "if the old man turns out a humbug, you may do what you please. I wash my hands of the matter" (136). M. Nioche does turn out a humbug, but Newman cannot altogether wash his hands of the matter, since Valentin's pursuit of Noémie turns out to place him in jeopardy. Newman's loyalty thus shifts from M. Nioche to his friend Valentin, both of whom need protection from Noémie. As Valentin tells Newman, "For the girl herself, you may be at rest. I don't know what harm she may do to me, but I certainly can't hurt her" (136). Given M. Nioche's lack of paternal power, Noémie is loosed upon the market, where it is men who need protection from her. It is worth keeping in mind that Newman proves no more capable of protecting Valentin from her than he has of protecting M. Nioche.

In the case of Madame de Cintré, the cause of paternal impotence is somewhat clearer. Not only is her father dead, but he was hastened to his grave precisely because he had prohibited his wife's sale of his daughter in marriage. Again, as in the story of M. Nioche's decline, money is identified with women, but here the relation is direct and causal. Madame de Bellegarde usurps the power of the father in order to transform her daughter into a commodity whose sale will replenish the family coffers. Left without her father's protection and obliged to obey a mercenary mother, Claire falls into the flow of exchange value. Valentin cannot save her from this fate, and Urbain is complicit in forcing it upon her. With the death of the father, the family is corrupted from within by the ambition of the mother.

Once freed by widowhood from this victimization, Claire tries to protect herself by striking a bargain with her mother, whose every command she agrees to obey save one, the command to marry again. Thus does she hope to preserve her rewon status as not for sale. But without paternal protection, she remains vulnerable. From her first appearance in the novel, if we credit Mrs. Tristram's interpretations, Claire is being harassed by her mother, who apparently regards her bargain with her daughter in the same light that she regards her word of honor to Newman—as a strategy, not a promise. In any case, Claire's continued vulnerability results less from her mother's dishonesty than from the pecuniary interest it serves. For what renders Claire's exemption from commodity status fragile is that she is too valuable *not* to be sold. Up to a point, Claire's very expensiveness serves to protect her; her mother's ambition, after all, is of a high order, and there are few men with sufficient millions even to make a bid. But when Newman proves able to meet her price and Claire consents to marry him, Madame de Bellegarde presumably considers all promises suspended and the auction again open. In the absence of her father's power to protect her, Claire is left in the same position that Noémie occupies; she must "be converted into specie" or face up to "burying herself alive" (53).

Gerda Lerner has recently argued that one of the earliest forms in which two classes of women were distinguished is expressed in Middle Assyrian Law 40, which designates who can and cannot be veiled. As Lerner decodes the law, it reveals that respectable women are those "protected by their men," whereas unrespectable women are those left "unprotected."[10] Although Lerner's interest in this law leads her analysis in a somewhat different direction, and although the society the law served is quite alien to nineteenth-century Paris, I think the distinction she identifies can shed light on James's diagnosis of Parisian society as the scene of paternal powerlessness. For that scene reveals a world in which a patriarchal nobility has been undermined by the corrosive force of capitalism. No doubt the aging marquis had been a rake, but what killed him was not his sins but his wife's greed. Valentin is also a bit of a rake, but a fine fellow nevertheless, and what kills him is, effectively, Noémie's greed. The duel he fights over her, as she puts it, "will make her fortune" (207). Noémie and Madame de Bellegarde are sellers on the market, and Claire is sold there, but all have been reduced to functions of the cash nexus, and by the same forces that have already undermined paternal power.

A major social transformation from patriarchy to capitalism has taken place beneath the surface of Parisian society as James represents it, and its consequences are most vividly expressed in the threat that transformation poses to the traditional distinction between two classes of women. When fathers command authority, they can both control and protect their daughters. Under these conditions, it is possible to mark off respectable from unrespectable

[10]"The Origin of Prostitution in Ancient Mesopotamia," *Signs* 11 (Winter 1986):253.

women, since the former *are* protected. But as traditional patriarchal power is displaced by the commercial power of the marketplace, this distinction breaks down. Women cannot be protected, but neither can they be controlled. Even the ethereal Claire repudiates her mother's authority in the end. Most significantly with respect to James's problems as a novelist, under these transformed conditions the two classes of women cannot be distinguished. It is testimony to the central role of women as the decisive form of all value in this scenario that when this distinction breaks down, the very concept of value is thrown into doubt.

At the highest level of abstraction, of course, women have always been forms of exchange value.[11] James's novel is not written at that level, of course. Rather, he has simply appropriated a set of novelistic conventions, traceable to *Clarissa* on the one hand and to *Moll Flanders* on the other, and put them into play in accord with his plot demands, but these demands force him to the edge of an abyss. In sum, when patriarchy breaks down, and with it the distinction between women under and not under male control and protection, all women are left unprotected and uncontrolled. The only distinction remaining is that between those who are for sale and those who are not, and this difference in turn begins to blur.

Thus, I propose, did James dig a hole in his path. His need to portray Newman as cruelly wronged led him to see more deeply into the corruption of French society than his idea had led him to expect. Having made his hero's moral status dependent upon his adherence to a moral value traditionally vested in women, he found himself forced to cover up the vacuum left by the absence of such value.

Accordingly, in the novel James is compelled to erect a set of defenses against the progressively unfolding revelation of an absence of value. Valentin's demonstrated honor as an ally of Newman to the bitter end is the most powerful of these defenses, since Valentin is the sole male member of the Bellegarde family who embodies a genuine moral imagination. Yet once beguiled by the charms of Noémie, Valentin is doomed by the very principles of honor that have elevated him above his family. As a stay against the confusion of values displayed around him, Valentin lacks force, to say the least. As both he and Claire point out to Newman, Valentin has nothing to do. Regarded by his elder brother and his mother as the black sheep of the family, he is in fact the last, along with Claire, of what Newman sees as the fine and noble strain in the family bloodline. His death testifies to the hollowness of his concept of honor in a world that can provide no place for its survival. Yet, like his sister, Valentin does at least function as a symbol of the moral value that ought to inhere in the "highest civilization," and his friendship with Newman

---

[11]Cf. Gayle Rubin, "The Traffic in Women: Notes on the 'Political Economy' of Sex," in *Toward an Anthropology of Women*, ed. Rayna R. Reiter (New York: Monthly Review Press, 1975), pp. 57–210.

helps to authenticate the latter's aspiration to believe in something besides money getting.

Another defense James develops against the erosion of value takes the form of lowering his sights from "honor" to "respectability." Respectability is further identified as English, rather than French, largely through its association with Mrs. Bread. As Claire's surrogate mother and Newman's surrogate partner in a rather ludicrous midnight tryst, Mrs. Bread stands in for the missing lover and refers us to a solid English culture for evidence of the familial loyalties missing in Paris.[12] As her name all too blatantly suggests, she is an arbitrary symbol of solid and unpretentious virtue.

The chief indicator of both of these characters' virtue, however, is their admiration for Newman, whose moral stature itself must provide the keystone for the arch James builds to cover the gap his novel has exposed. Seen, as the preface suggests James finally regarded him, as the ultimate defense against the disappearance of authentic value, Newman requires closer scrutiny.

4

We can begin to observe what is most curious about Newman's behavior as moral exemplar by comparing his response to Madame de Bellegarde's mistreatment of him with Valentin's response to Stanislas Kapp's "offence" (209). The two scenes follow each other in chapters 17 and 18. No doubt we heartily agree with Newman's judgment that Valentin is "too good to go and get [his] throat cut for a prostitute" (211–12). In trying to dissuade Valentin from this "wretched theatrical affair," Newman expresses himself in terms that epitomize American common sense and masculine force: "Because your great-grandfather was an ass, is that any reason why you should be? . . . I think I could manage him yet." Valentin replies, "you can't invent anything that will take the place of satisfaction for an insult" (211).

Although it is clear enough that Valentin's duel with the "sanguineous" son of a "rich brewer of Strasbourg" is a most pathetic "remnant" of the "high-tempered time" to which Valentin refers it, it is also clear, or rather proves so in the following chapter, that Newman *is* unable to "invent" anything to take the duel's place as "satisfaction for an insult" (211). If Valentin gets his "throat cut for a prostitute," he at least avenges his honor as a man. "A man," as he explains to Newman, "can't back down before a woman" (209). Yet Newman does just that. Confronted by Madame de Bellegarde's repudiation, he feels "sick, and suddenly helpless," and emerges from her house "too stunned and wounded for consecutive action" (219, 220). Although the major contrast established in these two chapters is that between Valentin's authentic honor

---

[12]Cf. William Veeder, *Henry James: The Lessons of the Master* (Chicago: University of Chicago Press, 1975), pp. 118–19.

and his family's lack of it, Newman's ineffective response to what is manifestly an insult as well as a betrayal conjures forth a secondary contrast between him and Valentin as masculine figures.

In both scenes, Newman protests "violently," but with utterly no effect (211). Furthermore, in the second, Newman himself calls attention to the fact that Claire's mother has "frightened her, . . . bullied her, . . . *hurt* her" (218). So he is not only backing down before one woman, he is failing to protect another. Newman's behavior here strikingly lacks the masculine force he has claimed to possess when he says to Valentin, "If a man hits you, hit him back; if a man libels you, haul him up" (211). Of course, Madame de Bellegarde is not a man, but the "authority" she invokes in her confrontation with Newman makes her as hard as the "stone" to which Newman compares Noémie when he insists to Valentin, "I don't call her a woman" (215, 209). His straightforward statement in chapter 17 about how to respond to mistreatment figures as part of Newman's healthy and direct, distinctively American, perspective. But it rings a bit false in retrospect, as Newman stands there vainly insisting to the Bellegardes, "A man can't be used in this fashion" (217). Clearly, he can be. Clearly, he has been.

Such an account of Newman's impotence may seem churlish and unfair, and in a sense it is. Newman has no choice, really, but to back down at this point, particularly in view of Claire's behavior. Yet it is precisely the fact that he has no choice, the fact that the plot dictates that he have none, that is noteworthy, since it is that which makes him impotent. If this is true, then his final repudiation of revenge is the more telling. Before turning to that subject, let me clarify the point at issue here.

If the Bellegardes mistreat Newman, he could readily protest that James has done the same, for Newman is not only slated for failure by his assigned task of desiring to acquire the unacquirable, he is also placed in a role that threatens to feminize him. Let me emphasize the terms "role" and "threaten," for Newman is virtually the only vigorous and robust male hero James was ever to create in a novel, a notable fact that might be explained on psychological and biographical grounds. But I am not concerned here with the nest of questions surrounding James's own sexual anxieties, rich and provocative as these have become in recent years.[13] In other words, I am concerned not with James's expressed or repressed attitudes toward sex, but with his representational use of gender. From this point of view, Newman's exceptional status as an unequivocally masculine hero may be seen as the kind of exception that proves a rule, the rule that is instituted in *The Portrait of a Lady*. For what

---

[13]The most provocative treatment of these issues is Eve Kosofsky Sedgwick's "The Beast in the Closet: James and the Writing of Homosexual Panic," in *Sex, Politics, and Science in the Nineteenth-Century Novel*, ed. Ruth Bernard Yeazell (Baltimore: Johns Hopkins University Press, 1986). A contrasting view may be found in Alfred Habegger, *Gender, Fantasy and Realism in American Literature* (New York: Columbia University Press, 1982).

led James to transform his innocent American into what he promised Howells would be a "female Newman"[14] can be inferred from examining the extent to which Newman's role in *The American*—his role as distinguished from the virtually innate masculinity with which James tries to invest him as a character—threatens to feminize him.

If we return now to the issue of Newman's final revenge, we can first observe that he more than makes up for his pathetic retreat in chapter 18. He confronts Madame de Bellegarde and her son Urbain together in the Parc Monceau and, "tingling . . . with passion," thoroughly enjoys presenting them with his evidence and torturing them with the threat of exposure (281). As if this were not enough, he is visited the next day by the ever diligent Urbain, who has summoned up in the interim more ingenuity than he had displayed the previous day in claiming that Newman's evidence is a forgery. At the close of this second interview, Newman exclaims, "Well, I ought to be satisfied now!" (288). But such satisfaction as he has gained turns to disgust when he tries to make good on his threats. Calling upon the "comical duchess," he is suddenly faced with "the folly of his errand," having "morally . . . turned a sort of somersault" (289, 291). His satisfaction, when it finally arrives, is the "strange satisfaction" that descends on him later as he stands outside of the "dumb, deaf, inanimate" walls of Claire's living tomb on the rue d'Enfer and gives her up as lost forever (305).

Thus is the necessary resolution imposed and Newman redeemed as a moral hero, but in terms that undermine his masculinity. That James feels the pressure exerted by this problem is clear from the amount of conventional satisfaction he affords Newman before he is forced into his moral somersault. In the scene in the park, Newman enjoys "all the vengeance" he wants, as he later tells Mrs. Tristram, since he is sure he has provoked fear in Madame de Bellegarde (309). Her remarkable courage in the face of such fear even provokes his respect: "You're a mighty plucky woman," he tells her. "It's a great pity you have made me your enemy. I should have been one of your greatest admirers" (285). In effect, Newman has fought a duel here and come away with his honor intact. It is only after Urbain visits him the next day that Newman's satisfaction starts to disintegrate, as James lays the ground for Newman's final repudiation of his vengeful threat. In short, the scene in the park has served to reaffirm Newman's masculinity as forcefully as possible at the last moment available to James before his hero's moral ascendance is negotiated. Once Newman turns away in moral disgust and derives his "satisfaction" from accepting loss rather than avenging insult, his masculinity is again threatened, as it had been earlier when he retreated from Madame de Bellegarde's drawing room. For no matter how absurd Valentin's duel may have been, the code of honor it represents is allied with masculinity. Indeed,

---

[14]"To William Dean Howells," October 24, 1876, in Edel, ed., *Henry James: Letters*, Vol. II, p. 72.

from the opening presentation of M. Nioche, that "exquisite image of shabby gentility," to the description of Valentin's rooms with their "faded tapestries," their "rusty arms and ancient panels and platters," their "floors muffled in the skins of beasts," the novel relentlessly associates masculinity with the forms of a patriarchal past, no matter how moth-eaten and decayed it has become. Newman's own "gilded saloons on the Boulevard Haussmann," by contrast, associate him with a modern, commercially defiled world, as does his taste for garish splendor (22, 96).

As Newman sees it, his quest for revenge has led him "very near being an ass," a condition he has already associated with Valentin's great-grandfather and the code of honor his dueling tradition maintains. It is not clear, however, how one *avoids* being an ass *without* such traditions. As he leaves the duchess's house, Newman wonders "whether, after all, he was not an ass not to have discharged his pistol" (292). Newman knows how to use a pistol; as he has told Valentin, "I wish it were pistols. . . . I could show you how to lodge a bullet" (209). Yet James does allow Newman to discharge his pistol in the scene in the park. If, as Newman believes, "words were acts," the words he utters to Madame de Bellegarde are violent ones: "Looking her straight in the eyes," he says, "You killed your husband" (281–2). Nevertheless, as the closing scene of the novel reveals, it is by no means clear that Newman has lodged any bullets. Newman admits that the Bellegardes have not been "humbled," but he insists that "they were afraid." It is Mrs. Tristram, however, who has the final word. She explains that the Bellegardes were "probably" not frightened, after all, but bluffed Newman on the basis of their "confidence" in his "good nature." When Newman "instinctively" turns to see if his evidence has burned up, he is in effect reaching again for his pistol.

James is still trying to mediate here between the demands of his plot and the threat it poses to his hero's masculinity, and this is about the best he can do. For the plot has called from the outset for Newman's victimization. "Beguiled and betrayed," as James calls him in the preface, Newman is already situated by James's idea in the traditional role of a woman seduced and betrayed, and what makes him vulnerable is precisely that "good nature" on which Mrs. Tristram claims that the Bellegardes rely. Repeatedly invoked as his identifying trait, this good nature is what makes Newman want to observe the necessary customs, to resist quarreling with Claire's family, and to dissuade Valentin from fighting the duel. When Claire tells him, "you are too good-natured," she passes judgment on his refusal to respond with any apparent vigor to Urbain's dislike of him (159). Perhaps this is one of those "delicate clues" to Claire's conduct, for here she seems actually to want Newman to fight for her.

Newman's good nature is most crudely exploited by the young marquise when she proposes that he take her into the demimonde. As she puts it, "All I ask of you is to give me your arm; you are less compromising than anyone else. I don't know why, but you are" (202). What makes Newman "less compromising than anyone else" is presumably his status as an American who stands outside the world of class gradations that Urbain's wife finds so restricting. Yet her proposition, by taking advantage of Newman's detached social position, has the effect of transforming it into that of the courtesan, whose ability to float above class distinctions and to move freely across all social boundaries is exemplified by Noémie Nioche. Of course, Noémie and the young marquise are themselves mirror images of one another. The marquise "reminded Newman of his friend, Mademoiselle Nioche; this was what that much-obstructed young lady would have liked to be" (121). If Noémie floats across class boundaries by emulating the model embodied in the marquise, the latter young woman would like to enjoy a similar freedom. Their aspirations converge. Yet this convergence cannot entirely obscure another, between Noémie and Newman, which the marquise's proposal suggests. She wishes to enjoy social freedom without "undue risk" to her reputation, but in propositioning Newman, she is not only indifferent to his but eager to exploit its lack of definition. Newman's agreement to oblige her only after his marriage serves to underscore the impropriety implicit in her request. When the planned marriage falls through, the marquise resorts to another outsider, Lord Deepmere, whose respect for propriety in any case is rather less acute than Newman's.

Newman's good nature operates as a signifier of his Americanness, but it also turns out to signify an incipiently female vulnerability. Once we begin to observe such contradictions at the center of his character, they become manifest at the representational surface of the novel as well. For example, when James introduces Newman as "a powerful specimen of an American," he associates the fact that "he never smoked" with an American image of "health and strength." It is not because Newman is careful to preserve such health that he does not smoke. On the contrary, "he had been assured . . . that cigars were excellent for the health" and was "quite capable of believing it," but his health, as James is taking pains to point out, is of that inherently robust kind "which the owner does nothing to 'keep up' " (18). As a representative American, Newman is unreflective and un-self-conscious, traits that poor Mr. Babcock finds quite distressing. Newman is in fact too much the robust and healthy American male for Mr. Babcock, but as Newman remarks in his letter to Mrs. Tristram, he is too much the "Methodist . . . old lady" for his English traveling companion (76). Meanwhile, Newman's temperateness as a nonsmoker, introduced as a mark of his American vigor, marks him off from the sexually charged male world in which Valentin and Mr. Tristram are always smoking or asking if it is allowed. Newman's gilded rooms strike Valentin as too large for smoking, whereas his own small abode is suffused with the scent of tobacco mixed with perfume. Apparently, American masculinity lacks not only force, but sexual energy as well.

The cross-signals of a threatened masculinity inscribed in such signs of Newman's Americanness register a tension built into James's treatment of his hero that is already visible in the opening description of him. Christopher Newman is seated in the Louvre, "staring at Murillo's beautiful moon-borne Madonna" after a wearying day of looking "out all the pictures to which an asterisk was affixed . . . in his Baedeker." Described as "long, lean, and muscular," Newman is carefully associated with masculine "vigour" and "toughness," traits underscored by James's remark that Newman "had often performed great physical feats which left him less jaded than his tranquil stroll through the Louvre" (17). Newman is, in short, a vigorous American male, comically afflicted with an "aesthetic headache" brought on by his atypical "exertions" as an aesthetic spectator, and yet the pose in which he comes into view for us as readers conflicts strikingly with this fact. "Reclining at his ease" on a "great circular divan," a "commodious ottoman," and in "serene possession of its softest spot," the "jaded" Newman is identified not only with "weak-kneed lovers of the fine arts" but also with what those arts themselves would have displayed as a feminine pose. A man looking at a painting of a woman, Newman is simultaneously a man posed as a woman. Indeed, one might compare his posture to that of the courtesan in Manet's "Olympia."

The vulnerability inscribed in Newman's pose is signaled by James's effort to protect him when he remarks, "We have approached him, perhaps, at a not especially favourable moment; he is by no means sitting for his portrait" (19). Yet that is precisely what Newman is doing by unwittingly obliging the "observer" James conjures forth to take his measure as American. Accordingly, James must take pains to save Newman, as male gazer and subject, from being absorbed by the pose James has placed him in, as female object of a male gaze. Thus it is stressed that Newman is persistently looking at women, whether they be pictures, copies, or copyists.

We might give many examples of other narrative sites at which Newman's masculinity is threatened, but the point I wish to make is that it cannot avoid being threatened from the moment James undertakes to develop his idea. By creating a "female Newman" in Isabel Archer, James solved not only this problem but also the more blatant one he took note of in the preface. That is, by making his American a woman, he appropriated the right gender for a protagonist doomed to victimization at the hands of a corrupt European civilization. Further, if moral value had turned up missing at the site of the novel's generic type, the female object of desire, he restored that value in a new type, the female subject of desire, and invested her with value himself, a value adumbrated by the consciousness she develops.

In order for that development to be displayed, of course, Isabel too must be "beguiled and betrayed"; her consciousness blossoms forth in the midnight vigil in chapter 42 of *The Portrait of a Lady*, where she realizes for the first time that she has been deceived. In other words, James remains committed to a moral economy of loss, but Isabel Archer's demonstration of moral superiority through loss does not threaten her gender identity. It confirms it.

Further, the moral economy of loss to which Newman's "strange satisfaction" is inadequately referred, with Isabel Archer becomes fully operational. Newman has lost Claire, but we cannot know what, exactly, that loss means, since Claire remains a virtual blank. But we know quite well what Isabel Archer has lost—her freedom. As the female subject of desire, Isabel marries an Osmond whom she regards as a kind of transcendent gentleman, a natural aristocrat with whom she will enjoy sharing a supreme freedom. But when he proves a sham, the values Isabel has mistakenly projected onto him are not thrown into doubt, nor is her dream of freedom exposed as itself without foundation. Married for her money, she has not been reduced to money, since she has been accorded an identity grounded in the "beautiful circuit and subterfuge of [her] thought and [her] desire," and her failed marriage only sets in relief what has been lost—the freedom to realize that identity in the world. In Isabel's consciousness, James finds a site on which to locate value.

Aestheticism and *The Portrait* of a Lady

Jonathan Freedman

Like *Roderick Hudson*, *The Portrait of a Lady* inscribes a historically specific response to aestheticism. It is important to remember that when James arrived in London in 1880 to finish the novel, the aesthetic craze was at its height. Aestheticism had at that very moment moved from a coterie concern to a public sensation. Oscar Wilde's notoriety had reached its apogee: having come down from Oxford some two years previously, Wilde threw himself into the round of dinner parties and soirees, enthralling many and shocking the rest with his calculated outrageousness. His fame, and that of his set, extended beyond the range of dinner-party gossip. No fewer than three plays brought aestheticism to the attention of the West End public. James Albery's inept *Where's the Cat?*, a more successful farce, *The Colonel*, by the mediocre but prolific Frank Burnand, and, of course, Gilbert and Sullivan's *Patience* all opened in 1881, the latter two to spectacular public response. And, seemingly every week, *Punch* launched satirical lampoons at the aesthetes, sometimes in prose, sometimes in cartoons, most from the hand of George Du Maurier.

Aestheticism thus formed the subject matter of the plays James was seeing, the newspapers and periodicals he was reading, and, undoubtedly, the parties he was attending. It was becoming part of his professional life as well. James met Du Maurier when the latter's lampoons of the aesthetes were at their peak of popularity, and entered into protracted negotiations with him over the illustrations to *Washington Square*. And the issue of *Macmillan's* in which *Portrait* was first published was preceded immediately by one containing a venomous attack on aestheticism, entitled "The New Renaissance; or, The Gospel of Intensity," by the conservative art critic Harry Quilter; the novel's second installment was followed immediately by William Michael Rossetti's response to Quilter's assault.

It is not surprising, therefore, that aestheticism was also becoming part of James's own novel, largely through the vehicle of the malevolent Gilbert Osmond. Indeed, the representation of Osmond is thoroughly grounded in this historical moment—far more thoroughly than critics have acknowledged.[1] Osmond resembles not only the idle American expatriate connoisseurs in Italy—of whom there were certainly enough by 1881, as James learned on his journeys there—but also the English aesthetes he was meeting, gossiping about, seeing at the theater. "What is life but an art? Pater has said that so well, somewhere" says a fatuous young American named Louis Leverett in James's 1879 story, *A Bundle of Letters;*[2] so does Gilbert Osmond, when he tells Isabel that one "ought to make one's life a work of art."[3] Osmond's taste for Japanese china and his collection of bric-a-brac place him directly in the context of the "aesthetic craze" of the late 1870's, since it was precisely these objects that the aesthetic movement prized and that its members (especially Rossetti and Whistler) collected. To nail down the association and understand its point, we need turn only to Lord Warburton's comment on what Isabel bitterly calls Osmond's "genius for upholstery"—"there is a great rage for that sort of thing now": Osmond, as collector and interior designer alike, is identified with the rage or mania whose apotheosis James was witnessing in London (588). Moreover, as Richard Ellmann has reminded us, James slyly signals the connection between Osmond and the epigone of aestheticism, Oscar Wilde: the poem Osmond sends to Isabel as part of his perverse courtship, *Rome Revisited,* subtly alludes to Wilde's *Rome Unvisited*—published, along with the rest of Wilde's poems, in 1881, to a chorus of critical catcalls.[4]

Noting the precision with which Osmond's historical provenance is established helps us appreciate what James called in *The Art of Fiction* the novel's "solidity of specification," but it does something more important as well. It helps us understand not only that Osmond is partially composed in response to the aesthetes whose careers James was witnessing as he wrote the novel, but also that he is depicted along the satirical lines James was reading in magazines or seeing at the theater. Indeed, far more than being a reflection of the "real" Oscar Wilde or any of the other "real" aesthetes James knew, the

[1]See, as examples of the sporadic discussion of this grounding, Richard Ellmann, "Henry James Among the Aesthetes," in *Proceedings of the British Academy,* vol. 69 (London: Oxford University Press, 1984), and Sara Stambaugh, "The Aesthetic Movement and *The Portrait of a Lady,*" *Nineteenth-Century Fiction* 30 (1976):495–510.

[2]Henry James, *The Complete Tales of Henry James,* ed. Leon Edel, 12 vols. (Philadelphia: Lippincott, 1962–64), 4:441.

[3]Henry James, *The Portrait of a Lady,* in *Henry James: Novels, 1881–1886,* ed. William Stafford (New York: Library of America, 1985), p. 507. Further citations in the text will refer to this edition.

[4]Ellmann, "Henry James Among the Aesthetes," p. 215. Sara Stambaugh's contention that Oscar Wilde's mother, "Speranza," served as a model for Osmond's mother strikes me as more tenuous.

representation of Osmond mirrors and mimics the satirical attacks on these
aesthetes launched largely, but not exclusively, by Du Maurier and the rest of
the *Punch* coterie. Their satirical portraits of the aesthete focused formulai-
cally, even obsessively, on a limited number of issues, and James follows out
the lines of this satire quite faithfully. As represented by the *Punch* satirists,
the aesthete is, above all else, indolent. He is languid, weary, enervated,
bored; he prefers inaction to action, passivity to assertion, all things decaying
to those robust and healthy. His very demeanor implies his enervation: the
characteristic pose of a Du Maurier aesthete is a cultivated slouch, and even
the sunflowers and pansies he holds in his hands droop. Moreover, the
aesthete believes in his own enervation. Extending Pater's praise for "*being* as
distinct from *doing*—a certain disposition of the mind" as the ground of value,
the Du Maurier aesthete establishes his moral superiority on the basis of his
perfected being and being alone, and urges others to imitate his self-satisfied
indolence. In the cartoon *Maudle on the Choice of a Profession* (1881), for
example, Du Maurier's aesthete Maudle (who had come to look, as of 1881,
exactly like Oscar Wilde) slouches in the direction of Mrs. Brown, "a Philis-
tine from the country," to drawl his appreciation of her would-be artist son.
"*Why* should he be an artist?" asks Maudle. "Well, he must be *something!*"
replies Mrs. Brown. "Why should he *be* anything?" responds Maudle. "Why
not let him remain for ever content to *exist beautifully?*"[5]

Snobbery is the basis as well of the second ground of satire: the aesthete is
a creature of inexplicable enthusiasms and eccentric tastes whose values the
aesthete and the aesthete alone is capable of identifying while asserting them
to be transcendentally valid. Chinoiserie, medieval Italian painting, peacock's
feathers, and dadoes: all are objects of delight to the aesthete and of confusion
to the other members of his world, since the qualities that make such objects
"aesthetic" are impossible to define except in vague, and thus ultimately
absurd, terms. As Bunthorne, in Gilbert's *Patience*, says:

> If you're anxious for to shine in the high aesthetic line as a man of culture
>   rare,
> You must get up all the germs of the transcendental terms, and plant them
>   everywhere.
> You must lie upon the daisies and discourse in novel phrases of your
>   complicated state of mind,
> The meaning doesn't matter if it's only idle chatter of a transcendental kind.
>   And every one will say
>   As you walk your mystic way,
> "If this young man expresses himself in terms too deep for *me*,
> Why, what a very singularly deep young man this deep young man must be!"[6]

5*Punch* 80 (Feb. 12, 1881): 62.
6W. S. Gilbert, *Plays and Poems of W. S. Gilbert* (New York: Random House, 1932), pp. 199–
200. Further citations in the text will refer to this edition.

The aesthete's exaltation of taste, in other words, represents an expression of his or her will to power; and, in the terms of the social struggle in which these characters are frequently engaged, will to social power—a means of intimidating their gullible audience with recondite enthusiasms and dilettantish predilections. Moreover, there is something unnatural or perverse in the aesthete's tastes. He or she is, literally, a commodity fetishist; libidinal energies are deflected from healthy and normal outlets onto art objects, which are thus worshipped in a perverse and unhealthy manner. The most famous example of this habit of thought is Du Maurier's famous cartoon, *The Six-Mark Teapot* (1880). There, an "aesthetic bridegroom" and an "intense bride"—the term "intense" served in these satires, as it did for Quilter, as a virtual synonym for "aesthetic"—gaze reverently at a blue china teapot: "It is quite consummate, is it not?" asks the leering male (it is difficult to tell whether he is leering at the teapot or the bride); "It is, indeed! Oh, Algernon, let us live up to it!" replies his bride, a look of rapt aesthetic devotion on her face.[7]

Finally, as far as the satirists are concerned, the aesthete is a phony, a fraud, a mountebank. Some ulterior motive was necessary to explain their bizarre affectations, their mysterious enthusiasms. Such a motive was not hard to find: self-promotion, self-advancement, and pecuniary self-aggrandizement, particularly the self-aggrandizing attempts of those who by birth or wealth or both are excluded from high society to make their way into its confines. Streyke, in *The Colonel*, worms his way into the good graces of the Forester family in order to marry off his cousin and make his own fortune; when he is unmasked, we learn that the nephew is really an apothecary's assistant, not a struggling young artist, and that "the gifted master, Lambert Streyke" himself is really an accountant turned confidence man. The applications of aestheticism's valorization of the pose to the fine art of social climbing were no less obvious to Du Maurier. Throughout this period, Du Maurier's cartoons consistently portrayed aesthetes as *parvenus* seeking to climb the social ladder. In 1880, for example, his aesthete Postlethwaite avers that "the Lily had carried me through my first season, the Primrose through my second . . . what Flower of Flowers is to carry me through my next?" In 1876, one Swellington Spiff expresses the hope that his china collection will help him meet a duke.[8] Some of the more gullible members of Du Maurier's high society may be fooled by these aesthetes, but the social act Du Maurier's cartoons inscribe is that of the public revelation of their hypocrisy and fraudulence. Indeed, in one of the final cartoons in the Du Maurier aesthete series, Maudle and Postlethwaite and their favorite hostess, the *parvenue* Mrs. Cimabue Brown, learn that their fame is due to *Punch* and *Punch* alone; the title of the cartoon, and the act it seeks to perform, is "Frustrated Social Ambition."

[7] *Punch* 79 (Oct. 30, 1880): 194.
[8] These examples were suggested to me by Leonée Ormond, *George Du Maurier* (Pittsburgh, Pa.: University of Pittsburgh Press, 1969), p. 307.

The representation of Osmond conforms to these outlines with striking accuracy. In the first description of Osmond, James not only emphasizes the artifice of his appearance—his "thin, delicate, sharply-cut face," the "beard, cut in the manner of the portraits of the sixteenth century"—but also his resemblance to one of Du Maurier's cartoon figures. The description of Osmond he offers here is strikingly similar to the thin, pale, and indolent "aesthetic bachelors" Du Maurier drew: "he had a light, lean, lazy-looking figure, and was apparently neither tall nor short" (425).[9] Throughout this scene, it is precisely Osmond's aestheticist languor that is emphasized:

"What epithet would properly describe me?" [Osmond asks Madame Merle].
"You are indolent. For me that is your worst fault."
"I am afraid it is really my best."
"You don't care," said Madame Merle, gravely.
"No; I don't think I care much. What sort of fault do you call that?" (435)

We can note here not only that Osmond's indolence places him in the aestheticist tradition, but that the rhetoric he uses to announce it does so as well. The paradoxical reversal of terms of value—"I am afraid it is really my best"—is, of course, a recognizable characteristic of Oscar Wilde's epigrammatic wit; and Osmond's paradoxical praise for his own capacities of indolence anticipates almost precisely Wilde's assertion that "to do nothing at all is the most difficult thing in the world, the most difficult and the most intellectual."[10]

The representation of Osmond shares other direct affinities with popular satires on aestheticism. Like Maudle, Osmond proclaims himself to be a creature beyond the mere exigencies of vocational choice: "I could do nothing. I had no prospects, I was poor, and I was not a man of genius . . . I was simply the most fastidious young gentleman living" (463). Osmond's career, of course, *is* his fastidiousness; he is solely a creature of taste, "the incarnation of taste," as Ralph Touchett puts it—partially the tastes of the aesthetic era, although not exclusively so; moreover, further like Du Maurier or Gilbert, the novel demystifies his fine taste, viewing it as nothing more than a form of affected pretension (547). As in Du Maurier's satires, it is only the naive characters who see Osmond's taste as rich, rare, and extraordinary. Osmond may be, as Isabel believes early in their courtship, "the man who had the best taste in the world," but those with greater sophistication think otherwise

---

[9]In the New York edition, James extends the comparison between Osmond and the aesthete by noting: "He was dressed as a man dresses who takes little other trouble about it than to have no vulgar things." *Novels and Tales of Henry James*, 26 vols. (New York: Charles Scribner's Sons, 1907–9), 3:329. This edition hereafter cited as NY.

[10]Oscar Wilde, *The Artist as Critic: Critical Writings of Oscar Wilde*, ed. Richard Ellmann (New York: Random House, 1968), pp. 233, 381. Osmond tends to the epigrammatic throughout the novel, as, for example, with the comment later in this scene: "I prefer women like books—very good and not too long" (NY, 3:331). And here, too, his aestheticist tendency to conflate his life as a connoisseur and his life as a lover is what the epigram emphasizes.

(631). Lord Warburton, as we have already seen, identifies Osmond's taste as a product of the more ephemeral sort of fashion; Ned Rosier is even more unsparing. "It's papa's taste; he has so much," Pansy tells him; "he had a good deal, Rosier thought; but some of it was bad" (574). As indeed it is: when Rosier walks his way through Osmond's collection, he notes for us, through the delicate modulations of the *style indirect libre*, the aesthetic gaucherie represented by the "big cold Empire clock" in Gilbert's living room, the diminished imagination registered by his collection of miniatures (574). As the novel progresses, Osmond's taste becomes progressively, even incrementally, diminished. When the reader first encounters him, Osmond is sketching the Alps and expressing quiet contentment over his "discovering . . . a sketch by Coreggio on a panel daubed over by some inspired idiot"; by the end of the novel, having been endowed with the greatest possible acquisitive scope by Isabel's wealth, he realizes the requirements of his imagination by collecting miniatures and sketching a gold coin (463). Osmond is finally attacked by the novel on the same ground on which Oscar Wilde was attacked by his critics: he is nothing more than an "aesthetic sham," or, in Ralph's words, a "sterile dilettante" (547).

More than the critique of his taste links Osmond to the satirical portraits of the aesthetes. He, like them, is finally portrayed by the novel as being nothing more than a social climber, a parvenu—even an American!—who seeks to use his aesthetic sensibilities, particularly as manifested in his choice of a wife, to mount the social ladder. Like Du Maurier's aesthetes, his stance of fastidious disdain for the social milieu is finally revealed to be only a highly developed form of hypocrisy. Ralph Touchett puts the revelation of Gilbert's worldliness for us most eloquently when, late in the novel, he realizes that

> under the guise of caring only for intrinsic values, Osmond lived exclusively for the world. Far from being its master, as he pretended to be, he was its very humble servant, and the degree of its attention was his only measure of success. He lived with his eye on it, from morning till night, and the world was so stupid it never suspected the trick. Everything he did was *pose*—*pose* so deeply calculated that if one were not on the lookout one mistook it for impulse. Ralph had never met a man who lived so much in the land of calculation. His tastes, his studies, his accomplishments, his collections, were all for a purpose. His life on his hill-top in Florence had been a *pose* of years. His solitude, his ennui, his love for his daughter, his good manners, his bad manners, were so many features of a mental image constantly present to him as a model of impertinence and mystification. His ambition was not to please the world, but to please himself by exciting the world's curiosity and then declining to satisfy it. It made him feel great to play the world a trick. (597–98)

Indeed, Ralph's critique repeats precisely the terms of denigration employed by the popular satirists of aestheticism. For them, too, the aesthete's bizarre "tastes, his studies, his accomplishments, his collections" serve only a "social purpose." Gilbert's Bunthorne, whose "medievalism's affectation / Born of a morbid love of admiration" (199), or the Du Maurier aesthetes who attempt to crash high society by means of their aesthetic refinement are all shown to possess the combination of indifference and obsessive consideration for the social sphere Osmond displays. "What is it to be an Aesthete?" asked Frederic Harrison, who then proceeds to give a virtual paraphrase of Ralph's condemnation of Osmond. "Is it not to air one's zeal for Art, not out of genuine love of beauty, but out of fashion and love of display, in order to be like our neighbours or to be unlike our neighbours, in the wantonness of a noisy life and a full pocket?"[11] Gilbert and Du Maurier and Harrison would all agree that the most galling feature of the aesthete was the curious admixture of "impertinence and mystification" Ralph defines as the essence of Osmondism. All join Ralph and, by extension, James, in the satirical rejection of the aesthete, in his expulsion from the social and moral community he seeks to join.

I don't mean to stress the satirized side of Osmond's character at the expense of its other components, particularly that aspect critics have tended to focus on: his massive egotism, his manipulative coldness—those qualities in Osmond that cause Isabel to think of him as possessing "the evil eye," the "faculty for making everything wither that he touched," the qualities that make Osmond resemble the villain of a Gothic romance (629, 628). But I also think that it is an aspect of James's representational strategy we should not ignore. That the novel also invites us to view Osmond satirically has consequences not otherwise graspable if we view him in terms of the Gothic (or even Hawthornean) romance paradigm. For it brings Osmond into a recognizably social world. Instead of asking us to view Osmond and Osmondism as representing a nearly supernatural form of evil (James's version of "motiveless malignity"), or as a psychological allegory of the causes and consequences of such evil, it invites us to understand the social dimensions of his behavior: to understand its role in the power games of the human community, to understand the ubiquity, even the banality of such games. Instead of asking us to view his character in isolation, James's satire demands that we view the links between Osmond's form of behavior and that of the other characters in the novel. The notorious ambivalence of satire, its tendency to break down precisely the moral boundaries it has sought to establish, affects this novel as well. As we are asked to view Osmond as a vehicle of malevolence, we are also led to notice the form of behavior he so spectacularly exemplifies in all the characters who surround him—even, or especially, those characters at whose expense he is satirized. In this, James uses satire for ends precisely the opposite of those for which we saw it deployed in *Roderick Hudson*. Instead of seeking to discriminate between an aesthete and those with whom he is

---

[11]Frederic Harrison, "The Aesthete," rpt. in *The Choice of Books and Other Literary Pieces* (London: Macmillan, 1886), p. 291. Harrison's representative aesthete—whom he dubs Young Osric, an obvious thrust at Wilde—is also recognizably Osmondian.

surrounded, James here uses a satirized aestheticism to complicate these relations: in this novel aestheticism is understood as being an endemic—indeed epidemic—contagion, ultimately infecting even the author himself.

We see this contagion most clearly in the novel's portrayal of Ralph Touchett. As virtually all critics of the novel have noted, there are numerous troubling similarities between Isabel's benefactor and her bane, and their common connoisseurship is at the center of them. R. P. Blackmur puts the matter with his customary suavity when he writes that "everyone tampers with Isabel, and it is hard to say whether her cousin Ralph Touchett, who had arranged the bequest, or the Prince, Gilbert Osmond, who marries her because of it, tampers the more deeply."[12] The link between the two inheres in more than just their common "tampering," however: it extends to the very perceptual systems that underlie such acts. Gilbert views Isabel, as he views everyone in his narrow world, as an objet d'art, a potential "figure in his collection of choice objects" (501). Osmond's particular form of what we might call the aestheticizing vision is marked both by the distance of the contemplative observer, coolly evaluating the people he encounters with an assumed—if fraudulent—disinterestedness, and by the ruthlessness with which he seeks to make them into testimonies to his taste. Such a vision carries with it an implicit notion of both self and other. In Gilbert's form of vision, the self is understood to be a smug, observing entity, a private and self-satisfied "point of view," while all others are treated as objects of this contemplative vision, to be either appreciated or rejected but always transformed into signs of the supreme taste of the observer. Gilbert's aestheticizing vision, in other words, might also be said to be a reifying vision. Despite the nobility of his rhetoric, Osmond perceives all the others he encounters as detached, deadened objects of his purely passive perception, and seeks to make those who refuse to be so into such beautiful objects.[13] And when Ralph first meets Isabel, he first resists, and then succumbs to a similar impulse:

> If his cousin were to be nothing more than an entertainment to him, Ralph was conscious that she was an entertainment of a high order. "A character like that," he said to himself, "is the finest thing in nature. It is finer than the finest work of art—than a Greek bas-relief, than a great Titian, than a Gothic cathedral. It is very pleasant to be so well treated where one least looked for it. I had never been more blue, more bored, than for a week before she came; I had never expected less that something agreeable would happen. Suddenly, I receive a Titian, by the post, to hang on my wall—a Greek bas-relief to stick over my chimney piece. The key of a beautiful edifice is thrust into my hand, and I am told to walk in and admire." (254)

[12]R. P. Blackmur, "*The Portrait of a Lady*," in *Studies in Henry James*, ed. Veronica Makowksy (New York: New Directions, 1983), p. 193.
    [13]It is at this point that I need to acknowledge my greatest debt to Carolyn Porter, *Seeing and Being: The Plight of the Participant Observer in Emerson, James, Adams, and Faulkner* (Middletown, Conn.: Wesleyan University Press, 1981).

At first, Ralph sees Isabel as a character of pure "nature" who possesses a vital energy of her own, whose "play" transcends that of any work of art. Isabel transcends all the mental structures Ralph erects to define her, all the images he conjures up to describe her. But he is not able to sustain this vision of Isabel for long. Soon, he subtly but unmistakably metamorphoses her into that which he had previously claimed she transcended—a work of art. By so doing, he begins inadvertently to show Osmondian characteristics. Having defined the mystery that is Isabel as a painting or bas-relief, he attempts imaginatively to collect her. For after he has mentally transformed Isabel into a particularly beautiful but nevertheless static portrait of a lady, the next logical step is to hang her on the wall of his mental portrait gallery. To translate from the novel's metaphorical language back into the grammar of its plot: Ralph endows Isabel with a fortune (much as one would endow an art museum) in order to continue to contemplate her—to "gratif[y] my imagination" (382).

I mention these well-known passages not to inculpate Ralph, but rather to suggest how unwittingly he falls into Gilbert's aestheticizing vision. This judgment must be calibrated rather delicately, for many critics fall into the traps of wholly idealizing Ralph (as we are clearly meant to do, up to a certain point) or condemning him (as we are also meant to do, but again only up to a certain point). Neither approval nor condemnation, however, does justice to the tragic machine James creates out of the inevitability and the insidiousness of the process of aestheticization. Such acts are inevitable for Ralph because they are a cognitive necessity. It is impossible for even so subtle a consciousness as Ralph's to tolerate a phenomenon like Isabel, which remains so resolutely resistant to definition. Despite his own desire to do otherwise, Ralph is forced by the very structure of his perception to reify and then aestheticize Isabel, to treat her with the detached but appreciative vision of the discerning connoisseur. The novel clearly demonstrates the negative consequences of such an aestheticizing vision—even so generous a vision as one that compares Isabel to a Titian. Ralph thinks he can respond to Isabel as he would to a work of art, with energetic detachment and consummate disinterestedness. But he is forced to discover that this is impossible, for she is neither a painting nor a bas-relief but only an extremely naive human being—prey, like all humans, to making ill-considered decisions. Isabel challenges his disinterestedness by doing what paintings cannot: by growing and changing along the idiosyncratic lines of her own character. And—in one of the bitterest ironies of this endlessly ironic book—she will exercise this freedom by marrying the one man who attempts what Ralph only imagines: to turn her into a beautiful but static and immobile work of art.

For Isabel suffers precisely the same kind of aestheticist contagion as Ralph. She, too, shares a good many of the more problematic qualities of Osmond's aestheticism, albeit in a more benign shape, and it is precisely these qualities that cause her to fall under his control. Isabel's aestheticism is signaled by James through the application of much of the characteristic language of the British aesthetic movement to his descriptions of Isabel, particularly those early in the novel. Indeed, James runs through most of the famous, if not notorious, catchphrases of the Conclusion to *The Renaissance* in depicting her. We learn that Isabel possesses a "delicate . . . flame-like spirit"; that she responds to Lord Warburton with a "quickened consciousness"; that she enjoys a number of aesthetic "pulsations" in St. Peter's; and, late in the novel, that she muses over the "infinite vista of a multiplied life" with which she first encountered Osmond (242, 257, 485, 629). To a certain extent, James employs this language to describe the eagerness with which the young Isabel partakes of the Paterian endeavor of "drain[ing] the cup of experience," a propensity Osmond appeals to in his protracted seduction: "Go everywhere," he said at last, in a low, kind voice, "do everything; get everything out of life" (345, 508). But as in the case of Ralph, Isabel's aestheticism is more deeply ingrained, and more ultimately problematic, than it appears at first glance. Isabel possesses an aestheticizing vision of her own and, as with Ralph, this vision is understood as something of a cognitive necessity. For when Isabel first meets Osmond, her reaction to him, as was Ralph's to her, is one of utter confusion:

> His pictures, his carvings and tapestries were interesting; but after a while Isabel became conscious that the owner was more interesting still. He resembled no one she had ever seen; most of the people she knew might be divided into groups of half-a-dozen specimens. There were one or two exceptions to this; she could think, for instance, of no group that would contain her Aunt Lydia. There were other people who were, relatively speaking, original—original, as one might say, by courtesy—such as Mr. Goodwood, as her cousin Ralph, as Henrietta Stackpole, as Lord Warburton, as Madame Merle. But in essentials, when one came to look at them, these individuals belonged to types which were already present to her mind. Her mind contained no class which offered a natural place to Mr. Osmond—he was a specimen apart. (458–59)

As in the case of Ralph, Isabel's cognitive difficulties are caused by Osmond's failure to conform to any of her preexisting mental categories. But Isabel's mistakes are even more extensive. What Isabel fails to realize is that Gilbert's ambiguousness is a result of his limitations, not a sign of the subtlety or fineness of his character. She cannot see that her failure to place Osmond is utterly appropriate: that, having no positive qualities of his own, he can only be defined in terms of negation. This is how virtually every character in the book defines Gilbert. Madame Merle introduces him to Isabel in the language of negation: "No career, no name, no position, no fortune, no past, no future, no anything" (393). After meeting Osmond for the first time in Rome, Ralph identifies him to Warburton by name. "What is he besides?" Warburton asks. "Nothing at all," Ralph replies (495). Gilbert himself proposes to Isabel with a declaration that, like all of Gilbert's statements, is at once literally true and deeply false: "I have neither fortune, nor fame, nor extrinsic advantages of any kind. So I offer nothing" (509–10).

Isabel commits the error of mistaking Gilbert's passivity for mystery, his fastidiousness for subtlety, his indifference for reserve. And she responds to the mystery of his poverty in the same way as Ralph responded to that of her plentitude: by mentally transforming him into a work of art that could meet the requirements of her imagination. This process, again like the one Ralph undertakes with her, reaches a climax in a moment of mental *ekphrasis*, a moment at which she imagines Osmond as a finely drawn "picture":

> She had carried away an image from her visit to his hill-top which her subsequent knowledge of him did nothing to efface and which happened to take her fancy particularly—the image of a quiet, clever, sensitive, distinguished man, strolling on a moss-grown terrace above the sweet Val d'Arno, and holding by the hand a little girl whose sympathetic docility gave a new aspect to childhood. The picture was not brilliant, but she liked its lowness of tone, and the atmosphere of summer twilight that pervaded it. (476)

Indeed, there is even a greater portion of aestheticism in Isabel's response to her mental picture than in Ralph's to his. She explicitly adopts the attitude he unconsciously falls into, that of the connoisseur, for she stands back from her image of Osmond to nod her approval of its "lowness of tone" and the "atmosphere of summer twilight that pervaded it." Her subsequent actions extend this incipient Osmondism. Having so appreciated her own mental image of this "specimen apart," Isabel proceeds to try to add it to her own collection. Just as the greatest triumph of Gilbert's career as a collector was "discovering . . . a sketch by Coreggio on a panel daubed over by some inspired idiot," so Isabel fancies that she alone is capable of identifying the true value of the artwork that is Osmond (463). The result, needless to say, is disastrous. Her unwittingly Osmondian tendency to see Osmond as he sees himself—as a rare and fine work of art—leads to her equally unwitting Osmondian attempt to collect Osmond. By seeking to marry "the man who had the best taste in the world" for what she sees as "an indefinable beauty about him—in his situation, in his mind, in his face," Isabel finds herself transformed into a mere extension of that taste, an object for cultivated appreciation possessing "nothing of her own but her pretty appearance" (631, 632). Seeking to collect a collector, she finds herself collected.

My purpose in stressing these parallels is not merely to inculpate Isabel, but rather to suggest the universality of aestheticism in the novel. Aestheticism of one sort or another is a donnée of *The Portrait of a Lady*, a piece of perceptual equipment James issues each of his characters. In doing so, he suggests how a "sterile dilettante" like Osmond can exert so powerful a force. The plot of the novel is so constructed that Osmond's aestheticism causes Isabel's and Ralph's to rebound against them. We have seen this effect in the way that Osmond's designs on Isabel force Ralph to face the consequences of his own disingenuously disinterested vision of her; Osmond confronts Ralph with a grotesque parody of his own attempt to achieve a detached, aestheticized vision of Isabel and blatantly enacts the appropriating reification delicately implicit in Ralph's perception. We may see it even more clearly in Isabel's marriage, in which Osmond's aestheticism corresponds to her naive aestheticist propensities in just enough ways to trap her irrevocably.

Through the first two-thirds of the book, then, we witness a movement that seeks to include all characters—even (or especially) the most sensitive and richly aware characters—in a form of belief and behavior that is satirized, but not expunged, by Osmond. This movement reaches a climax at the beginning of chapter 37, when we see through the eyes of yet another aesthete, Ned Rosier, Isabel "framed in the gilded doorway . . . the picture of a gracious lady" (570). Ned sees Isabel as Ralph had unconsciously seen her and as Osmond consciously wishes to see her: a static, reified art object. But at this moment, the problematic powers of aestheticism seem to have extended even further. For by reminding us that Isabel has been converted, or has converted herself, into a person whose "function" is to "represent" her husband, James is also reminding us of the affinities between aestheticism and his own representational endeavor (597). For insofar as the novel claims to be a "portrait of a lady"—a detached, objective account of Isabel's experience—it aligns itself with the possibilities it has thoroughly criticized: with the purely disinterested aestheticizing vision of Ralph, and the ironic detachment and masked will to power of Osmond. Indeed, it would seem that Gilbert, not Ralph, would most successfully figure James's own authorial aestheticism, since Ralph's irony is qualified by deep imaginative sympathy and since his stance of disinterested observation is abandoned as early as chapter 22, and since Gilbert, not Ralph, is most intensely interested in transforming Isabel into a representation of himself.

The exploration of the problematic dimension of aestheticism reaches its climax, then, with Rosier's identification of Isabel as a portrait of a lady. At this moment, it appears that all the novel's characters and even its author are somehow implicated in one form or another of Gilbert's malevolent aestheticism, just as Roderick and Rowland were in *Roderick Hudson* and just as all the characters of *The Author of Beltraffio* will be. But this same moment also initiates a countermovement. If in the first two-thirds of the novel James is interested in linking divergent characters to Osmond, in its final part, he attempts to differentiate between them and Gilbert. If the novel suggests that even the most noble, if naive, examples of the aestheticizing vision are fatally flawed, then James's alternatives are clear: either he needs to abandon or alter his fictional project entirely, or he needs to find a way to repurify the aesthetic itself, to demonstrate that perceptual and experiential responses like intense observation and the aestheticizing vision might prove redeemable, if not redemptive. And, needless to say, it is this latter path that he chooses.

We may observe the first step in this process by noting the increasing interest the novel gives to discriminating between Osmond and the other characters. The most spectacular instance of this discrimination is its portrayal of the relation between Osmond and Madame Merle. During the first two-thirds of the novel, we have been asked to note their commonality: we have witnessed their combined interest in acquiring a fortune for Gilbert and a mother for Pansy by marrying Osmond to Isabel. More important, we have encountered the view of the world that can make such plots possible. Madame Merle, like Osmond, perceives herself and all those around her as things to be arranged or manipulated, and is thus able to adjust her own appearances the better to shape the actions of others in order to achieve her ends. But in the last third of the novel we discover that the two can—indeed, must—be distinguished from each other. Gilbert is finally the only character who can fully exemplify the reified self that Madame Merle so eloquently defines. This discovery opens the way to more of the novel's ironies, for, just as Gilbert uses the implicit aestheticism of Isabel Archer against her, so he employs Madame Merle's reified vision of the self to reify Madame Merle herself.

The kinds of identifications and discriminations we are asked to make between these two characters are among the subtlest and most complicated in the novel. To cite but one example, Gilbert and Madame Merle are initially united, but ultimately distinguished, by their concern for appearances. We have seen the deep duplicity of this concern throughout the novel, for we have witnessed the ways they present Mrs. Touchett, Isabel, and society at large with artfully arranged poses: Madame Merle as disinterested friend and "the cleverest woman in the world"; Osmond as devoted father and aloof aesthete who cares nothing for the opinion of the world (759). But as soon as we understand the "horror" (as Madame Merle calls it) these facades are constructed to conceal, we are asked to distinguish between their desires (389). Gilbert's concern for propriety and love of convention are shown to be one small part of his obsessive concern for "the world" and that world's opinion of him. Madame Merle's concern, while superficially similar, is ultimately antithetical to his. Her "worship of appearances" is motivated not by her love of convention or her concern for propriety but rather by her fear of the discovery of her adulterous secret. Further, this divergence between Madame Merle and her former lover provides the grounds for the final break in their relation. For, as the Countess Gemini informs Isabel, Madame Merle's "worship of appearances" became "so intense that even Osmond himself got tired of it" (751). In other words, the very ground on which stands the relation she seeks so desperately to conceal is ultimately destroyed by the tenacity with which she is compelled to conceal it.

Just as we are asked to discriminate between the attitudes of Osmond and Madame Merle toward "the world," we are also asked to differentiate between their values and perceptions throughout the rest of the novel. We are initially inclined to grant Madame Merle a stature that is denied Osmond. For one thing, Madame Merle is ultimately distinguished from the reifying aestheticism with which she has been associated for much of the novel, and Osmond alone is left to bear its taint. This particular discrimination is suggested in a number of ways throughout the last third of *Portrait*, but one of the more important is made by Isabel herself. Late in the novel, just after her ride on the Campagna, Isabel broods over Madame Merle's role in arranging her marriage, and she remembers "the wonder" of her strong "desire" for the "event." "There were people who had the match-making passion, like the votaries of art for art," Isabel reflects, "but Madame Merle, great artist as she was, was scarcely one of these" (725). This passage, of course, reflects Isabel's increasingly bitter view of Madame Merle; after all, she has just applied "the great historical epithet of *wicked*" to her "false" friend (725). And the identification of Madame Merle as a "great artist" associates art with the sinister manipulation of others. But Isabel's observation reminds us that Madame Merle does indeed seem to be granted some of the less equivocal powers of the artist, and that her qualities are therefore to be distinguished from Osmond's sterile aestheticism. Madame Merle possesses in abundance the positive qualities James habitually associated with the artist—a rich sensibility, a subtlety, a complex and ultimately tragic capacity for deep emotion— along with the admittedly less positive side of the Jamesian artist—the ability to manipulate poses and create surfaces to achieve equivocal ends. As a result of this identification, Madame Merle's stature seems to increase. We are led to view her, along with Isabel, as someone who has been trapped and betrayed by circumstance and convention, and who has therefore been forced to employ even (especially) her most positive qualities for mere manipulation—and failed manipulation at that.

Sympathetic as the novel asks us to be toward Madame Merle, however, we also acknowledge that in the final divergence between her and Osmond it traps her in its own relentlessly ironic logic. She may transcend her own definition of the self as a mere collection of reified qualities, but Gilbert does not, and his amoral aestheticism finally punishes her in a chillingly appropriate manner. If Madame Merle, along with Gilbert, has turned Isabel into a deadened object of her will—in Isabel's own words, into "a dull, unreverenced tool"—so Madame Merle finally discovers, she too has been used by Osmond as a mere tool, to be discarded when she is no longer useful to him (759). This dimension of their relation becomes clear in their final scene together, in which a cracked cup becomes horrifically emblematic of their relations. Madame Merle's "precious object" is established as a symbol of their relation when Gilbert sunders that relation at the same moment as he discovers "a small crack" in the cup (730). By the end of the scene, when Madame Merle turns again to her own object, it takes on an even more resonant meaning: "After he had left her, Madame Merle went and lifted from the mantel-shelf the attenuated coffee-cup in which he had mentioned the existence of a crack; but she looked at it rather abstractedly. 'Have I been so vile all for nothing?' she murmured to herself" (731).

The scene is delicate and subtle, and, as many critics have noted, it adumbrates the symbolistic later James, the James of *The Golden Bowl*.[14] But it is important to observe that the scene is also savagely satiric, and that its satire here too is again cognate with that of popular satires on aestheticism. The notion of representing human relations in terms of crockery is one which, as we have seen, exercised the moral indignation of the *Punch* satirists from the time of Du Maurier's famous 1880 cartoon on the subject of living up to one's teapot. Here, too, the aesthete's propensity to reify his relations in trivializing terms is imaged by these satiric means. But the calculated whimsy of this early cartoon is replaced in James's text by an unsparing irony: the aesthete not only demonstrates his reifying vision, but also the aesthetic flaws of the object of his contemplation. In doing so, the development of James's satire and that of Du Maurier parallel each other with uncanny accuracy. On May 14, 1881, there appeared in *Punch* a mordant sketch, probably by Du Maurier, entitled *Philistia Defiant,* "in which aestheticism, assisted by a Teapot, is the cause of a division between friends."[15] In the sketch, a Mrs. Vamp invites a friend, Betsinda Grig, to her "High-Art boudoir in South Kensington," in order to appreciate, admire, adore, and ultimately "live up to" a newly acquired antique teapot, with a small crack in it. After a long speech in praise of the teapot, Betsinda replies, "with drawlingly deliberate acerbity, 'It's dreadfully cracked, and horribly ugly; if *that's* what you mean by Unutterably Utter and all the rest of it. And, upon my word, Sara, I think you must be living up—or down—to it, for you seem to get more decidedly cracked and more utterly ugly every day.' "

My point in mentioning this sketch is not to point to a "source" for James's scene, but rather to suggest how in this scene he finds his satirical energies developing along lines parallel to those of Du Maurier. Indeed, James outdoes the increasing acidulousness of Du Maurier's satire. In James's hands, a "deliberate acerbity" works to punish not only the reifying aesthete, but his reified victim as well. It is precisely Madame Merle's own reified vision of the self as a collection of things that is turned against her, for she has become to Gilbert nothing more than the appurtenance she believes the self to be. She is of no more consequence to him than an exquisite cup, to be discarded if and when flaws are discovered in it. And, to complete the irony, we realize in her moment of self-discovery, at her own "murmured" threnody to her love for Gilbert and her lament for what she has done in the name of that love, that Osmond rejects her for precisely the passionate emotion and keen intelligence she displays in her moment of horrified recognition. In short, all the qualities that make her more than a mere object are precisely those that cause Osmond to discard her as one.

[14]The best explication of it may be found in Laurence Holland, *The Expense of Vision: Essays on the Craft of Henry James* (Princeton, N. J.: Princeton University Press, 1964), p. 48.
[15]*Punch* 80 (May 14, 1881): 221.

The most important discrimination established in the last third of the novel, however, is that between Isabel and Osmond. For as Isabel grasps the flaws of her aestheticizing vision and begins to move beyond this form of apprehension, she progresses into a heightened and purified form of aestheticism—a form of aestheticism superficially similar to, but ultimately distinguishable from, the reifying aestheticism of an Osmond. It's true that Osmondian language tends to be associated with the representation of her own thought processes—as, for example, when she too rejects Madame Merle. The effect of Madame Merle's unexpectedly appearing at Pansy's convent is compared by Isabel to a "sort of reduplication"; this hint of an aestheticizing temper is carried further when Isabel sees Madame Merle's uncertainty "as distinctly as if it had been a picture on the wall" (756–57, 759). Indeed, Isabel might be said to approach Osmondism here—however justifiably—since her action in this scene, like Osmond's throughout the novel, is to withdraw, to retreat into being "silent still—leav[ing] Madame Merle in this unprecedented situation" (759). But Isabel's aestheticizing imagination leads her in a wholly different direction than does Osmond's. In this scene, her refusal directly to confront Madame Merle still grants her an essential otherness, still allows her her own scope of action—grants Madame Merle the opportunity to judge herself, to do "a kind of proud penance" (767).

What is true of Isabel's behavior in this scene is true of her perceptual apparatus as well. As her aestheticizing vision moves beyond the reifying aestheticism so thoroughly implicated in Osmondism, it progresses to a higher form of aestheticism—if "aesthetic" is understood as informed by the original sense of *aesthesis*, as a heightening or perfection of the act of perception. The most extended exercise in such heightened vision is provided in the most famous moment in the novel—the moment James claimed to have been most proud of—Isabel's silent reverie in chapter 42. That chapter is of the utmost importance for our endeavor, for it provides an example of a form of perception structurally different from that we have seen associated with Gilbert throughout the novel and in which we can implicate every other character. Isabel's visions in this scene are important because they are so intense and because they are so personal. Like Osmond's aestheticizing vision, they are fully grounded in the self, but they are ultimately antithetical to Osmond's. Her flickering visions in chapter 42 do not partake of Osmond's narcissistic attempt to force the objects in the world to serve as objects for his detached contemplation. Rather, unlike Osmond, Isabel achieves a moment of her own vision experienced in, of, and for itself; a moment of vision that is fully detached from the world of objects but that helps her to understand the nature of that world. And, I would suggest, the homology between Isabel's vision and that of Paterian *aesthesis* may be seen more clearly when we juxtapose chapter 42 with the Conclusion to *The Renaissance*. Both Pater and James privilege a special moment at which, under conditions of high intensity, "a quickened, multiplied consciousness" comes into powerful visionary being. It is quite true that there are significant dissimilarities between the circumstances under which such an intense vision may come into being and the uses to which it can be put. For James, the "quickened consciousness" is (as it is always for James) attached to high emotional drama, while for Pater such a consciousness is activated through many forms of intense experience—"great passions" including, among others, both the "ecstasy and sorrow of love" and (first among equals) "the poetic passion, the desire of beauty, the love of art for art's sake."[16] But my point here is that for both James and Pater the moment at which consciousness exercises itself in heightened vision is valuable in and of itself—is the ultimate end, the perfect end. Pater's aesthete and James's heroine both achieve a perfect moment of intense vision which, for their authors, is the highest—perhaps the only—consummation possible in a world shadowed over by death and human failure.

This valorization of *aesthesis*, of what James calls in the Preface to the novel "the mere still lucidity" of Isabel's mental vision, suggests one way that the novel recuperates a form of aestheticism (NY, 3:xxi). But it is precisely by means of this recuperation that critics have taken James to task for being an aesthete in the negative sense of the word. Here, the achievement of a form of transcendence by means of consciousness and consciousness alone would seem, at the very best, to associate James with a naive form of reification, and at the very worst to identify him as an arrogant connoisseur of consciousness. For this moment seems to define the transcendent self as fundamentally contemplative, passive, inert, to remove that self from any real contact with others, from any possibility of action, indeed, from history itself; it would thus seem to imprison Isabel in the prison house of consciousness as thoroughly as Osmond imprisons her in the Palazzo Roccanera. Isabel, Michael Gilmore writes, "chooses a freedom that is mental rather than experiential, a freedom uncontaminated by sensuous engagement with the world." James, he adds ominously, "makes a similar choice for his art."[17]

James, however, anticipates—and sidesteps—this critique. For there is another moment in the novel at which the aestheticizing vision is deployed, and to ends that are different from either those we see with Osmond or those we see in chapter 42. I am referring to the scene, a few chapters later, of Isabel's lonely ride on the Campagna. For we encounter in this passage yet another variant of the mode of perception Isabel shares with Osmond. As a tourist, as an observing traveler, Isabel would seem to fall into the detached, contemplative mode of Osmond; moreover she seems to perform the Osmondian task of aestheticizing the natural world she encounters, of responding to it as to a work of art:

16Walter Pater, *The Works of Walter Pater*, 8 vols. (London: Macmillan, 1900–1), 1: 238, 239.
17Michael Gilmore, "The Commodity World of *The Portrait of a Lady*," *New England Quarterly* 59 (1986):73.

The carriage, passing out of the walls of Rome, rolled through narrow lanes, where the wild honeysuckle had begun to tangle itself in the hedges, or waited for her in quiet places where the fields lay near, while she strolled further and further over the flower-freckled turf, or sat on a stone that had once had a use, and gazed through the veil of her personal sadness at the splendid sadness of the scene—at the dense, warm light, the far gradations and soft confusions of colour, the motionless shepherds in lonely attitudes, the hills where the cloud-shadows had the lightness of a blush. (724)

While this exercise of the aestheticizing vision may seem superficially similar to Gilbert's, it is ultimately antithetical to his vision and value system alike. Isabel may sit in Osmond's position of the detached aesthetic observer, viewing the Campagna spread out before her like a painted landscape—all motion arrested, its figures fixed in "lonely attitudes," its colors and gradations displayed in the rich muted colors of an artist's palette—but she does not seek to detach herself from that scene. For the "profound sympathy" between Isabel's perception and the objects she encounters is repeatedly suggested in this passage, often by verbal repetition or by transfer of qualities from the Campagna to Isabel's life; "the sadness of landscape" reflecting her "sadness of mood," the "lonely attitudes" of the shepherds reflecting her own sense of loneliness and betrayal. As she "rest[s] her weariness upon things that had crumbled for centuries," as she "drop[s] her secret sadness into the silence of lonely places," Isabel comes to recognize the "haunting sense of the continuity of the human lot" (723–24). Having learned from Rome, a "place where people had suffered," of the commonality of her own suffering, she rejoins the human community—not the corrupt community of Roman society that Gilbert and Madame Merle inhabit, but a more fully human community of shared suffering (724). Rather than possessing a reifying vision of landscape as irrevocably other, as alien and mute objects unconnected to human emotions and events and coldly to be appreciated as such, Isabel achieves at this moment a humanizing vision in which her individual "sadness" and the sadness of the scene connect to form an image of commonality and community, not one of alienation and superiority. If in chapter 42 Isabel moves beyond her superficial Paterian aestheticism into the more valuable mode of Paterian *aesthesis*, so here she moves beyond a superficial form of aestheticizing vision into a richer, more meaningful one: one that emphasizes her own embeddedness in historical process, her own participation in the human community—in short, the very "sensuous engagement with the world" whose absence Gilmore decries.

It is this version of the aestheticist vision that provides James with his most deeply treasured, and most arduously won, triumph. For this moment of detached yet meaningful perception provides a way out of the artistic impasse James has created for himself. Isabel's vision provides a more positive model for the stance of the detached author than does Osmond's, one that can lead to a sense of communion, not solipsism; to sympathy, not superiority. James signals this, I think, by the very abstemiousness with which he treats Isabel's dilemma at the end of the novel. If James is like Osmond in enmeshing Isabel in a plot whose goal is to aestheticize her, to transform her into a static, frozen portrait of a lady (the literary equivalent of the murderous aestheticization performed by the Duke in Browning's *My Last Duchess*), he can demonstrate himself to be a non-Osmondian author only by opening up the plot: by refusing the consolation of closure, whether comic, ironic, or tragic. It is in response to this problematic, I am suggesting, that James ends his novel with an interpretive mystery—and one of the most famous cruxes in American literature: the question of Isabel's mysteriously motivated return to Osmond. Certainly, the novel supplies by implication many reasons for this return: her loyalty to Pansy, her affirmation of convention and of social forms, her affirmation of the value of renunciation.[18] But the novel carefully refuses to choose between these various explanations. Further, it ends without giving any further indication of the success or failure of Isabel's course of action, thereby precluding any final judgment of the wisdom or folly of her choice.

It is this narrative silence that provides the final repudiation of the reifying aestheticism associated with Osmond and of the narrative problematics it initiates. James's narrative voice here may be detached, but it is hardly unsympathetic. Indeed, its failure to pass any final judgment on Isabel may be taken as an acknowledgment of James's authorial sympathy rather than as an indication of his ironic distance. For by this silence, James reminds the reader of the values that Osmond's reifying aestheticism ignores: a respect for the fundamentally mysterious otherness of human beings. The mystery with which the novel concludes indicates James's authorial acknowledgment of the otherness of others, for this gesture acknowledges Isabel's ability to transcend any one vision that tries to fix or define her—even the author's own ostensibly omniscient vision. By granting Isabel such resonant ambiguity, in other words, James endows Isabel with the powers Rossetti endows Jenny or—more relevantly—those Isabel grants Madame Merle. For the effect of this conclusion is to enable Isabel to step beyond the narrative frame within which she is enclosed, to move out of the "Portrait of a Lady"; it is—in a phrase James added to Isabel's final vision of Madame Merle in the New York edition—"like suddenly, and rather awfully, seeing a painted picture move" (NY, 4:375).

18To Gilmore, however, none of these explanations is sufficient; rather, Isabel "spurns the chance of leaving Osmond for the more rarefied liberation of 'motionlessly *seeing*'" (73). This strikes me as perhaps the least credible of possible explanations, since it ignores entirely the possibility that Isabel might be returning as an active participant in her marriage, particularly with respect to Pansy's future—an interesting omission for so strenuously moralizing a critic as Gilmore to make.

The Princess Casamassima

Lionel Trilling

I

In 1888, on the second of January, which in any year is likely to be a sad day, Henry James wrote to his friend William Dean Howells that his reputation had been dreadfully injured by his last two novels. The desire for his productions, he said, had been reduced to zero, editors no longer asked for his work, they even seemed ashamed to publish the stories they had already bought. But James was never without courage. "However, I don't despair," he wrote, "for I think I am now really in better form than I ever have been in my life and I propose yet to do many things." And then, no doubt with the irony all writers use when they dare to speak of future recognition, but also, surely, with the necessary faith, he concludes the matter: "Very likely too, some day, all my buried prose will kick off its various tombstones at once."

And so it happened. The "some day" has arrived and we have been hearing the clatter of marble as James's buried prose kicks off its monuments in a general resurrection. On all sides James is being given the serious and joyous interest he longed for in his lifetime.

One element of our interest must be the question of how some of James's prose ever came to be buried at all. It is not hard to understand why certain of James's books did not catch the contemporary fancy. But the two books on which James placed the blame for his diminishing popularity were *The Bostonians* and *The Princess Casamassima*, and of all James's novels these are the two which are most likely to make an immediate appeal to the reader of today. That they should not have delighted their contemporary public, but on the contrary should have turned it against James, makes a lively problem in the history of taste.[1]

From Lionel Trilling, *The Liberal Imagination* (New York: Viking Press, 1950), 55–71, 77–88. Copyright © 1950 by Lionel Trilling. Reprinted by permission of the Estate of Lionel Trilling. This selection omits a portion of the original on pp. 71–77.

[1]Whoever wishes to know what the courage of the artist must sometimes be could do no better than to read the British reviews of *The Bostonians* and *The Princess Casamassima*. In a single year James brought out two major works; he thought they were his best to date and expected great things of them; he was told by the reviewers that they were not really novels at all; he was scorned and sneered at and condescended to and dismissed. In adjacent columns the ephemeral novels of the day were treated with gentle respect. The American press rivaled the British in the vehemence with which it condemned *The Bostonians*, but it was more tolerant of *The Princess Casamassima*.

In the masterpieces of his late years James became a difficult writer. This is the fact and nothing is gained for James by denying it. He himself knew that these late works were difficult; he wished them to be dealt with as if they were difficult. When a young man from Texas—it was Mr. Stark Young— inquired indirectly of James how he should go about reading his novels, James did not feel that this diffidence was provincial but happily drew up lists which would lead the admirable young man from the easy to the hard. But the hostility with which *The Bostonians* and *The Princess Casamassima* were received cannot be explained by any difficulty either of manner or intention, for in these books there is none. The prose, although personally characteristic, is perfectly in the tradition of the nineteenth-century novel. It is warm, fluent, and on the whole rather less elaborate and virtuose than Dickens' prose. The motives of the characters are clear and direct—certainly they are far from the elaborate punctilio of the late masterpieces. And the charge that is sometimes made against the later work, that it exists in a social vacuum, clearly does not pertain here. In these novels James is at the point in his career at which society, in the largest and even the grossest sense, is offering itself to his mind with great force. He understands society as crowds and police, as a field of justice and injustice, reform and revolution. The social texture of his work is grainy and knotted with practicality and detail. And more: his social observation is of a kind that we must find startlingly prescient when we consider that it was made some sixty years ago.

It is just this prescience, of course, that explains the resistance of James's contemporaries. What James saw he saw truly, but it was not what the readers of his time were themselves equipped to see. That we now are able to share his vision required the passage of six decades and the events which brought them to climax. Henry James in the eighties understood what we have painfully learned from our grim glossary of wars and concentration camps, after having seen the state and human nature laid open to our horrified inspection. "But I have the imagination of disaster—and see life as ferocious and sinister": James wrote this to A. C. Benson in 1896, and what so bland a young man as Benson made of the statement, what anyone then was likely to make of it, is hard to guess. But nowadays we know that such an imagination is one of the keys to truth.

It was, then, "the imagination of disaster" that cut James off from his contemporaries and it is what recommends him to us now. We know something about the profound disturbance of the sexual life which seems to go along with hypertrophy of the will and how this excess of will seems to be a response to certain maladjustments in society and to direct itself back upon them; D. H. Lawrence taught us much about this, but Lawrence himself never attempted a more daring conjunction of the sexual and the political life than Henry James succeeds with in *The Bostonians*. We know much about misery and downtroddenness and of what happens when strong and gifted personalities are put at a hopeless disadvantage, and about the possibilities of extreme violence, and about the sense of guilt and unreality which may come to members of the upper classes and the strange complex efforts they make to find innocence and reality, and about the conflict between the claims of art and of social duty—these are among the themes which make the pattern of *The Princess Casamassima*. It is a novel which has at its very center the assumption that Europe has reached the full of its ripeness and is passing over into rottenness, that the peculiarly beautiful light it gives forth is in part the reflection of a glorious past and in part the phosphorescence of a present decay, that it may meet its end by violence and that this is not wholly unjust, although never before has the old sinful continent made so proud and pathetic an assault upon our affections.

II

The Princess Casamassima belongs to a great line of novels which runs through the nineteenth century as, one might say, the very backbone of its fiction. These novels, which are defined as a group by the character and circumstance of their heroes, include Stendhal's *The Red and the Black*, Balzac's *Père Goriot* and *Lost Illusions*, Dickens' *Great Expectations*, Flaubert's *Sentimental Education*; only a very slight extension of the defini- tion is needed to allow the inclusion of Tolstoi's *War and Peace* and Dos- toevski's *The Idiot*.

The defining hero may be known as the Young Man from the Provinces. He need not come from the provinces in literal fact, his social class may constitute his province. But a provincial birth and rearing suggest the simplicity and the high hopes he begins with—he starts with a great demand upon life and a great wonder about its complexity and promise. He may be of good family but he must be poor. He is intelligent, or at least aware, but not at all shrewd in worldly matters. He must have acquired a certain amount of education, should have learned something about life from books, although not the truth.

The hero of *The Princess Casamassima* conforms very exactly to type. The province from which Hyacinth Robinson comes is a city slum. "He sprang up at me out of the London pavement," says James in the preface to the novel in the New York Edition. In 1883, the first year of his long residence in England, James was in the habit of prowling the streets, and they yielded him the image "of some individual sensitive nature or fine mind, some small obscure creature whose education should have been almost wholly derived from them, capable of profiting by all the civilization, all the accumulation to which they testify, yet condemned to see things only from outside—in mere quickened consideration, mere wistfulness and envy and despair."

Thus equipped with poverty, pride, and intelligence, the Young Man from the Provinces stands outside life and seeks to enter. This modern hero is connected with the tales of the folk. Usually his motive is the legendary one of setting out to seek his fortune, which is what the folktale says when it means that the hero is seeking himself. He is really the third and youngest son of the woodcutter, the one to whom all our sympathies go, the gentle and misunderstood one, the bravest of all. He is likely to be in some doubt about his parentage; his father the woodcutter is not really his father. Our hero has, whether he says so or not, the common belief of children that there is some mystery about his birth; his real parents, if the truth were known, are of great and even royal estate. Julien Sorel of *The Red and the Black* is the third and youngest son of an actual woodcutter, but he is the spiritual son of Napoleon. In our day the hero of *The Great Gatsby* is not really the son of Mr. Gatz; he is said to have sprung "from his Platonic conception of himself," to be, indeed, "the son of God." And James's Hyacinth Robinson, although fostered by a poor dressmaker and a shabby fiddler, has an English lord for his real father.

It is the fate of the Young Man to move from an obscure position into one of considerable eminence in Paris or London or St. Petersburg, to touch the life of the rulers of the earth. His situation is as chancy as that of any questing knight of medieval romance. He is confronted by situations whose meanings are dark to him, in which his choice seems always decisive. He understands everything to be a "test." Parsifal at the castle of the Fisher King is not more uncertain about the right thing to do than the Young Man from the Provinces picking his perilous way through the irrationalities of the society into which he has been transported. That the Young Man be introduced into great houses and involved with large affairs is essential to his story, which must not be confused with the cognate story of the Sensitive Young Man. The provincial hero must indeed be sensitive, and in proportion to the brassiness of the world; he may even be an artist; but it is not his part merely to be puzzled and hurt; he is not the hero of *The Way of All Flesh* or *Of Human Bondage* or *Mooncalf.* Unlike the merely sensitive hero, he is concerned to know how the political and social world are run and enjoyed; he wants a share of power and pleasure and in consequence he takes real risks, often of his life. The "swarming facts" that James tells us Hyacinth is to confront are "freedom and ease, knowledge and power, money, opportunity, and satiety."

The story of the Young Man from the Provinces is thus a strange one, for it has its roots both in legend and in the very heart of the modern actuality. From it we have learned most of what we know about modern society, about class and its strange rituals, about power and influence and about money, the hard fluent fact in which modern society has its being. Yet through the massed social fact there runs the thread of legendary romance, even of downright magic. We note, for example, that it seems necessary for the novelist to deal in transformation. Some great and powerful hand must reach down into the world of seemingly chanceless routine and pick up the hero and set him down in his complex and dangerous fate. Pip meets Magwitch on the marsh; a felon-godfather Pierre Bezuhov unexpectedly inherits the fortune that permits this uncouth young man to make his tour of Russian society;

powerful unseen forces play around the proud head of Julien Sorel to make possible his astonishing upward career; Rastignac, simply by being one of the boarders at the Maison Vauquer which also shelters the great Vautrin, moves to the very center of Parisian intrigue; James Gatz rows out to a millionaire's yacht, a boy in dungarees, and becomes Jay Gatsby, an Oxford man, a military hero.

Such transformations represent, with only slight exaggeration, the literal fact that was to be observed every day. From the late years of the eighteenth century through the early years of the twentieth, the social structure of the West was peculiarly fitted—one might say designed—for changes in fortune that were magical and romantic. The upper-class ethos was strong enough to make it remarkable that a young man should cross the borders, yet weak enough to permit the crossing in exceptional cases. A shiftless boy from Geneva, a starveling and a lackey, becomes the admiration of the French aristocracy and is permitted by Europe to manipulate its assumptions in every department of life: Jean Jacques Rousseau is the father of all the Young Men from the Provinces, including the one from Corsica.

The Young Man's story represents an actuality, yet we may be sure that James took special delight in its ineluctable legendary element. James was certainly the least primitive of artists, yet he was always aware of his connection with the primitive. He set great store by the illusion of probability and verisimilitude, but he knew that he dealt always with illusion; he was proud of the devices of his magic. Like any primitive storyteller, he wished to hold the reader against his will, to *enchant*, as we say. He loved what he called "the story as story"; he delighted to work, by means of the unusual, the extravagant, the melodramatic, and the supernatural, upon what he called "the blessed faculty of wonder"; and he understood primitive story to be the root of the modern novelist's art. F. O. Matthiessen speaks of the fairytale quality of *The Wings of the Dove*; so sophisticated a work as *The Ambassadors* can be read as one of those tales in which the hero finds that nothing is what it seems and that the only guide through the world must be the goodness of his heart.

Like any great artist of story, like Shakespeare or Balzac or Dickens or Dostoevski, James crowds probability rather closer than we nowadays like. It is not that he gives us unlikely events but that he sometimes thickens the number of interesting events beyond our ordinary expectation. If this, in James or in any storyteller, leads to a straining of our sense of verisimilitude, there is always the defense to be made that the special job of literature is, as Marianne Moore puts it, the creation of "imaginary gardens with real toads in them." The reader who detects that the garden is imaginary should not be led by his discovery to a wrong view of the reality of the toads. In settling questions of reality and truth in fiction, it must be remembered that, although the novel in certain of its forms resembles the accumulative and classificatory sciences, which are the sciences most people are most at home with, in certain other of its forms the novel approximates the sciences of experiment. And an experiment is very like an imaginary garden which is laid out for the express purpose of supporting a real toad of fact. The apparatus of the researcher's bench is not nature itself but an artificial and extravagant contrivance, much like a novelist's plot, which is devised to force or foster a fact into being. This seems to have been James's own view of the part that is played in his novels by what he calls "romance." He seems to have had an analogy with experiment very clearly in mind when he tells us that romance is "experience liberated, so to speak; experience disengaged, disembroiled, disencumbered, exempt from the conditions that usually attach to it." Again and again he speaks of the contrivance of a novel in ways which will make it seem like illegitimate flummery to the reader who is committed only to the premises of the naturalistic novel, but which the intelligent scientist will understand perfectly.

Certainly *The Princess Casamassima* would seem to need some such defense as this, for it takes us, we are likely to feel, very far along the road to romance, some will think to the very point of impossibility. It asks us to accept a poor young man whose birth is darkly secret, his father being a dissipated but authentic English lord, his mother a French courtesan-seamstress who murders the father; a beautiful American-Italian princess who descends in the social scale to help "the people"; a general mingling of the very poor with persons of exalted birth; and then a dim mysterious leader of revolution, never seen by the reader, the machinations of an underground group of conspirators, an oath taken to carry out an assassination at some unspecified future day, the day arriving, the hour of the killing set, the instructions and the pistol given.

Confronted by paraphernalia like this, even those who admire the book are likely to agree with Rebecca West when, in her exuberant little study of James, she tells us that it is "able" and "meticulous" but at the same time "distraught" and "wild," that the "loveliness" in it comes from a transmutation of its "perversities"; she speaks of it as a "mad dream" and teases its vast unlikelihood, finding it one of the big jokes in literature that it was James, who so prided himself on his lack of naïveté, who should have brought back to fiction the high implausibility of the old novels which relied for their effects on dark and stormy nights, Hindu servants, mysterious strangers, and bloody swords wiped on richly embroidered handkerchiefs.

Miss West was writing in 1916, when the English naturalistic novel, with its low view of possibility, was in full pride. Our notion of political possibility was still to be changed by a small group of quarrelsome conspiratorial intellectuals taking over the control of Russia. Even a loyal Fabian at that time could consider it one of the perversities of *The Princess Casamassima* that two of its lower-class characters should say of a third that he had the potentiality of becoming Prime Minister of England; today Paul Muniment sits in the Cabinet and is on the way to Downing Street. In the thirties the book was much admired by those who read it in the light of knowledge of our own radical movements; it then used to be said that although James had dreamed up an impossible revolutionary group he had nonetheless managed to derive from it some notable insights into the temper of radicalism; these admirers grasped the toad of fact and felt that it was all the more remarkably there because the garden is so patently imaginary.

Yet an understanding of James's use of "romance"—and there is "romance" in Hyacinth's story—must not preclude our understanding of the striking literary accuracy of *The Princess Casamassima*. James himself helped to throw us off the scent when in his preface to the novel he told us that he made no research into Hyacinth's subterranean politics. He justified this by saying that "the value I wished most to render and the effect I wished most to produce were precisely those of our not knowing, of society's not knowing, but only guessing and suspecting and trying to ignore, what 'goes on' irreconcilably, subversively, beneath the vast smug surface." And he concludes the preface with the most beautifully arrogant and truest thing a novelist ever said about his craft: "What it all came back to was, no doubt, something like *this* wisdom—that if you haven't, for fiction, the root of the matter in you, haven't the sense of life and the penetrating imagination, you are a fool in the very presence of the revealed and assured; but that if you *are* so armed, you are not really helpless, not without your resource, even before mysteries abysmal." If, to learn about the radical movement of his time, James really did no more than consult his penetrating imagination—which no doubt was nourished like any other on conversation and the daily newspaper—then we must say that in no other novelist did the root of the matter go so deep and so wide. For the truth is that there is not a political event of *The Princess Casamassima*, not a detail of oath or mystery or danger, which is not confirmed by multitudinous records.

III

We are inclined to flatter our own troubles with the belief that the late nineteenth century was a peaceful time. But James knew its actual violence. England was, to be sure, rather less violent than the Continent, but the history of England in the eighties was one of profound social unrest often intensified to disorder. In March of 1886, the year in which *The Princess Casamassima* appeared in book form, James wrote to his brother William of a riot in his street, of ladies' carriages being stopped and the "occupants hustled, rifled, slapped, and kissed." He does not think that the rioters were unemployed workingmen, more likely that they were "the great army of roughs and thieves." But he says that there is "immense destitution" and that "everyone is getting poorer—from causes which, I fear, will continue." In the same year he wrote to Charles Eliot Norton that the state of the British upper class seems to be "in many ways very much the same rotten and *collapsible* one of the French aristocracy before the revolution."

James envisaged revolution, and not merely as a convenience for his fiction. But he imagined a kind of revolution with which we are no longer familiar. It was not a Marxian revolution. There is no upsurge of an angry proletariat led by a disciplined party which plans to head a new strong state. Such a revolution has its conservative aspect—it seeks to save certain elements of bourgeois culture for its own use, for example, science and the means of production and even some social agencies. The revolutionary theory of *The Princess Casamassima* has little in common with this. There is no organized mass movement; there is no disciplined party but only a strong conspiratorial center. There are no plans for taking over the state and almost no ideas about the society of the future. The conspiratorial center plans only for destruction, chiefly personal terrorism. But James is not naïvely representing a radical Graustark; he is giving a very accurate account of anarchism.

In 1872, at its meeting in The Hague, the First International voted the expulsion of the anarchists. Karl Marx had at last won his long battle with Bakunin. From that point on, "scientific socialism" was to dominate revolutionary thought. Anarchism ceased to be a main current of political theory. But anarchism continued as a force to be reckoned with, especially in the Latin countries, and it produced a revolutionary type of great courage and sometimes of appealing interest. Even in decline the theory and action of anarchism dominated the imagination of Europe.

It is not possible here to give a discriminating account of anarchism in all its aspects; to distinguish between the mutation which verges on nihilism and that which is called communist-anarchism, or between its representatives, Sergei Nechayev, who had the character of a police spy, and Kropotkin or the late Carlo Tresca, who were known for their personal sweetness; or to resolve the contradiction between the violence of its theory and action and the gentle world toward which these are directed. It will have to be enough to say that anarchism holds that the natural goodness of man is absolute and that society corrupts it, and that the guide to anarchist action is the desire to destroy society in general and not merely a particular social form.

When, therefore, Hyacinth Robinson is torn between his desire for social justice and his fear lest the civilization of Europe be destroyed, he is dealing reasonably with anarchist belief. "The unchaining of what is today called the evil passions and the destruction of what is called public order" was the consummation of Bakunin's aim which he defended by saying that "the desire for destruction is at the same time a creative desire." It was not only the state but all social forms that were to be demolished according to the doctrine of *amorphism*; any social form held the seeds of the state's rebirth and must therefore be extirpated. Intellectual disciplines were social forms like any other. At least in its early days anarchism expressed hostility toward science. Toward the arts the hostility was less, for the early leaders were often trained in the humanities and their inspiration was largely literary; in the nineties there was a strong alliance between the French artists and the anarchist groups. But in the logic of the situation art was bound to come under the anarchist fire. Art is inevitably associated with civil peace and social order and indeed with the ruling classes. Then too any large intense movement of moral-political action is likely to be jealous of art and to feel that it is in competition with the full awareness of human suffering. Bakunin on several occasions spoke of it as of no account when the cause of human happiness was considered. Lenin expressed something of the same sort when, after having listened with delight to a sonata by Beethoven, he said that he could not listen to music too often. "It affects your nerves, makes you want to say stupid, nice things, and stroke the heads of people who could create such beauty while living in this vile hell. And you mustn't stroke anyone's head— you might get your hand bitten off." And similarly the Princess of James's novel feels that her taste is but the evidence of her immoral aristocratic existence and that art is a frivolous distraction from revolution.

The nature of the radicals in *The Princess Casamassima* may, to the modern reader, seem a distortion of fact. The people who meet at the Sun and Moon to mutter their wrongs over their beer are not revolutionists and scarcely radicals; most of them are nothing more than dull malcontents. Yet they represent with complete accuracy the political development of a large part of the working class of England at the beginning of the eighties. The first great movement of English trade unionism had created an aristocracy of labor largely cut off from the mass of the workers, and the next great movement had not yet begun; the political expression of men such as met at the Sun and Moon was likely to be as fumbling as James represents it.

James has chosen the occupations of these men with great discrimination. There are no factory workers among them; at that time anarchism did not attract factory workers so much as the members of the skilled and relatively sedentary trades: tailors, shoemakers, weavers, cabinetmakers, and ornamental-metal workers. Hyacinth's craft of bookbinding was no doubt chosen because James knew something about it and because, being at once a fine and a mechanic art, it perfectly suited Hyacinth's fate, but it is to the point that bookbinders were largely drawn to anarchism.

When Paul Muniment tells Hyacinth that the club of the Sun and Moon is a "place you have always overestimated," he speaks with the authority of one who has connections more momentous. The anarchists, although of course they wished to influence the masses and could on occasion move them to concerted action, did not greatly value democratic or quasi-democratic mass organizations. Bakunin believed that "for the international organization of all Europe one hundred revolutionists, strongly and seriously bound together, are sufficient." The typical anarchist organization was hierarchical and secret. When in 1867 Bakunin drew up plans of organization, he instituted three "orders": a public group to be known as the International Alliance of Social

Democracy; then above this and not known to it the Order of National Brothers; above this and not known to it the Order of International Brothers, very few in number. James's Muniment, we may suppose, is a National Brother.

For the indoctrination of his compact body of revolutionists, Bakunin, in collaboration with the amazing Sergei Nechayev, compiled *The Revolutionary Catechism*. This vade mecum might be taken as a guidebook to *The Princess Casamassima*. It instructs the revolutionist that he may be called to live in the great world and to penetrate into any class of society: the aristocracy, the church, the army, the diplomatic corps. It tells how one goes about compromising the wealthy in order to command their wealth, just as the Princess is compromised. There are instructions on how to deal with people who, like James's Captain Sholto, are drawn to the movement by questionable motives; on how little one is to trust the women of the upper classes who may be seeking sensation or salvation—the Princess calls it reality—through revolutionary action. It is a ruthless little book: eventually Bakunin himself complains that nothing—no private letter, no wife, no daughter—is safe from the conspiratorial zeal of his co-author Nechayev.

The situation in which Hyacinth involves himself, his pledge to commit an assassination upon demand of the secret leadership, is not the extreme fancy of a cloistered novelist, but a classic anarchist situation. Anarchism could arouse mass action, as in the riots at Lyon in 1882, but typically it showed its power by acts of terror committed by courageous individuals glad to make personal war against society. Bakunin canonized for anarchism the Russian bandit Stenka Razin; Balzac's Vautrin and Stendhal's Valbayre (of *Lamiel*) are prototypes of anarchist heroes. Always ethical as well as instrumental in its theory, anarchism conceived assassination not only as a way of advertising its doctrine and weakening the enemy's morale, but also as punishment or revenge or warning. Of the many assassinations or attempts at assassination that fill the annals of the late years of the century, not all were anarchist, but those that were not were influenced by anarchist example. In 1878 there were two attempts on the life of the Kaiser, one on the King of Spain, one on the King of Italy; in 1880 another attempt on the King of Spain; in 1881 Alexander II of Russia was killed after many attempts; in 1882 the Phoenix Park murders were committed, Lord Frederick Cavendish, Secretary for Ireland, and Undersecretary Thomas Burke being killed by extreme Irish nationalists; in 1883 there were several dynamite conspiracies in Great Britain and in 1885 there was an explosion in the House of Commons; in 1883 there was an anarchist plot to blow up, all at once, the Emperor Wilhelm, the Crown Prince, Bismark, and Moltke. These are but a few of the terroristic events of which James would have been aware in the years just before he began *The Princess Casamassima*, and later years brought many more.

Anarchism never established itself very firmly in England as it did in Russia, France, and Italy. In these countries it penetrated to the upper classes. The actions of the Princess are not unique for an aristocrat of her time, nor is she fabricating when she speaks of her acquaintance with revolutionists of a kind more advanced than Hyacinth is likely to know. In Italy she would have met on terms of social equality such notable anarchists as Count Carlo Cafiero and the physician Enrico Malatesta, who was the son of a wealthy family. Kropotkin was a descendant of the Ruriks and, as the novels of James's friend Turgenev testify, extreme radicalism was not uncommon among the Russian aristocracy. In France in the eighties and still more markedly in the nineties there were artistic, intellectual, and even aristocratic groups which were closely involved with the anarchists.

The great revolutionary of *The Princess Casamassima* is Hoffendahl, whom we never see although we feel his real existence. Hoffendahl is, in the effect he has upon others, not unlike what is told of Bakunin himself in his greatest days, when he could enthrall with his passion even those who could not understand the language he spoke in. But it is possible that James also had the famous Johann Most in mind. Most figured in the London press in 1881 when he was tried because his newspaper, *Freiheit*, exulted in the assassination of the Czar. He was found guilty of libel and inciting to murder and sentenced to sixteen months at hard labor. The jury that convicted him recommended mercy on the ground that he was a foreigner and "might be suffering violent wrong." The jury was right—Most had suffered in the prisons of Germany after a bitter youth. It is not clear whether he, like James's Hoffendahl, had had occasion to stand firm under police torture, but there can be no doubt of his capacity to do so. After having served his jail sentence, he emigrated to America, and it has been said of him that terrorist activities in this country centered about him. He was implicated in the Haymarket Affair and imprisoned for having incited the assassin of President McKinley; Emma Goldman and Alexander Berkman were his disciples, and they speak of him in language such as Hyacinth uses of Hoffendahl. It is worth noting that Most was a bookbinder by trade.

In short, when we consider the solid accuracy of James's political detail at every point, we find that we must give up the notion that James could move only in the thin air of moral abstraction. A writer has said of *The Princess Casamassima* that it is "a capital example of James's impotence in matters sociological." The very opposite is so. Quite apart from its moral and aesthetic authority, *The Princess Casamassima* is a brilliantly precise representation of social actuality. . . .

V

We must not misunderstand the nature of Hyacinth's tragic fate. Hyacinth dies sacrificially, but not as a sacrificial lamb, wholly innocent; he dies as a human hero who has incurred a certain amount of guilt.

The possibility of misunderstanding Hyacinth's situation arises from our modern belief that the artist is one of the types of social innocence. Our competitive, acquisitive society ritualistically condemns what it practices— with us money gives status, yet we consider a high regard for money a debasing thing and we set a large value on disinterested activity. Hence our cult of the scientist and the physician, who are presumed to be free of the acquisitive impulses. The middle class, so far as it is liberal, admires from varying distances the motives and even the aims of revolutionists: it cannot imagine that revolutionists have anything to "gain" as the middle class itself understands gain. And although sometimes our culture says that the artist is a subversive idler, it is nowadays just as likely to say that he is to be admired for his innocence, for his activity is conceived as having no end beyond itself except possibly some benign social purpose, such as "teaching people to understand each other."

But James did not see art as, in this sense, innocent. We touch again on autobiography, for on this point there is a significant connection between James's own life and Hyacinth's.

In Chapter xxv of *A Small Boy and Others*, his first autobiographic volume, James tells how he was initiated into a knowledge of style in the Galerie d'Apollon of the Louvre. As James represents the event, the varieties of style in that gallery assailed him so intensely that their impact quite transcended aesthetic experience. For they seemed to speak to him not visually at all but in some "complicated sound" and as a "deafening chorus"; they gave him what he calls "a general sense of glory." About this sense of glory he is quite explicit. "The glory meant ever so many things at once, not only beauty and art and supreme design, but history and fame and power, the world in fine raised to the richest and noblest expression."

Hazlitt said that "the language of poetry naturally falls in with the language of power," and goes on to develop an elaborate comparison between the processes of the imagination and the processes of autocratic rule. He is not merely indulging in a flight of fancy or a fashion of speaking; no stancher radical democrat ever lived than Hazlitt and no greater lover of imaginative literature, yet he believed that poetry has an affinity with political power in its autocratic and aristocratic form and that it is not a friend of the democratic virtues. We are likely not to want to agree with Hazlitt; we prefer to speak of art as if it lived in a white bungalow with a garden, had a wife and two children, and were harmless and quiet and cooperative. But James is of Hazlitt's opinion; his first great revelation of art came as an analogy with the triumphs of the world; art spoke to him of the imperious will, with the music of an army with banners. Perhaps it is to the point that James's final act of imagination, as he lay dying, was to call his secretary and give her as his last dictation what purported to be an autobiographical memoir by Napoleon Bonaparte.

But so great an aggression must carry some retribution with it, and as James goes on with the episode of the Galerie d'Apollon, he speaks of the experience as having the effect not only of a "love-philtre" but also of a "fear-philtre." Aggression brings guilt and then fear. And James concludes the episode with the account of a nightmare in which the Galerie figures; he calls it "the most appalling and yet most admirable" nightmare of his life. He dreamed that he was defending himself from an intruder, trying to keep the door shut against a terrible invading form; then suddenly there came "the great thought that I, in my appalled state, was more appalling than the awful agent, creature or presence"; whereupon he opened the door and, surpassing the invader for "straight aggression and dire intention," pursued him down a long corridor in a great storm of lightning and thunder; the corridor was seen to be the Galerie d'Apollon. We do not have to presume very far to find the meaning in the dream, for James gives us all that we might want; he tells us that the dream was important to him, that, having experienced art as "history and fame and power," his arrogation seemed a guilty one and represented itself as great fear which he overcame by an inspiration of straight aggression and dire intention and triumphed in the very place where he had had his imperious fantasy. An admirable nightmare indeed. One needs to be a genius to counterattack nightmare; perhaps this is the definition of genius.

When James came to compose Hyacinth's momentous letter from Venice, the implications of the analogue of art with power had developed and become clearer and more objective. Hyacinth has had his experience of the glories of Europe, and when he writes to the Princess his view of human misery is matched by a view of the world "raised to the richest and noblest expression." He understands no less clearly than before "the despotisms, the cruelties, the exclusions, the monopolies and the rapacities of the past." But now he recognizes that "the fabric of civilization as we know it" is inextricably bound up with this injustice; the monuments of art and learning and taste have been reared upon coercive power. Yet never before has he had the full vision of what the human spirit can accomplish to make the world "less impracticable and life more tolerable." He finds that he is ready to fight for art—and what art suggests of glorious life—against the low and even hostile estimate which his revolutionary friends have made of it, and this involves of course some reconciliation with established coercive power.

It is easy enough, by certain assumptions, to condemn Hyacinth and even to call him names. But first we must see what his position really means and what heroism there is in it. Hyacinth recognizes what very few people wish to admit, that civilization has a price, and a high one. Civilizations differ from one another as much in what they give up as in what they acquire; but all civilizations are alike in that they renounce something for something else. We do right to protest this in any given case that comes under our notice and we do right to get as much as possible for as little as possible; but we can never get everything for nothing. Nor, indeed, do we really imagine that we can. Thus, to stay within the present context, every known theory of popular revolution gives up the vision of the world "raised to the richest and noblest expression." To achieve the ideal of widespread security, popular revolutionary theory condemns the ideal of adventurous experience. It tries to avoid doing this explicitly and it even, although seldom convincingly, denies that it does it at all. But all the instincts or necessities of radical democracy are against the superbness and arbitrariness which often mark great spirits. It is sometimes said in the interests of an ideal or abstract completeness that the choice need not be made, that security can be imagined to go with richness and nobility of expression. But we have not seen it in the past and nobody really strives to imagine it in the future. Hyacinth's choice is made under the pressure of the counterchoice made by Paul and the Princess; their "general rectification" implies a civilization from which the idea of life raised to the richest and noblest expression will quite vanish.

There have been critics who said that Hyacinth is a snob and the surrogate of James's snobbery. But if Hyacinth is a snob, he is of the company of Rabelais, Shakespeare, Scott, Dickens, Balzac, and Lawrence, men who saw the lordliness and establishment of the aristocrat and the gentleman as the proper condition for the spirit of man, and who, most of them, demanded it for themselves, as poor Hyacinth never does, for "it was not so much that he wished to enjoy as that he wished to know; his desire was not to be pampered but to be initiated." His snobbery is no other than that of John Stuart Mill when he discovered that a grand and spacious room could have so enlarging an effect upon his mind; when Hyacinth at Medley had his first experience of a great old house, he admired nothing so much as the ability of a thing to grow old without loss but rather with gain of dignity and interest; "the spectacle of long duration unassociated with some sordid infirmity or poverty was new to him; for he had lived with people among whom old age meant, for the most part, a grudged and degraded survival." Hyacinth has Yeats's awareness of the dream that a great house embodies, that here the fountain of life "overflows without ambitious pains,"

> And mounts more dizzy high the more it rains
> As though to choose whatever shape it wills
> And never stoop to a mechanical
> Or servile shape, at others' beck and call.

But no less than Yeats he has the knowledge that the rich man who builds the house and the architect and artists who plan and decorate it are "bitter and violent men" and that the great houses "but take our greatness with our violence" and our "greatness with our bitterness."[2]

By the time Hyacinth's story draws to its end, his mind is in a perfect equilibrium, not of irresolution but of awareness. His sense of the social horror of the world is not diminished by his newer sense of the glory of the world. On the contrary, just as his pledge of his life to the revolutionary cause

---

[2]"Ancestral Houses" in *Collected Poems*. The whole poem may be read as a most illuminating companion-piece to *The Princess Casamassima*.

had in effect freed him to understand human glory, so the sense of the glory quickens his response to human misery—never, indeed, is he so sensitive to the sordid life of the mass of mankind as after he has had the revelation of art. And just as he is in an equilibrium of awareness, he is also in an equilibrium of guilt. He has learned something of what may lie behind abstract ideals, the envy, the impulse to revenge and to dominance. He is the less inclined to forgive what he sees because, as we must remember, the triumph of the revolution presents itself to him as a certainty and the act of revolution as an ecstasy. There is for him as little doubt of the revolution's success as there is of the fact that his mother had murdered his father. And when he thinks of revolution, it is as a tremendous tide, a colossal force; he is tempted to surrender to it as an escape from his isolation—one would be lifted by it "higher on the sun-touched billows than one could ever be by a lonely effort of one's own." But if the revolutionary passion thus has its guilt, Hyacinth's passion for life at its richest and noblest is no less guilty. It leads him to consent to the established coercive power of the world, and this can never be innocent. One cannot "accept" the suffering of others, no matter for what ideal, no matter if one's own suffering be also accepted, without incurring guilt. It is the guilt in which every civilization is implicated.

Hyacinth's death, then, is not his way of escaping from irresolution. It is truly a sacrifice, an act of heroism. He is a hero of civilization because he dares do more than civilization does: embodying two ideals at once, he takes upon himself, in full consciousness, the guilt of each. He acknowledges both his parents. By his death he instructs us in the nature of civilized life and by his consciousness he transcends it.

VI

Suppose that truth be the expression, not of intellect, nor even, as we sometimes now think, of will, but of love. It is an outmoded idea, and yet if it has still any force at all it will carry us toward an understanding of the truth of *The Princess Casamassima*. To be sure, the legend of James does not associate him with love; indeed, it is a fact symptomatic of the condition of American letters that Sherwood Anderson, a writer who himself spoke much of love, was able to say of James that he was the novelist of "those who hate." Yet as we read *The Princess Casamassima* it is possible to ask whether any novel was ever written which, dealing with decisive moral action and ultimate issues, makes its perceptions and its judgments with so much loving-kindness.

Since James wrote, we have had an increasing number of novels which ask us to take cognizance of those whom we call the underprivileged. These novels are of course addressed to those of us who have the money and the leisure to buy books and read them and the security to assail our minds with accounts of the miseries of our fellow men; on the whole, the poor do not read about the poor. And in so far as the middle class has been satisfied and gratified by the moral implications of most of these books, it is not likely to admire Henry James's treatment of the poor. For James represents the poor as if they had dignity and intelligence in the same degree as people of the reading class. More, he assumes this and feels no need to insist that it is so. This is a grace of spirit that we are so little likely to understand that we may resent it. Few of our novelists are able to write about the poor so as to make them something more than the pitied objects of our facile sociological minds. The literature of our liberal democracy pets ¡and dandles its underprivileged characters, and, quite as if it had the right to do so, forgives them what faults they may have. But James is sure that in such people, who are numerous, there are the usual human gradations of understanding, interest, and good- ness. Even if my conjecture about the family connection of the novel be wholly mistaken, it will at least suggest what is unmistakably true, that James could write about a workingman quite as if he were as large, willful, and complex as the author of *The Principles of Psychology*. At the same time that everything in the story of *The Princess Casamassima* is based on social difference, everything is also based on the equality of the members of the human family. People at the furthest extremes of class are easily brought into relation because they are all contained in the novelist's affection. In that context it is natural for the Princess and Lady Aurora Langrish to make each other's acquaintance by the side of Rosy Muniment's bed and to contend for the notice of Paul. That James should create poor people so proud and intelligent as to make it impossible for anyone, even the reader who has paid for the privilege, to condescend to them, so proud and intelligent indeed that it is not wholly easy for them to be "good," is, one ventures to guess, an unexpressed, a never-to-be-expressed reason for finding him "impotent in matters sociological." We who are liberal and progressive know that the poor are our equals in every sense except that of being equal to us.

But James's special moral quality, his power of love, is not wholly com- prised by his impulse to make an equal distribution of dignity among his characters. It goes beyond this to create his unique moral realism, his particular gift of human understanding. If in his later novels James, as many say he did, carried awareness of human complication to the point of virtuosity, he surely does not do so here, and yet his knowledge of complication is here very considerable. But this knowledge is not an analytical one, or not in the usual sense in which that word is taken, which implies a cool dissection. If we imagine a father of many children who truly loves them all, we may suppose that he will see very vividly their differences from one another, for he has no wish to impose upon them a similarity which would be himself; and he will be quite willing to see their faults, for his affection leaves him free to love them, not because they are faultless but because they are they; yet while he sees their faults he will be able, from long connection and because there is no reason to avoid the truth, to perceive the many reasons for their actions. The discriminations and modifications of such a man would be enormous, yet the moral realism they would constitute would not arise from an analytical intelligence as we usually conceive it but from love.

The nature of James's moral realism may most easily be exemplified by his dealings with the character of Rosy Muniment. Rosy is in many ways similar to Jenny Wren, the dolls' dressmaker of *Our Mutual Friend*; both are crippled, courageous, quaint, sharp-tongued, and dominating, and both are admired by the characters among whom they have their existence. Dickens unconsciously recognizes the cruelty that lies hidden in Jenny, but consciously he makes nothing more than a brusque joke of her habit of threatening people's eyes with her needle. He allows himself to be deceived and is willing to deceive us. But James manipulates our feelings about Rosy into a perfect ambivalence. He forces us to admire her courage, pride, and intellect and seems to forbid us to take account of her cruelty because she directs it against able-bodied or aristocratic people. Only at the end does he permit us the release of our ambivalence—the revelation that Hyacinth doesn't like Rosy and that we don't have to is an emotional relief and a moral enlightenment. But although we by the author's express permission are free to dislike Rosy, the author does not avail himself of the same privilege. In the family of the novel Rosy's status has not changed.

Moral realism is the informing spirit of *The Princess Casamassima* and it yields a kind of social and political knowledge which is hard to come by. It is at work in the creation of the character of Millicent Henning, whose strength, affectionateness, and warm sensuality move James to the series of remarkable prose arias in her praise which punctuate the book; yet while he admires her, he knows the particular corruptions which our civilization is working upon her, for he is aware not only of her desire to pull down what is above her but also of her desire to imitate and conform to it and to despise what she herself is. Millicent is proud of doing nothing with her hands, she despises Hyacinth because he is so poor in spirit as to consent to *make* things and get dirty in the process, and she values herself because she does nothing less genteel than exhibit what others have made; and in one of the most pregnant scenes of the book James involves her in the peculiarly corrupt and feeble sexuality which is associated in our culture with exhibiting and looking at luxurious objects.

But it is in the creation of Paul Muniment and the Princess that James's moral realism shows itself in fullest power. If we seek an explanation of why *The Princess Casamassima* was not understood in its own day, we find it in the fact that the significance of this remarkable pair could scarcely have emerged for the reader of 1886. But we of today can say that they and their relationship constitute one of the most masterly comments on modern life that has ever been made.

In Paul Muniment a genuine idealism coexists with a secret desire for personal power. It is one of the brilliances of the novel that his ambition is never made explicit. Rosy's remark about her brother, "What my brother really cares for—well, one of these days, when you know you'll tell me," is perhaps as close as his secret ever comes to statement. It is conveyed to us by his tone, as a decisive element of his charm, for Paul radiates what the sociologists, borrowing the name from theology, call *charisma*, the charm of power, the gift of leadership. His natural passion for power must never become explicit, for it is one of the beliefs of our culture that power invalidates moral purpose. The ambiguity of Paul Muniment has been called into being by the nature of modern politics in so far as they are moral and idealistic. For idealism has not changed the nature of leadership, but it has forced the leader to change his nature, requiring him to present himself as a harmless and self-abnegating man. It is easy enough to speak of this ambiguity as a form of hypocrisy, yet the opposition between morality and power from which it springs is perfectly well conceived. But even if well conceived, it is endlessly difficult to execute and it produces its own particular confusions, falsifications, and even lies. The moral realist sees it as the source of characteristically modern ironies, such as the liberal exhausting the scrupulosity which made him deprecate all power and becoming extravagantly tolerant of what he had once denounced, or the idealist who takes license from his ideals for the unrestrained exercise of power.

The Princess, as some will remember, is the Christina Light of James's earlier novel, *Roderick Hudson*, and she considers, as Madame Grandoni says of her, "that in the darkest hour of her life, she sold herself for a title and a fortune. She regards her doing so as such a terrible piece of frivolity that she can never for the rest of her days be serious enough to make up for it." Seriousness has become her ruling passion, and in the great sad comedy of the story it is her fatal sin, for seriousness is not exempt from the tendency of ruling passions to lead to error. And yet it has an aspect of heroism, this hunt of hers for reality, for a strong and final basis of life. "Then it's real, it's solid!" she exclaims when Hyacinth tells her that he has seen Hoffendahl and has penetrated to the revolutionary holy of holies. It is her quest for reality that leads her to the poor, to the very poorest poor she can find, and that brings a light of joy to her eye at any news of suffering or deprivation, which must surely be, if anything is, an irrefrangible reality. As death and danger are— her interest in Hyacinth is made the more intense by his pledged death, and she herself eventually wants to undertake the mortal mission. A perfect drunkard of reality, she is ever drawn to look for stronger and stronger drams.

Inevitably, of course, the great irony of her fate is that the more passionately she seeks reality and the happier she becomes in her belief that she is close to it, the further removed she is. Inevitably she must turn away from Hyacinth because she reads his moral seriousness as frivolousness; and inevitably she is led to Paul who, as she thinks, affirms her in a morality which is as real and serious as anything can be, an absolute morality which gives her permission to devaluate and even destroy all that she has known of human good because it has been connected with her own frivolous, self-betraying past. She cannot but mistake the nature of reality, for she believes it is a thing, a position, a finality, a bedrock. She is, in short, the very embodiment of the modern will which masks itself in virtue, making itself appear harmless, the will that hates itself and finds its manifestations guilty and is able to exist only if it operates in the name of virtue, that despises the variety and modulations of the human story and longs for an absolute humanity, which is but another way of saying a nothingness. In her alliance with Paul she constitutes a striking symbol of that powerful part of modern culture that exists by means of its claim to political innocence and by its false seriousness—the political awareness that is not aware, the social consciousness which hates full consciousness, the moral earnestness which is moral luxury.

The fatal ambiguity of the Princess and Paul is a prime condition of Hyacinth Robinson's tragedy. If we comprehend the complex totality that James has thus conceived, we understand that the novel is an incomparable representation of the spiritual circumstances of our civilization. I venture to call it incomparable because, although other writers have provided abundant substantiation of James's insight, no one has, like him, told us the truth in a single luminous act of creation. If we ask by what magic James was able to do what he did, the answer is to be found in what I have identified as the source of James's moral realism. For the novelist can tell the truth about Paul and the Princess only if, while he represents them in their ambiguity and error, he also allows them to exist in their pride and beauty: the moral realism that shows the ambiguity and error cannot refrain from showing the pride and beauty. Its power to tell the truth arises from its power of love. James had the imagination of disaster and that is why he is immediately relevant to us; but together with the imagination of disaster he had what the imagination of disaster often destroys and in our time is daily destroying, the imagination of love.

Surveillance in *The Princess Casamassima*

Mark Seltzer

I

"We do not suffer from the spy mania here," George R. Sims observes in his monograph on the London underworld, *The Mysteries of Modern London*; in this "free land," he argues, it is "not our custom to take violent measures" against the secret agents of the nether world. The freedom from violence that Sims celebrates, however, carries a rider that he at once suggests and disavows, and the "spy mania" reappears in a somewhat different guise: "The system of observation is as perfect as can be. . . . every foreign anarchist and terrorist known to the police—and I doubt if there is one in our midst who is not—is shadowed." London's "freedom" is guaranteed by the existence of an unlimited policing and by the dissemination of elaborate methods of police surveillance. An intense watchfulness generalizes the spy mania that Sims has discounted, and for the violence of the law is substituted a more subtle and more extensive mode of power and coercion: a power of observation and surveillance, and a seeing that operates as a more effective means of overseeing. Nor is it merely, in Sims's account, the agents of secret societies and criminals of the underworld who are shadowed by this perfect system of observation. London itself is constituted as a secret society, and everyday life is riddled with suggestions of criminality and encompassed by an incriminating surveillance:

> In the 'buses and the trams and the trains the silent passengers sit side by side, and no man troubles about his neighbour. But the mysteries of modern London are represented in the crowded vehicle and in the packed compartment. The quiet-looking woman sitting opposite you in the omnibus knows the secret that the police have been seeking to discover for months. The man who politely raises his hat because he touches you as he passes from his seat would, if the truth were known, be standing in the dock of the Old Bailey to answer a capital charge.

Originally published as "*The Princess Casamassima*: Realism and the Fantasy of Surveillance," *Nineteenth-Century Fiction*, 35, no. 4 (March 1981), 506–34. Copyright © 1981 by the Regents of the University of California. Reprinted by permission of the author and the Regents. This selection reproduces portions of the text as slightly revised by the author for his *Henry James and the Art of Power* (Ithaca, N.Y.: Cornell University Press, 1984), 25–34, and 39–58.

The melodrama of the secret crime and the secret life passes "side by side with all that is ordinary and humdrum in the monotony of everyday existence." And since there are "no mysteries of modern London more terrible than its unrecorded ones," "silence" can only imply a more nefarious criminality; and not to have been brought to book by the police can only invoke a suspicion of mysteries more insidious and of a criminality more threatening in its apparent innocence and ordinariness.[1]

If Sims's vision of the London streets is marked by a fantastic paranoia, it is also a remarkable piece of police work, an attempt to "book" London's unrecorded mysteries and to supplement the official police record through an unrestricted lay policing. Discovering mysteries everywhere, Sims places all of London under suspicion and under surveillance. Nor is Sims's vision untypical of the manner in which London is seen and recorded in the late nineteenth century. The extensive documentation that accumulates about London from the mid-century on displays an interesting paradox. On the one hand, from George W. M. Reynolds's *The Mysteries of London* (1845–1848) to Sims's *The Mysteries of Modern London* (1906), London was reproduced as an impenetrable region of mystery; on the other, as this proliferating literature itself testifies, London was subjected to an unprecedented and elaborate scrutiny and surveillance. The sense of the city as an area of mystery incites an intensive policing, a police work not confined to the institutions of the law (although the expansion of the London police and detective forces was "a landmark in the history of administration")[2] but enacted also through an "unofficial" literature of detection: by the reports of tourists from the "upper world" and by the investigations of an exploratory urban sociology, particularly the work of Henry Mayhew, Charles Booth, and B. Seebohm Rowntree. It is played out also in the "discovery" of the city, and its underworld, by the realist and naturalist novelists.

Henry James's eccentric contribution to the literature of London exploration is *The Princess Casamassima*, his vision of the "sinister anarchic underworld" of London. "Truly, of course," James observes in his preface to the novel, "there are London mysteries (dense categories of dark arcana) for every spectator." *The Princess Casamassima* is a novel about the mysteries of London, about spies and secret societies, and it is also a novel about spectatorship, about seeing and being seen. James offers an obligingly simple account of the novel's origin: "This fiction proceeded quite directly, during the first year of a long residence in London, from the habit and the interest of walking the streets." "The attentive exploration of London," he suggests, ". . . fully explains a large part" of the novel; one walked "with one's eyes greatly open," and this intense observation provoked "a mystic solicitation, the

[1]George R. Sims, *The Mysteries of London* (London: C. Arthur Pearson, 1906), 81, 10, 8.
[2]Francis Sheppard, *London, 1808–1870: The Infernal Wen* (Berkeley: University of California Press, 1971), 36.

urgent appeal, on the part of everything, to be interpreted."³ It is the insistent continuity between secrecy and spectatorship, between the "mysteries abysmal" of London and the urgent solicitation to interpretation, that I want to focus on in this study of *The Princess Casamassima.* More precisely, I want to explore two questions that this continuity poses. First, what does it mean to walk the streets of London at this time, and how does this street walking function as a metonymy for the ways in which London is seen by James and his contemporaries? Second, how do the content and the techniques of representation in James's novel reproduce the London spy mania and the coercive network of seeing and power that characterize the literature of London mysteries?

Critics of *The Princess Casamassima* have traditionally located its politics in James's representation of London anarchist activities and have largely dismissed the novel's political dimension by pointing to James's lack of knowledge about these activities. The critical impulse has been to rescue the significance of the text by redirecting attention away from its ostensible political subject to its techniques, and these techniques have been seen to be at odds with the novel's political references. Manfred Mackenzie has recently summarized this depoliticization of the text, claiming that James, "because of his prior or primary American association . . . , cannot participate in any conventional modes of European social power, only in 'seeing,' or 'knowledge,' or 'consciousness.' "⁴

But can "seeing" and "power" be so easily opposed in this literature, and are the politics of *The Princess Casamassima* separable from its techniques, from its ways of seeing and ways of knowing? What I hope to demonstrate is that *The Princess Casamassima* is a distinctly political novel but that James's analysis of anarchist politics is less significant than the power play that the narrative technique itself enacts. This is not to say that the politics of the novel are confined to its techniques: the institutions of the law and its auxiliaries, primarily the prison and the police, function as explicit topics in the text. But beyond these explicit and local representations of policing power, there is a more discreet kind of policing that the novel engages, a police work articulated precisely along the novel's line of sight.

³Henry James, *The Princess Casamassima* (New York: Scribner's, 1908), 1:xxi, vii, v. Subsequent references to the novel and to the preface are to this edition (vols. 5 and 6 of the New York Edition) and appear in parentheses in the text.

⁴Manfred Mackenzie, *Communities of Honor and Love in Henry James* (Cambridge: Harvard University Press, 1976), 3. See also Lionel Trilling, *The Liberal Imagination* (New York: Viking, 1950), 92; Irving Howe, *Politics and the Novel* (Cleveland: Meridian Books, 1957), 146; John Goode, "The Art of Fiction: Walter Besant and Henry James," in *Tradition and Tolerance in Nineteenth-Century Fiction,* ed. David Howard, John Lucas, and John Goode (London: Routledge, 1966), 280; and Lvall H. Powers, *Henry James and the Naturalist Movement* (East Lansing: Michigan State University Press, 1971), 119.

II

If a relation between seeing and power becomes evident in the literature of the London underworld, it asserts itself not because the writer acknowledges the relation but, rather, because he works so carefully to disavow it. Sims, for instance, denies the existence of a "spy mania" on two counts: first, by separating police surveillance from an exercise of power, and second, by attempting to draw a line between his own acts of espionage and those of the police. Sims insists that he does not require a police escort in his wanderings through the London streets: "I have never asked for their assistance in my journeyings into dark places."[5] Nevertheless, he is uneasily aware of the incriminating cast of his prowling and publication of the London netherworld. In his earlier *How the Poor Live* and *Horrible London* (1883), he notes that "it is unpleasant to be mistaken, in underground cellars where the vilest outcasts hide from the light of day, for detectives in search of their prey."[6] Techniques of "disinterested" information gathering are unpleasantly mistaken for exercises of social control.

Additionally, Sims attempts to defend himself from another kind of "mistake," a misreading that would similarly put his motives in question. He introduces his text with a series of disclaimers: "It is not my object in these pages to bring out the sensational features of police romance"; my task "has for its object not the gratifying of a morbid curiosity, but the better understanding of things as they are." But if Sims seeks to tell "only the truth . . . , a plain unvarnished tale," his account, again, everywhere takes the form of what he protests against. If he will reveal only the truth, it is because the "truth is stranger than any written tale could ever hope to be"; and he proceeds to detail the underworld of East London as "the romances of the 'Mysterious East.' "[7] His motives and, by implication, the motives of his audience cannot be separated from a morbid curiosity-mongering.

Sims's works sensationalize the mysteries beneath the humdrum surface and posit lurid secrets to be detected; they incite and cultivate a fascination with the underworld that converts it into a bizarre species of entertainment. On the one side, putting the underworld into discourse takes the form of a certain detective work, on the other, the purveying of a sensational entertainment. It is between these two poles—policing and entertainment—that Sims wishes to situate his texts, disclaiming both his (mis)identification as a detective and his exploitation of an intrusive voyeurism. Sims tries to open up a narrow space—called "things as they are"—to evade the charge of violating

[5]Sims, *The Mysteries of Modern London*, 12.
[6]Cited in Jack Lindsay, Introduction to Jack London, *The People of the Abyss* (1903; reprint of 1st ed., London: Journeyman Press, 1977), 7.
[7]Sims, *The Mysteries of Modern London*, 9–14.

what he sees and reports. But this space is eroded from both sides: watching cannot be freed from an act of violation, from a conversion of the objects of his investigation into, as he expresses it, the "victims of my curiosity."[8]

The double bind in which Sims finds himself, and the alibis he offers to extricate himself, recur frequently in other representations of the London underworld. This literature is always, in effect, playing on the twin senses of "bringing to book," making it difficult to disentangle publication from incrimination, and foregrounding the police work always latent in the retailing of London mysteries. James Greenwood, in his *Low-Life Deeps: An Account of the Strange Fish to be Found There* (1881), feels compelled, like Sims, to offer apologies for his intrusions into the underworld: "The extraordinary endurance of popular interest in the 'Orton imposture' . . . will perhaps be regarded as sufficient justification for here reproducing what was perhaps the most conclusive evidence of the man's guilt at the time, or since brought to light." Greenwood, however, does more than reproduce the evidence and respond, after the fact, to popular demand. His own investigations have in fact produced the confession and its accompanying popularity. Greenwood has brought Orton to book in the double sense that I have indicated: "I am glad to acknowledge that the confession of 'brother Charles' was obtained by me, the more so when I reflect on the vast amount of patience and perseverance it was found necessary to exercise in order to bring the individual in question to book." The impostor Orton is turned over, in a single gesture, to the reading public and to the police. And what follows Greenwood's self-congratulatory acknowledgement of his agency is Orton's signed confession—the signature juridically reproduced at the close of Greenwood's chapter—serving both as an entertainment in the popular interest and as an instrument of indictment.[9]

Greenwood's gesture toward justification is a momentary confession on his own part of the "power of writing" that he exercises; his documentation of London mysteries, in *Low-Life Deeps* and in his earlier *The Wilds of London* (1874), is also a kind of victimization. More often, however, the victimization is less explicit; the function of supplying an entertainment is more obvious than any overt police action. James, we recall, speaks of "mysteries . . . for every spectator," and it is as a spectacle that the underworld is most frequently represented. Furthermore, James's formulation—"mysteries . . . for every spectator" rather than "spectators for every mystery"—points to the constitutive power that the spectator exerts. The watcher produces, and not merely reproduces, what he sees and puts the underworld on stage as a theatrical entertainment.

The "staging" of the underworld is evident in Daniel Joseph Kirwan's *Palace and Hovel* (1870). Kirwan is an unselfconscious curiosity seeker and

---

8Ibid., 12.

9James Greenwood, *Low-Life Deeps: An Account of the Strange Fish to be Found There* (London: Chatto, 1881), 95.

desires simply "to see something interesting." Presenting a series of underworld "scenes," he records, for example, a visit to a thieves' den, and his
account is typical in the way it manages to convert a potentially threatening
encounter into a moment of theater. His desire to be entertained is immediately gratified: each of the thieves Kirwan interrogates presents himself as an
out-of-work entertainer, and each in turn performs for Kirwan's amusement.
Crude and prefaced with excuses, the performances are clearly extemporized;
the criminals have readily adopted the roles that Kirwan has implicitly assigned and have cooperated to produce the spectacle he wants to see. The underworld, quite literally, appears as a sort of underground theater. And the
play is a power play in another sense as well. Kirwan, like most tourists
of the nether regions, is accompanied and protected by a police detective, and
the detective has supplied the cue for the performance that results. Before
admitting the visitors, the "master of the mansion" has asked whether it is
"bizness or pleasure," adding that "hif hits business you must 'elp yourself."
"O, pleasure by all means," the detective replies.[10] The displacement of
poverty and crime into theater, of business into pleasure, is clearly marked,
and the performers are willing to confine themselves to the roles of a beggars'
opera in order to escape a more definitive confinement.

The metaphor of the theater also pervades Sims's *The Mysteries of Modern
London.* His intent is to take the reader "behind the scenes": "When the
interior of a house is set upon the stage, the fourth wall is always down in
order that the audience may see what is going on. In real life the dramas
within the domestic interior are played with the fourth wall up. . . . care is
taken that no passer-by shall have a free entertainment. I am going to take the
fourth wall down to-day."[11] Indeed, this is not "free entertainment" but the
basis of a literary industry; poverty, conspiracy, criminality are purchasable
spectacles, at once opened to the public and reduced and distanced as theater.
" 'Do show me some cases of unmitigated misery,' is a request said to have
been made by a young lady in search of sensation," Mrs. Bernard Bosanquet
records in *Rich and Poor* (1896), her study of the slums.[12] The request might
easily be that of James's Princess, who "liked seeing queer types and exploring
out-of-the-way social corners" (2:234).

But if Sims's fantasy of disclosure—his taking down of the fourth wall—has
an immediate theatrical reference, it refers also to another sort of fantasy. The
source of Sims's passage might well be the familiar passage in Dickens's
Dombey and Son in which the author imagines "a good spirit who would take
the house-tops off . . . and show a Christian people what dark shapes issue

---

[10]Daniel Joseph Kirwan, *Palace and Hovel; or, Phases of London Life,* ed. A. Allan (1870:
reprint ed., London: Abelard-Schuman, 1963), 27.

[11]Sims, *The Mysteries of Modern London,* 141.

[12]Mrs. Bernard Bosanquet, *Rich and Poor* (London: Macmillan, 1896), 5.

from amidst their homes."[13] There is, however, a more immediate source than this fantasy of a providential supervision, a possible source that makes unmistakable the nexus of policing and entertainment I have been tracing: "If we could fly out of that window hand in hand, hover over this great city, gently remove the roofs, and peep in at the queer things which are going on, the strange coincidences, the plannings, the cross-purposes, the wonderful chain of events . . . , it would make all fiction, with its conventionalities and foreseen conclusions, most stale and unprofitable."[14] The speaker is Sherlock Holmes, in A. Conan Doyle's tale "A Case of Identity," precisely the "police romance" that Sims begins by disavowing and precisely the form that most insistently manifests the twin operations of vision and supervision, of spectatorship and incrimination, that the literature of the underworld engages. The impulse to explore and disclose the underworld in detective fiction becomes indistinguishable from a fantasy of surveillance; in the figure of the detective seeing becomes the mode of power par excellence. . . .

III

The most evident feature of the discourses of the city that I have been tracing is an insistent watchfulness, a "spy mania," which appears at once as a form of entertainment and as a police action. The twin sites of this obsessive surveillance are the theater and the prison. *The Princess Casamassima* invokes this discursive scenario. James recalled his initial sense of the novel as a self-implicating network of watchers: "To find [Hyacinth's] possible adventure interesting I had only to conceive his watching the same public show, the same innumerable appearances, I had watched myself, and of his watching very much as I had watched" (1:vi). This specular relation is reproduced throughout the novel, explicitly in the figures of the police spy and secret agent, whose disguised presence is always suspected, but also in the more ordinary exchanges of sight in the novel. In *The Princess Casamassima*, seeing and being seen always implicitly involve an actual or potential power play. Hyacinth, typically, promises "himself to watch his playmate [Millicent] as he had never done before. She let him know, as may well be supposed, that she had her eye on *him*, and it must be confessed that as regards the exercise of a right of supervision he had felt himself at a disadvantage ever since the night at the theatre" (2:65). Seeing makes for a "right of supervision" and a power of coercion; it is the nexus of seeing and power that I now want to examine in *The Princess Casamassima*.

Hyacinth dates his "disadvantage" from the "night at the theatre," and it

[13]Charles Dickens, *Dombey and Son*, New Oxford Illustrated Dickens (London: Oxford University Press, 1950), chap. 47.
[14]A. Conan Doyle, *The Sherlock Holmes Illustrated Omnibus* (New York: Schocken, 1976), 31.

does not take much interpretive pressure to see that a pervasive theatricality runs through the novel. The governing mode of interaction between characters involves a series of performances: the characters engage in the "entertainment of watching" (1:307) as they are alternately recruited "for supplying such entertainment" (1:210). Muniment commandeers Hyacinth "for Rosy's entertainment" (1:253) as Hyacinth is brought to Medley by the Princess because his "*naïveté* would entertain her" (2:19). The Princess especially is repeatedly referred to in theatrical terms as an "actress" performing on the "*mise-en-scène* of life" (1:268), and her imitation of a small bourgeoise provides Hyacinth with "the most finished entertainment she had yet offered him" (2:186).

The insistent theatricality of the novel refers less to any "dramatic analogy" than to the reciprocal watchfulness that invests every relation in the novel. The theater scenes in the novel enact an indifferent interchange of audience and play as objects of observation. The theater is the privileged point of vantage for an "observation of the London world" (1:189), and if, as Hyacinth notes, "one's own situation seem[ed] a play within the play" (1:208), it is because one is both spectator and spectacle. It is in the theater that Hyacinth discovers that he is being watched, that he has been spotted by Sholto and the Princess, herself "overshadowed by the curtain of the box, drawn forward with the intention of shielding her from the observation of the house" (1:205). Hyacinth, in the balcony and not in the box, is not shielded from observation, and his vulnerable position indicates that, despite the exchanges of performance between characters, there is a certain asymmetry in this "entertainment of watching."

Hyacinth, "lacking all social dimensions was scarcely a perceptible person," and he is gratified that Sholto should "recognise and notice him" in the theater "because even so small a fact as this was an extension of his social existence" (1:192). The under classes "exist" only when they have become the object of regard of the upper classes. But there is a counterside to this visibility. For if to be seen is to exist, it is also to be objectified, fixed, and imprisoned in the gaze of the other. It is to be reduced to the status of a "favourable specimen" (1:257), to "studies of the people—the lower orders" (1:305). In the largest sense, to be seen is to be encompassed by a right of supervision.

To escape supervision, characters cultivate a style of secrecy, adopt disguises in order to see without being seen; and, indeed, seeing without being seen becomes the measure of power in the novel. Hyacinth insistently promotes the secret life, at times with a certain absurdity: "I don't understand everything you say, but I understand everything you hide," Millicent tells Hyacinth. "Then I shall soon become a mystery to you, for I mean from this time forth to cease to seek safety in concealment. You'll know nothing about me then—for it will be all under your nose" (2:332). If seeing is power, secrecy assumes a paramount value, and if beneath every surface a secret truth is suspected, to allow the "truth" to appear is consummately to disguise it.[15]

The relation between a theatrical secrecy and power is most evident in James's representation of the secret society. Invoking Sims's paranoid vision of London conspiracies, the secret society appears as an almost providential power because it is both pervasively present and invisible:

> The forces secretly arrayed against the present social order were pervasive and universal, in the air one breathed, in the ground one trod, in the hand of an acquaintance that one might touch or the eye of a stranger that might rest a moment on one's own. They were above, below, within, without, in every contact and combination of life; and it was no disproof of them to say it was too odd they should lurk in a particular improbable form. To lurk in improbable forms was precisely their strength. [2:275]

The spy mania is universal; the secret society, arrayed in improbable disguises, exercises a potentially unlimited surveillance, a potentially unlimited supervision.

There is another species of theater in *The Princess Casamassima* that makes even more explicit the nexus of seeing and power: the scene of the prison. Hyacinth's meeting with his mother in Millbank prison appears as another instance of reciprocal watchfulness: "They had too much the air of having been brought together simply to look at each other" (1:51). Mrs. Bowerbank, the jailer, scripts the encounter, staging a confrontation "scene" and managing the action as an entertainment, expressing "a desire to make the interview more lively" (1:52). She works to direct an occasion "wanting in brilliancy" and finally moves to "abbreviate the scene" (1:53, 56). The prison is a theater of power. Further, the jailer's visit to Pinnie sets the novel in motion; the novel opens under the shadow and gaze of the prison, "in the eye of the law" (1:7) and under "the steady orb of justice" (1:8). And most striking about Mrs. Bowerbank is not merely her representation of "the cold light of the penal system" and her "official pessimism" (1:14) but the way in which her unrelenting observation of Pinnie and Hyacinth is experienced as an accusation of guilt and as an arrest by the law. This "emissary of the law" (1:11) imprisons Pinnie in her gaze, and the dressmaker is "unable to rid herself of the impression that it was somehow the arm of the law that was stretched out to touch her" (1:13). When Hyacinth is produced for the jailer's "inspection," he asks: "Do you want to see me only to look at me?" (1:18). But "only" to be seen is already to be inscribed within a coercive power relation, to be placed under surveillance and under arrest. Mrs. Bowerbank's presence transforms the dressmaker's house into a prison house. The jailer appears as an "overruling providence" (1:46); her tone "seemed to refer itself to an iron discipline"

---

[15]Mackenzie discusses the "secret society" in *Communities of Honor and Love in Henry James*, 8–18.

(1:14), and Pinnie can only respond "guiltily" (1:8) to her questioning. Pinnie debates taking the "innocent child" to the prison and "defended herself as earnestly as if her inconsistency had been of a criminal cast" (1:11, 30). Indicted by Mrs. Bowerbank's observation, she attempts to shield herself, imagining the "comfort to escape from observation" (1:40), and distracts herself from the "case" "as a fugitive takes to by-paths" (1:22).

Pinnie, however, is not merely victimized and incriminated by the turn-key's legal eye. The jailer's visit disseminates an array of inquisitorial looks, recriminations, and betrayals, as the law stretches to include each character. But the characters are not merely victims; they in turn become "carriers" of the law. The more discreet and more insidious power of the law that Mrs. Bowerbank represents is the power to reproduce and extend the apparatus of surveillance and incrimination into situations that seem radically remote from crime, in the legal sense. The distribution of mechanisms of incrimination works not only to victimize those it stretches out to touch but more significantly to make its victims also its disseminators.

The opening scene of the novel is a concise instance of this "spreading" of the law, and a summary of the plot of the opening section is a summary of the displacement and extension of the techniques of penality that Mrs. Bowerbank incarnates. Pinnie, for instance, is not only incriminated by this emissary of the law: she herself becomes Mrs. Bowerbank's emissary. The jailer "would like to see" Hyacinth, and Pinnie undertakes to "look for the little boy," realizing at the same time that to make Hyacinth "visible" is also to bring him to judgment: as she expresses it, "if you could only wait to see the child I'm sure it would help you to judge" (1:3, 15).

To produce Hyacinth is to bring him to the law, and Pinnie both undertakes to produce him and proceeds to exercise a disciplinary authority of her own. As she obeys Mrs. Bowerbank's injunction to supply Hyacinth, she displaces the injunction onto his playmate, Millicent. She simultaneously places Millicent under the discipline of her observation—waiting "to see if her injunction would be obeyed"—and links this injunction with an appropriately reduced attribution of guilt—"you naughty little girl" (1:5). Millie, in turn, replies with a "gaze of deliberation" and with a refusal to "betray" Hyacinth to this extended arm of the law: "Law no, Miss Pynsent, I never see him" (1:6, 5). When Hyacinth appears, Pinnie repeats her accusation of Millicent: "Millicent 'Enning's a very bad little girl; she'll come to no good" (1:16). Hyacinth protests and tries to exculpate his friend from a betrayal in which he is implicated; his reply further suggests the displacements of guilt and responsibility that obsessively proliferate in this opening scene: "It came over him," he observes, "that he had too hastily shifted to her shoulders the responsibility of his unseemly appearance, and he wished to make up to her for this betrayal" (1:17).

These shifts and displacements of criminality and incrimination indicate a generalized extension of the power of watching and policing in the novel. In

The Princess Casamassima, police work is contagious, a contagion that James images as the transmission of a certain "dinginess" from one character to another: Hyacinth "hated people with too few fair interspaces, too many smutches and streaks. Millicent Henning generally had two or three of these at least, which she borrowed from her doll, into whom she was always rubbing her nose and whose dinginess was contagious. It was quite inevitable she should have left her mark under his own nose when she claimed her reward for coming to tell him about the lady who wanted him" (1:17). If Hyacinth has shifted onto Millicent the blame for his "unseemly appearance," leading to Pinnie's accusations of her, the shifting of blame and guilt corresponds to the shifting of a mark of "dinginess," the stigma of the slums.

The opening scene plays out, in an anticipatory and understated fashion, the diffusion of penality that traverses *The Princess Casamassima*. It is the prison that provides the model for the contagion. The first principle of the prison is isolation, confinement, but within the novel Millbank prison stands as the central and centering instance of this spread of criminality; the prison

> looked very sinister and wicked, to Miss Pynsent's eyes, and she wondered why a prison should have such an evil air if it was erected in the interest of justice and order—a builded protest, precisely, against vice and villany. This particular penitentiary struck her as about as bad and wrong as those who were in it; it threw a blight on the face of day, making the river seem foul and poisonous and the opposite bank, with a protrusion of long-necked chimneys, unsightly gasometers and deposits of rubbish, wear the aspect of a region at whose expense the jail had been populated. [1:42]

Vice and villainy are not confined by the *cordon sanitaire* of the prison; rather, the prison infects the surrounding area, disperses its "evil air," and blights the city. The prison spreads what it ostensibly protests against and is erected to delimit. The atmosphere of the prison extends from the local site of the prison into every area of the novel, and there is no escape from the contagion of criminality; as Pinnie notes, every "effort of mitigation . . . only involved her more deeply" (1:8).[16] "He had not done himself justice"; "she seemed to plead guilty to having been absurd"; "Hyacinth's terrible cross-questioning"; "he went bail for my sincerity": one might multiply these quotations indefinitely, and I abstract them from their local contexts because it is the multiplication of these references, in the most banal and "innocent" exchanges in the novel, that establishes a general context of policing and incrimination in *The Princess Casamassima*. The very ordinariness of the allusions indicates the extent to which a fantasy of supervision and police work infiltrates the novel.

---

[16]On the "Dickensian" theme of a contagious criminality, see, for instance: Michael Ignatieff, *A Just Measure of Pain: The Penitentiary in the Industrial Revolution, 1750–1850* (New York: Pantheon, 1978), 61.

"What do you mean, to watch me?" Hyacinth asks Mr. Vetch, and the question alludes to more than the fiddler's paternal overseeing of Hyacinth. The possibility that Mr. Vetch is a police spy has earlier been considered; the manner in which the possibility is dismissed extends rather than limits the spy mania that the novel reproduces: Hyacinth

> never suspected Mr. Vetch of being a governmental agent, though Eustache Poupin had told him that there were a great many who looked a good deal like that: not of course with any purpose of incriminating the fiddler. . . . The governmental agent in extraordinary disguises . . . became a very familiar type to Hyacinth, and though he had never caught one of the infamous brotherhood in the act there were plenty of persons to whom, on the very face of the matter, he had no hesitation in attributing the character. [1:108]

The secret agent lurks in improbable forms, and as in Sims's fantasies of the anarchic underworld, apparent innocence invites a suspicion of concealed criminality. This passage denies suspicion and the purpose of incrimination even as it attributes the character of the police spy indiscriminately. The attribution attaches, at one time or another, to virtually every character in the novel. To Captain Sholto, for instance: "Perhaps you think he's a spy, an *agent provocateur* or something of the sort." But Sholto's form is not improbable enough, a spy "would disguise himself more" (1:214). It attaches also to the Princess, who is suspected of being "an agent on the wrong side."

The Princess, Madame Grandoni tells the Prince, is "much entangled. She has relations with people who are watched by the police." "And is *she* watched by the police?" "I can't tell you; it's very possible—except that the police here isn't like that of other countries" (2:310). Indeed, the police here are not like they are elsewhere—they are everywhere. Just prior to this discussion, the Princess and Paul Muniment have left the house at Madeira Crescent on a conspiratorial mission that remains a narrative secret. The spies are themselves spied upon, as the narrative observer comments: "Meanwhile, it should be recorded, they had been followed, at an interval, by a cautious figure, a person who, in Madeira Crescent, when they came out of the house, was stationed on the other side of the street, at a considerable distance. On their appearing he had retreated a little, still however keeping them in sight" (2:301). James initially withholds the identity of the observer who has placed the conspirators under surveillance. His revelation of that identity takes a curious form: "The reader scarce need be informed, nevertheless, that his design was but to satisfy himself as to the kind of person his wife was walking with" (2:301). The disavowal of any need to inform the reader of the figure's identity only points to the reader's initial misidentification. The passage invites a "confusion" of domestic suspicions and police surveillance and indicates the extent to which all actions in the novel have come to resemble a police action. All characters in the novel are "in danger of playing the spy" (2:348).

There is no space free from the spy mania, from the infection of penality. Medley, the Princess's country-house retreat, provides no escape. The Princess there informs Hyacinth that "I've been watching you. I'm frank enough to tell you that. I want to see more—more—more!" (2:36). And if Hyacinth ceases "to be insignificant from the moment" the Princess sees him, he experiences his accession to significance as a subjection to "cross-examination" (2:35). A dispersed surveillance shadows Hyacinth, both in the Princess's watchfulness and in the supervision of his conduct "under the eye of the butler" (2:41). Medley is, for Hyacinth, the "real country," real nature, but nature itself participates in the general police action: "Never had the old oaks and beeches . . . witnessed such an extraordinary series of confidences since the first pair that sought isolation wandered over the grassy slopes and ferny dells beneath them" (2:46).

The witnessing eye of nature and the allusion to the providential supervision of the Garden indicate the thorough "naturalization" of mechanisms of surveillance and policing in *The Princess Casamassima*: nature itself appears to supplement the policing function. Mrs. Bowerbank early comments on Florentine's impending death by asserting that "if she lived a month [she] would violate (as Mrs. Bowerbank might express herself) every established law of nature" (1:14). James's parenthetical interpolation calls attention to the jailer's characteristic mode of expression, her linking of "nature" and the "law," her naturalizing of the penal apparatus. In *The Princess Casamassima*, the power of vision and supervision is not confined to the nominal agencies of the police: it is enforced by the "eyes of the world" (2:401). It is finally impossible to distinguish between the "eye of day and the observation of the police" (2:410).

IV

The spy mania and the incriminating techniques of policing and surveillance are not confined but contagious in *The Princess Casamassima*; the prison and the supervision and discipline it implies reappear at every turn in the novel. I have indicated the proposal of the prison as a model for the city at large in the work of the London sociologists, and I now want to take up the significance of this equation from a somewhat different perspective. Michel Foucault, in *Surveiller et punir*, his recent history of the rise of disciplinary practices, describes the extension of social mechanisms of surveillance and discipline into all areas of modern society. More specifically, he traces the reorganization of Western society around the model of the "punitive city": "Near at hand, sometimes even at the very centre of cities of the nineteenth century [stands] the monotonous figure, at once material and symbolic, of the power to punish"—the prison. The architectural figure of this social reorganization is Jeremy Bentham's Panopticon, a circular building, divided into cells, surrounding a central observation tower. The Panopticon operates through a controlling network of seeing and being seen: the inmate "is seen, but he does not see"; "in the central tower, one sees everything without ever being seen." The inmate is trapped in a "seeing machine," trapped in a state of conscious and constant visibility; as a result, he "inscribes in himself the power relation" in which he is caught up and "becomes the principle of his own subjection."[17]

London's Millbank prison was derived from Bentham's panopticon scheme. Convicts were accommodated in six pentagonal ranges that surrounded a central watchtower—the locus of a providential supervision that doubled also, and appropriately, as the prison chapel. James visited Millbank on a December morning in 1884 to collect notes for *The Princess Casamassima*. His description of the prison in the novel emphasizes the power of watching that the Panopticon employs. He records the "circular shafts of cells" ranged about a central observatory and, further, the "opportunity of looking at captives through grated peepholes," at the women with "fixed eyes" that Pinnie is "afraid to glance at" (1:47); the inmates are dressed in "perfect frights of hoods" (1:46). This last detail recalls the practice at Pentonville, where "all contact with other human beings, except the prison staff, was forbidden, and when convicts left their cells . . . , they wore masks with narrow eye-slits in order to prevent identification by their fellows."[18]

The Panopticon effects an exemplary conjunction of seeing and power, the conjunction that extends from the prison throughout *The Princess Casamassima*. "The panoptic schema," Foucault details, ". . . was destined to spread throughout the social body." Foucault discusses the dispersal of this schema in nineteenth-century society, its penetration into the factory, the workhouse, the reformatory, the school—into, in fact, all those institutions that, as we have seen, the urban colonizers deployed and cultivated. And further, the panoptic technique infiltrates "tiny, everyday" social practices, traverses and embraces those "minute social disciplines" apparently remote from the scene of the prison. Confiscating and absorbing "things of every moment," an everyday panopticism is finally universalized: "Police power must bear 'over everything.' "[19]

One final institutionalization of the panoptic technology remains to be considered. It has recently been suggested that Foucault's history might underwrite a radical revision of our sense of the "politics" of the novel, and the problem that I want now to take up, and which has been implicit all along, concerns the relation between these disciplinary techniques and the tech-

[17]Michel Foucault, *Surveiller et punir* (Paris: Gallimard, 1975); my citations are to the English translation by Alan Sheridan, *Discipline and Punish: The Birth of the Prison* (New York: Pantheon, 1977), 116, 200, 202, 207, 202–203. On the Panopticon, see also: Gertrude Himmelfarb, "The Haunted House of Jeremy Bentham," in her *Victorian Minds* (New York: Alfred A. Knopf, 1968).
[18]Sheppard, *London, 1808–1870: The Infernal Wen*, 375–77.
[19]Foucault, *Discipline and Punish*, 207, 213, et passim. See also Jacques Donzelot, *La police des familles* (Paris: Editions de Minuit, 1977).

niques of the novel, and more particularly of the realist and naturalist novel, which appears on the scene at the same time that the disciplinary society takes power.[20] Foucault suggests that the novel "forms part of that great system of constraint by which the West compelled the everyday to bring itself into discourse."[21] In what way may the realist novel be seen to participate in, and even to promote, a system of constraint?

It has been observed that "excellence of *vision* is the distinguishing mark of realism."[22] "To see" is the dominant verb in the realist text—"la gastronomie de l'oeil," as Balzac expressed it[23]—and realist fiction is preeminently concerned with seeing, with a seeing in detail. The proximity of this realist "seeing" to the overseeing and police work of detection becomes explicitly problematic and is most evident, of course, in the subgenre of realism that we have already glanced at, the fiction of detection.[24] In detective fiction, the relation between seeing and policing is taken for granted; literally, the range of the detective's vision is the range of his power. That power operates by placing the entire world of the text under scrutiny and under surveillance and invokes the possibility of an absolute supervision, in which everything may be comprehended and "policed" and in which the most trifling detail becomes potentially incriminating. Realistic fiction, in a more discreet and, for that reason, more comprehensive manner, deploys a similar tactic of detection; the techniques of surveillance and detection traverse the techniques of the realistic novel. Emerson, instancing Swift, notes "how realistic or materialistic in treatment of his subject" the novelist is: "He describes his fictitious persons as if for the police."[25] Indeed, detective fiction merely literalizes the realist representational scrutiny, its fascination with seeing and with the telling significance of detail, and lays bare *the policing of the real* that is the realist

[20]I am indebted especially to Leo Bersani, "The Subject of Power," *Diacritics* 7:3 (1977), 2–21; D. A. Miller, "From *roman-policier* to *roman-police*: Wilkie Collins's *The Moonstone*," *Novel* 13 (1980), 153–170; and Miller's "The Novel and the Police," *Glyph 8: Johns Hopkins Textual Studies* (Baltimore: Johns Hopkins University Press, 1981). See also: Jonathan Arac, *Commissioned Spirits: The Shaping of Social Motion in Dickens, Carlyle, Melville, and Hawthorne* (New Brunswick: Rutgers University Press, 1979), esp. chap. 1; Paul Foss, "The Lottery of Life," in *Michel Foucault: Power, Truth, Strategy*, ed. Meaghan Morris and Paul Patton (Sydney: Feral, 1979); Jeffrey Mehlman, *Revolution and Repetition: Marx/Hugo/Balzac* (Berkeley: University of California Press, 1977), 123–24; and Lennard J. Davis, "Wicked Actions and Feigned Words: Criminals, Criminality, and the Early English Novel," *Yale French Studies* 59 (1980), 106–18.

[21]Foucault, "The Life of Infamous Men," in *Michel Foucault: Power, Truth, Strategy*, 91.

[22]Mehlman, *Revolution and Repetition*, 124.

[23]Balzac, cited in Donald Fanger, *Dostoevsky and Romantic Realism* (Cambridge: Harvard University Press, 1965), 30.

[24]On the detective story, see Miller, "From *roman-policier* to *roman-police*: Wilkie Collins's *The Moonstone*"; and Pierre Macherey, *A Theory of Literary Production*, trans. Geoffrey Wall (London: Routledge, 1978), 18–36.

[25]Ralph Waldo Emerson, *English Traits*, in *The Selected Writings of Ralph Waldo Emerson*, ed. Brooks Atkinson (New York: Modern Library, 1950), 647.

project. "We novelists," writes Zola, "are the examining magistrates of men and their passions."[26]

The juridical expression of the aims of the realist novelist recurs frequently. There is, for instance, George Eliot's statement in *Adam Bede* (chapter 17) of the novelist's obligation to write "as if I were in the witness-box narrating my experience on oath" and Guy de Maupassant's avowal, in his preface to *Pierre et Jean*, to tell "la vérité, rien que la vérité, et toute la vérité."[27] And earlier, there is Lamb's comment that reading Defoe "is like reading evidence in a court of Justice" or Hazlitt's observation that Richardson "sets about describing every object and transaction, as if the whole had been given in on evidence by an eye-witness."[28] The convergence of the literary and the legal recurs also in attacks on the alleged illicitness and "illegality" of the realistic novel; thus W. S. Lilly, writing in 1885, asserts that, in the realist and naturalist novel, "everywhere at the bottom there is filth (*l'ordure*). Those proceedings in the courts of justice which from time to time bring it to the surface—like an abscess—are merely an experimental novel unfolding itself, chapter after chapter, before the public."[29] The realist novel is seen to proceed as a legal action. The realist novelist is the examining magistrate of everyday life.

There is a complementary movement in realistic fiction: toward a documentation of phenomena in precise detail, and toward a supervision of these phenomena. As Zola concisely expresses it, "the goal of the experimental method . . . is to study phenomena in order to control them."[30] The realists share, with other colonizers of the urban scene, a passion to see and document "things as they are," and this passion takes the form of a fantasy of surveillance, a placing of the tiniest details of everyday life under scrutiny. Is it not possible to discover in this fantasy of surveillance a point of intersection between the realist text and a society increasingly dominated by institutions of discipline, regularization, and supervision—by the dispersed networks of the "police"?

---

[26]Emile Zola, "The Experimental Novel," in *Documents of Modern Literary Realism*, ed. George J. Becker (Princeton: Princeton University Press, 1963), 168.

[27]George Eliot, *Adam Bede*, ed. Stephen Gill (Harmondsworth: Penguin, 1980), chap. 17; Guy de Maupassant, *Pierre et Jean* (New York: Scribner's, 1936), xxxvi.

[28]Charles Lamb and William Hazlitt cited in Ian Watt, *The Rise of the Novel* (Berkeley: University of California Press, 1957), 34.

[29]W. S. Lilly, "The New Naturalism," in *Documents of Modern Literary Realism*, ed. Becker, 277. Perhaps the most extraordinary indictment of the realist and naturalist novelists occurs in Max Nordau's influential *Degeneration* (New York: D. Appleton, 1895). Nordau classifies these novelists, preeminently Zola, in accordance with the classification of criminal types developed by the criminologist Cesare Lombroso, accuses them of "crime committed with pen and crayon" (p. 558), and calls for the institution of a "critical police" (p. 535) to return them to the law; at the same time, however, Nordau notes the resemblance between the realist text and the "police reports" (p. 489).

[30]Zola, "The Experimental Novel," 176.

There are a number of ways in which the relation between the novel and the law can be explored. There is, for instance, an intriguing resemblance between the realist typologies of character and the typologies proposed by the late nineteenth-century criminologists, chiefly Cesare Lombroso, a resemblance that Conrad exploits in *The Secret Agent*, another novel of the London spy mania.[31] More generally, one might note the encompassing control over character and action that the realist and naturalist doctrine of "determinism" secures. As Leo Bersani has recently suggested, the realist's method works to reduce "the events of fiction to a parade of sameness. For example, it would not be wholly absurd to suggest that a Balzac novel becomes unnecessary as soon as its exposition is over. The entire work is already contained in the presentation of the work, and the characters merely repeat in dialogue and action what has already been established about them in narrative summaries. Their lives mirror the expository portraits made of them at the beginning of the novel."[32]

The linear order and progression of the realistic novel enable the novel to "progress" only in a direction always preestablished. Indeed, it is as a "repetition" that Hyacinth experiences his every attempt to break with his origins and "antecedents," to break with his "naturalist" determinants of environment and heredity. His recruitment to assassinate the duke presents itself as "the idea of a *repetition*," as the "horror of the public reappearance, in his person, of the imbrued hands of his mother" (2:419). This "young man in a book" (1:xiv) expresses an interest in the "advanced and consistent realists" (1:315), but this "consistency," a key word in the novel, becomes another name for an entrapment in a (narrative) repetition.

In its fixing of consistent "types," and in its predictive control over narrative possibility, the realistic text gains a thorough mastery over its characters and their actions—a twin mastery of intelligibility and supervision. *The Princess Casamassima* has been regarded as James's primary excursion into the realistic or naturalistic mode.[33] The novel, in its choice of subjects and in its descriptive method, displays an affinity with the consistent realists, and certainly, it everywhere displays the fantasy of surveillance which, I have been suggesting, lies at the heart of the realist project. But we notice that this surveillance becomes in many ways the subject and not merely the mode of the novel, and such a foregrounding of the novel's tactics of supervision indicates, within limits that I will attempt to describe, James's exposure and

---

[31]On Conrad's use of Lombroso, see John E. Saveson, "Conrad, *Blackwood's*, and Lombroso," *Conradiana* 6 (1974), 57–62.

[32]Leo Bersani, *Baudelaire and Freud* (Berkeley: University of California Press, 1977), 121.

[33]Lyall H. Powers, in *Henry James and the Naturalist Movement*, claims that James had, by the mid-1880s, "made his peace" with the naturalists: "He had by this time come close to sharing fully the aesthetic persuasions of the Realist-Naturalist group" (p. 41). It is, rather, James's attempts to disaffiliate himself from the realist and naturalist "group," and from the politics that their method implies, that I emphasize here.

demystification of the realist mania for surveillance and his attempt to disown the policing that it implies.

Perhaps the most powerful tactic of supervision achieved by the traditional realist novel inheres in its dominant technique of narration—the style of "omniscient narration" that grants the narrative voice an unlimited authority over the novel's "world," a world thoroughly known and thoroughly mastered by the panoptic "eye" of the narration. The technique of omniscient narration, as is frequently noted, gives to the narrator a providential vision of the characters and action. It is the fantasy of such an absolute panopticism that we have previously traced in Sims's lifting of the fourth wall, and in Dickens's and Doyle's fantasy of "removing the roofs" and viewing the "queer things which are going on." In *The Princess Casamassima*, such omniscient vision is attributed to the master revolutionaries: "They know everything—everything. They're like the great God of the believers: they're searchers of hearts; and not only of hearts, but of all a man's life—his days, his nights, his spoken, his unspoken words. Oh they go deep and they go straight!" (2:383). Hoffendahl's God-like power is also the power of the omniscient narrator, a power of unlimited overseeing.

But if James inscribes in his text an image of comprehensive and providential supervision, the narrative method of the novel departs from this panoptic technique. As a number of critics have shown, and as James asserts in his preface to the novel, *The Princess Casamassima* marks a technical turning point in James's career: a turning away from the style of omniscient narration toward the technique of the "central recording consciousness" or "central intelligence." That technique displaces the authority of the narrative voice and disavows any direct interpretive authority over the action. It can be said that in *The Princess Casamassima*, omniscient authority is held up to scrutiny, and indicted, in being transferred to, or displaced upon, the masters of the revolution.

Can this supervisory power, however, be so easily disowned? In his preface, James imagines his observation of the underworld as a form of espionage: his vision of London is that of "the habitual observer . . . the pedestrian prowler" (1:xxi-xxii). But at the same time, he disclaims any violation or manipulation of the figures he "merely" observes: "I recall pulling no wires, knocking at no closed doors, applying for no 'authentic' information" (1:xxii). It is Hoffendahl, in the novel, who is the arch wire puller: "He had in his hand innumerable other threads" (2:55). And it is this puppeteering that James disavows. But having denied such a manipulative power, James proceeds to reclaim what he has dismissed: "To haunt the great city and by this habit to penetrate it, imaginatively, in as many places as possible—*that* was to be informed, *that* was to pull wires, *that* was to open doors" (1:xxii).

James distinguishes his "imaginative" penetration of the city from the manipulative vision and supervision of the conspiratorial plotters. The implication is clear: James would claim that his imaginative wire pulling is not an act of supervision, that his deep searching of hearts, of spoken and unspoken words, that his seeing and "haunting" of the city can be distinguished from the policing and spy mania that this haunting of the great city so closely resembles. It is just such a separation between "mere" seeing, consciousness, and knowledge and an exercise of power that I have been questioning. James offers the alibi of a "powerless" imagination to extricate himself from the charge of participating in the spy mania that the novel everywhere engages. But James would have no need to insist on the distinction if it were not already jeopardized, already threatened by the compelling resemblance between his haunting and perpetual prowling and the surveillance and policing from which he would disengage himself.

It becomes clear that the attempt on the part of the writers we have examined to disown the policing that they exercise can be seen as a "cover" for a more discreet and comprehensive policy of supervision, and it is as such a ruse that I think James's displacing of power and authority works. The recession of narrative supervision in *The Princess Casamassima* appears as one further "shifting of the shame," a displacing of responsibility, culpability, and, in the terms which the novel provides, criminality. The shifting of narrative authority makes reference to an uneasiness concerning the shame of power. If James's novel is systematically the story of a criminal continuity between seeing and power, this continuity is finally disowned. If James works toward a demystifying of the realist policing of the real, this police work is finally remystified, recuperated as the "innocent" work of the imagination.

From one point of view, the incompatibility of the novel and the subject of power is the "message" of *The Princess Casamassima*: the incompatibility of aesthetic and political claims leads to Hyacinth's suicide. Critics of the novel have restated this message, insisting, with approval or disapprobation, that the novel sacrifices its political references to technical preoccupations. In his preface, James himself observes that the underworld of London "lay heavy on one's consciousness" (1:vi). The phrase invites us to read "conscience" for "consciousness," and the substitution registers in miniature what has been seen as James's substitution in *The Princess Casamassima* of the ordeal of consciousness (that is, the work's technique) for matters of social conscience (its political subject). Thus it has been argued that "Hyacinth Robinson's sensitive consciousness is the mirror which controls the shape" of the novel, that James's "ignorance in the face of the reality, the great grey Babylon, which was nearest to him," compelled him to distort that reality by circumscribing it with a "controlling and bizarre consciousness," and that, finally, this technical preoccupation means that *The Princess Casamassima*'s "theme is not political at all."[34] As Leo Bersani points out, "it has been decided by 'politically

    [34]The quotations are from, respectively: J. M. Leucke, "*The Princess Casamassima*: Hyacinth's Fallible Consciousness," in *Henry James: Modern Judgments*, ed. Tony Tanner (London: Macmillan, 1969), 184; John Goode, "The Art of Fiction: Walter Besant and Henry James," 280, 279; J. A. Ward, *The Search for Form* (Chapel Hill: University of North Carolina Press, 1967), 115.

conscious' Anglo-American critics that James is a nonpolitical novelist."[35]

Critics of *The Princess Casamassima*, and of James's work generally, have restated the discontinuity that James himself proposed, enforcing a break between technique and subject, between ways of seeing and the subject of power. It is maintained that "in his quest for a quintessential social reality that was also an alien reality, James must necessarily have found himself recoiling upon the merely psychological and even epistemological, the merely imaginative—upon fantasy."[36] But if James's only "political novel" advertises a radical conflict between politics and the novel, there is, working against this simple polarization, a criminal continuity between the techniques of the novel and the social technologies of power that inhere in these techniques. It is in this rigorous continuity established in James's novels between seeing, knowing, and exercising power that the politics of the Jamesian text appears, and it is this continuity that I have been tracing in *The Princess Casamassima*.

James closes his preface to *The Princess Casamassima* by acknowledging an apparently disqualifying lack of knowledge about his ostensible subject. The setting of the novel is the anarchic underworld of London, but the scene of writing is far removed from the scene of the action: "I remember at any rate feeling myself all in possession of little Hyacinth's consistency, as I have called it, down at Dover during certain weeks that were none too remotely precedent to the autumn of 1885 and the appearance, in 'The Atlantic Monthly' again, of the first chapters of the story" (1:xx). Like the Princess, James appears to have "retired to a private paradise to think out the problem of the slums." But even here James obliquely acknowledges a continuity between this scene of light and culture and the policed underworld of London. The law reappears even in the midst of this private paradise: "There were certain sunny, breezy balconied rooms at the quieter end of the Esplanade of that cheerful castle-crested little town—now infinitely perturbed by gigantic 'harbour works,' but then only faded and over-soldiered and all pleasantly and humbly submissive to the law that snubs in due course the presumption of flourishing resorts" (1:xx). "Over-soldiered" and "humbly submissive to the law," in the diffused and extended sense that the novel has promoted, the scene of writing is a muted repetition of the scene of the novel. Reinscribed in the ordinary and everyday, the "police" are everywhere.

35Bersani, "The Subject of Power," 10.
36Mackenzie, *Communities of Honor and Love in Henry James*, 22.

The First Paragraph of *The Ambassadors*

Ian Watt

When I was asked if I would do a piece of explication at this conference, I was deep in Henry James, and beginning *The Ambassadors*: so the passage chose itself; but just what was explication, and how did one do it to prose? I take it that whereas explanation, from *explanare*, suggests a mere making plain by spreading out, explication, from *explicare*, implies a progressive unfolding of a series of literary implications, and thus partakes of our modern preference for multiplicity in method and meaning: explanation assumes an ultimate simplicity, explication assumes complexity.

Historically, the most developed tradition of explication is presumably that which developed out of medieval textual exegesis and became the chief method of literary instruction in French secondary and higher education in the late nineteenth century. *Explication de texte* in France reflects the rationalism of nineteenth-century Positivist scholarship. At its worst the routine application of the method resembles a sort of bayonet drill in which the exposed body of literature is riddled with etymologies and dates before being despatched in a harrowingly insensitive *résumé*. At its best, however, *explication de texte* can be solidly illuminating, and it then serves to remind us that a piece of literature is not necessarily violated if we give systematic attention to such matters as its author, its historical setting, and the formal properties of its language.

Practical Criticism, on the other hand, as it was developed at Cambridge by I. A. Richards, continues the tradition of the British Empiricists. Inductive rather than deductive, it makes a point of excluding linguistic and historical considerations, so as to derive—in appearance at least—all the literary values of a work empirically from the words on the page. In the last thirty years the emphasis of Practical Criticism on the autonomy of the text has revolutionised the approach to literary studies, and has proved itself a technique of supreme value for teaching and examining students; I myself certainly believe that its

From *Essays in Criticism* 10 (1960), 250–74. Reprinted by permission of the author and the editors of *Essays in Criticism*. (Originally entitled "The First Paragraph of *The Ambassadors*: An Explication.") Original acknowledgments have been omitted by the editor.

use should be expanded rather than curtailed. Yet, at least in the form in which I picked it up as a student and have later attempted to pass it on as a teacher, both its pedagogical effects and its basic methodological assumptions seem to me to be open to serious question. For many reasons. Its air of objectivity confers a spurious authority on a process that is often only a rationalisation of an unexamined judgment, and that must always be to some extent subjective; its exclusion of historical factors seems to authorise a more general anti-historicism; and—though this objection is perhaps less generally accepted—it contains an inherent critical bias in the assumption that the part is a complete enough reflection of the literary whole to be profitably appreciated and discussed in isolation from its context. How far this is true, or how far it can be made to appear so by a well-primed practitioner, is a matter of opinion; but it is surely demonstrable that Practical Criticism tends to find the most merit in the kind of writing which has virtues that are in some way separable from their larger context; it favours kinds of writing that are richly concrete in themselves, stylistically brilliant, or composed in relatively small units. It is therefore better suited to verse than to prose; and better suited to certain kinds of either than to others where different and less concentrated merits are appropriate, as in the novel.

As for its pedagogical effects—and here again I have mainly my own past experience in mind—Practical Criticism surely tends to sensitise us towards objects only within a certain range of magnitude: below that threshold it becomes subjective and impressionist, paying very little attention to the humble facts of the grammar and syntax of the words on the page; while, at the other extreme, it often ignores the larger meaning, and the literary and historical contexts of that meaning.

As a practical matter these restrictions may all be necessary for the pupil and salutary for the teacher; and I mention them mainly to justify my present attempt to develop the empirical and inductive methods of Practical Criticism in such a way as to deal with those elements in a literary text whose vibrations are so high or so low that we Ricardian dogs have not yet been trained to bark at them.

It is mainly in these penumbral areas, of course, that the French *explication de texte* habitually operates; but its analysis of grammar and of the literary and historical background are usually a disconnected series of discrete demonstrations which stop short of the unifying critical synthesis that one hopes for. Until fairly recently the same could have been said, and perhaps with greater emphasis, about the German tradition of literary scholarship, with its almost entirely independent pursuit of philology and philosophy. More recent trends in *Stilforschung* however—of which Wolfgang Clemen's *The Development of Shakespeare's Imagery* (Bonn, 1936), was an early example—come closer to, and indeed partly reflect, the more empirical Anglo-American models of literary criticism; while, even more promising perhaps for the study of prose, though seemingly quite independent of the influence of Practical Criticism, is the development, mainly from Romance philology, of what has come to be called 'stylistics'.

For my purposes, however, it remains not so much a method as a small group of isolated, though spectacular, individual triumphs. I yield to no one in my admiration for Leo Spitzer's *Linguistics and Literary History* (Baltimore, 1948), or for the continual excitement and illumination offered in Erich Auerbach's *Mimesis* (1946: trans. Willard Trask, Princeton, N.J., 1953); their achievements, however, strike me mainly as tributes to the historical imagination and philosophical understanding of the German mind at its best; I find their brilliant commentaries on words or phrases or passages essentially subjective; and if I am tempted to emulate the *bravura* with which they take off from the word on the page to leap into the farthest empyreans of *Kulturgeschichte,* I soon discover that the Cambridge east winds have condemned me to less giddy modes of critical transport.

Yet what other models are there to help one to analyse a paragraph of Jamesian prose? Some of the historical studies of prose style could, conceivably, be applied; but I am fearful of ending up with the proposition that James was a Ciceronian—with Senecan elements, of course, like everyone else. As for the new linguistics, the promises as regards literary analysis seem greater than the present rewards: the most practical consequence of my exposure to Charles Fries's *The Structure of English: An Introduction to the Construction of English Sentences* (New York, 1952), for example, was to deprive me of the innocent pleasure that comes from imagining you know the names of things. Structural linguistics in general is mainly (and rightly) concerned with problems of definition and description at a considerably more basic level of linguistic usage than the analysis of the literary effect of Henry James's grammatical particularities seems to require.

Perhaps the most promising signs of the gaps being filled have come from what are—in that particular area—amateurs: from Francis Berry's *Poets' Grammar* (London, 1958), or Donald Davie's *Articulate Energy* (London, 1955). But they don't help much with prose, of course, and they aren't basically concerned with grammatical structure in the ordinary sense; although Davie's notion that the principle of continuity in poetry is, after all, primarily grammatical and rational, at least lessens the separation between the stylistic domains of poetry and prose, and suggests some ways of studying how syntax channels expressive force.

Virtually helpless,[1] then, I must face the James passage alone as far as any fully developed and acceptable technique for explicating prose is concerned; but there seem to be good reasons why practical criticism should be supple-

[1]This was before the appearance of the English Institute's symposium *Style in Prose Fiction* (New York, 1959), which offers, besides two general surveys and a valuable bibliography of the field, stylistic studies of six novelists, including one by Charles R. Crow, of 'The Style of Henry James: *The Wings of the Dove.*'

mented by some of the approaches of French and German scholarship, and by whatever else will lead one from the words on the page to matters as low as syntax and as high as ideas, or the total literary structure.

I

Strether's first question, when he reached the hotel, was about his friend; yet on his learning that Waymarsh was apparently not to arrive till evening he was not wholly disconcerted. A telegram from him bespeaking a room 'only if not noisy', reply paid, was produced for the inquirer at the office, so that the understanding 5 they should meet at Chester rather than at Liverpool remained to that extent sound. The same secret principle, however, that had prompted Strether not absolutely to desire Waymarsh's presence at the dock, that had led him thus to postpone for a few hours his enjoyment of it, now operated to make him feel he could still wait without disappointment. They would dine together at the worst, 10 and, with all respect to dear old Waymarsh—if not even, for that matter, to himself—there was little fear that in the sequel they shouldn't see enough of each other. The principle I have just mentioned as operating had been, with the most newly disembarked of the two men, wholly instinctive—the fruit of a sharp sense that, delightful as it would be to find himself looking, after so much separation, into 15 his comrade's face, his business would be a trifle bungled should he simply arrange for this countenance to present itself to the nearing steamer as the first 'note' of Europe. Mixed with everything was the apprehension, already, on Strether's part, that it would, at best, throughout, prove the note of Europe in quite a sufficient degree.[2]

[2]Henry James, *The Ambassadors* (Revised Collected Edition, Macmillan: London, 1923). Since there are a few variants that have a bearing on the argument, it seems desirable to give a collation of the main editions; P is the periodical publication (*The North American Review*, clxxvi, 1903); IA the first American editon (Harper and Brothers, New York, 1903); IE the first English edition (Methuen and Co., London, 1903); N.Y., the 'New York Edition', New York and London, 1907–9 (the London Macmillan edition used the sheets of the American edition); CR the 'Collected Revised Edition', London and New York, 1921–31 (which uses the text of the New York Edition). It should perhaps be explained that the most widely used editions in England and America make misleading claims about their text: the 'Everyman' edition claims to use the text 'of the revised Collected Edition', but actually follows the Ist English edition in the last variant; while the 'Anchor' edition, claiming to be 'a faithful copy of the text of the Methuen first edition', actually follows the first American edition, including the famous misplaced chapters.

l.4.	reply paid NY, CR; *with the answer paid* P, IA, IE.
l.4.	*inquirer* P, IA, IE, CR; *enquirer* NY.
ll.4–5.	*understanding they* NY, CR; *understanding that they* P, IA, IE.
l.8.	*feel he* NY, CR; *feel that he* P, IA, IE.
l.11.	*shouldn't* CR, NY; *should not* P, IA, IE.
ll.13.	*newly disembarked,* all eds. except P: *newly-disembarked.*
ll.15–16.	*arrange for this countenance to present* NY, CR; *arrange that this countenance should present* P, IA, IE.
ll.16–17.	*'note', of Europe* CR; *'note', for him, of Europe* P, IA, IE; *'note', of Europe,* NY.
l.18.	*that it would* P, IA, NY, CR; *that he would* IE.

It seems a fairly ordinary sort of prose, but for its faint air of elaborate portent; and on second reading its general quality reminds one of what Strether is later to observe—approvingly—in Maria Gostrey: an effect of 'expensive, subdued suitability'. There's certainly nothing particularly striking in the diction or syntax; none of the immediate drama or rich description that we often get at the beginning of novels; and certainly none of the sensuous concreteness that, until recently, was regarded as a chief criterion of good prose in our long post-imagistic phase: if anything, the passage is conspicuously un-sensuous and un-concrete, a little dull perhaps, and certainly not easy reading.

The difficulty isn't one of particularly long or complicated sentences: actually they're of fairly usual length: I make it an average of 41 words; a little, but not very much, longer than James's average of 35 (in Book 2, ch. 2 of *The Ambassadors*, according to R. W. Short's count, in his very useful article 'The Sentence Structure of Henry James's *American Literature*, XVIII [March 1946], 71–88).[3] The main cause of difficulty seems rather to come from what may be called the delayed specification of referents: 'Strether' and 'the hotel' and 'his friend' are mentioned before we are told who or where they are. But this difficulty is so intimately connected with James's general narrative technique that it may be better to begin with purely verbal idiosyncrasies, which are more easily isolated. The most distinctive ones in the passage seem to be these: a preference for non-transitive verbs; many abstract nouns; much use of 'that'; a certain amount of elegant variation to avoid piling up personal pronouns and adjectives such as 'he', 'his' and 'him'; and the presence of a great many negatives and near-negatives.

By the preference for non-transitive verbs I mean three related habits: a great reliance on copulatives—'Strether's first question *was* about his friend'; '*was* apparently not to arrive': a frequent use of the passive voice—'*was* not wholly *disconcerted*'; 'a telegram . . . *was produced*'; 'his business *would be* a trifle *bungled*': and the employment of many intransitive verbs—'the understanding . . . remained . . . sound'; 'the . . . principle . . . operated to'. My count of all the verbs in the indicative would give a total of 14 passive, copulative or intransitive uses as opposed to only 6 transitive ones: and there are in addition frequent infinitive, participial, or gerundial uses of transitive verbs, in all of which the active nature of the subject-verb-and-object sequence is considerably abated—'on his learning'; 'bespeaking a room'; 'not absolutely to desire'; 'led him thus to postpone'.

This relative infrequency of transitive verbal usages in the passage is associated with the even more pronounced tendency towards using abstract nouns as subjects of main or subordinate clauses: 'question'; 'understanding'; 'the same secret principle'; 'the principle'; 'his business'. If one takes only the

---

[3]I am also indebted to the same author's 'Henry James's World of Images', *PMLA* LXVIII (Dec., 1953), 943–960.

main clauses, there are four such abstract nouns as subjects, while only three main clauses have concrete and particular subjects ('he' or 'they').[4]

I detail these features only to establish that in this passage, at least, there is a clear quantitative basis for the common enough view that James's late prose style is characteristically abstract; more explicitly, that the main grammatical subjects are very often nouns for mental ideas, 'question', 'principle', etc.; and that the verbs—because they are mainly used either non-transitively, or in infinitive, participial and gerundial forms,—tend to express states of being rather than particular finite actions affecting objects.

The main use of abstractions is to deal at the same time with many objects or events rather than single and particular ones: and we use verbs that denote states of being rather than actions for exactly the same reason—their much more general applicability. But in this passage, of course, James isn't in the ordinary sense making abstract or general statements; it's narrative, not expository prose; what need exploring, therefore, are the particular literary imperatives which impose on his style so many of the verbal and syntactical qualities of abstract and general discourse; of expository rather than narrative prose.

Consider the first sentence. The obvious narrative way of making things particular and concrete would presumably be 'When Strether reached the hotel, he first asked "Has Mr. Waymarsh arrived yet?" ' Why does James say it the way he does? One effect is surely that, instead of a sheer stated event, we get a very special view of it; the mere fact that actuality has been digested into reported speech—the question 'was about his friend'—involves a narrator to do the job, to interpret the action, and also a presumed audience that he does it for: and by implication, the heat of the action itself must have cooled off somewhat for the translation and analysis of the events into this form of statement to have had time to occur. Lastly, making the subject of the sentence 'question' rather than 'he', has the effect of subordinating the particular actor, and therefore the particular act, to a much more general perspective: mental rather than physical, and subjective rather than objective; 'question' is a word which involves analysis of a physical event into terms of meaning and intention: it involves, in fact, both Strether's mind and the narrator's. The narrator's, because he interprets Strether's act: if James had sought the most concrete method of taking us into Strether's mind—' "Has Mr. Waymarsh come yet?" I at once asked'—he would have obviated the need for the implied external categoriser of Strether's action. But James disliked the 'mere platitude of statement' involved in first-person narrative; partly, presumably, because it would merge Strether's consciousness into the narrative, and not isolate it for the reader's inspection. For such isolation, a more

---

[4]Sentences one and four are compound or multiple, but in my count I haven't included the second clause in the latter—'there was little fear': though if we can talk of the clause having a subject it's an abstract one—'fear'.

expository method is needed: no confusion of subject and object, as in first-person narration, but a narrator forcing the reader to pay attention to James's primary objective—Strether's mental and subjective state.

The 'multidimensional' quality of the narrative, with its continual implication of a community of three minds—Strether's, James's, and the reader's—isn't signalled very obviously until the fourth sentence—'The principle I have just mentioned as operating . . .'; but it's already been established tacitly in every detail of diction and structure, and it remains pervasive. One reason for the special demand James's fictional prose makes on our attention is surely that there are always at least three levels of development—all of them subjective: the characters' awareness of events; the narrator's seeing of them; and our own trailing perception of the relation between these two.

The primary location of the narrative in a mental rather than a physical continuum gives the narrative a great freedom from the restrictions of particular time and place. Materially, we are, of course, in Chester, at the hotel—characteristically 'the hotel' because a fully particularised specification—'The Pied Bull Inn' say—would be an irrelevant brute fact which would distract attention from the mental train of thought we are invited to partake in. But actually we don't have any pressing sense of time and place: we feel ourselves to be spectators, rather specifically, of Strether's thought processes, which easily and imperceptibly range forwards and backwards both in time and space. Sentence three, for example, begins in the past, at the Liverpool dock; sentence four looks forward to the reunion later that day, and to its many sequels: such transitions of time and place are much easier to effect when the main subjects of the sentences are abstract: a 'principle' exists independently of its context.

The multiplicity of relations—between narrator and object, and between the ideas in Strether's mind—held in even suspension throughout the narrative, is presumably the main explanation for the number of 'thats' in the passage, as well as of the several examples of elegant variation. There are 9 'thats'—only two of them demonstrative and the rest relative pronouns (or conjunctions or particles if you prefer those terms); actually there were no less than three more of them in the first edition, which James removed from the somewhat more colloquial and informal New York edition; while there are several other 'thats' implied—in 'the principle [that] I have just mentioned', for instance.

The number of 'thats' follows from two habits already noted in the passage. 'That' characteristically introduces relative clauses dealing not with persons but with objects, including abstractions; and it is also used to introduce reported speech—'on his learning that Waymarsh'—not 'Mr. Waymarsh isn't here'. Both functions are combined in the third sentence where we get a triple definition of a timeless idea based on the report of three chronologically separate events: 'the same secret principle that had prompted Strether not absolutely to desire Waymarsh's presence at the dock, that had led him thus to postpone for a few hours his enjoyment of it, now operated to make him feel that he could still wait without disappointment'.

Reported rather than direct speech also increases the pressure towards elegant variation: the use, for example, in sentence 1 of 'his friend', where in direct speech it would be 'Mr. Waymarsh' (and the reply—'*He* hasn't come yet'). In the second sentence—'a telegram . . . was produced for the inquirer'—'inquirer' is needed because 'him' has already been used for Waymarsh just above; of course, 'the inquirer' is logical enough after the subject of the first sentence has been an abstract noun—'question'; and the epithet also gives James an opportunity for underlining the ironic distance and detachment with which we are invited to view his dedicated 'inquirer', Strether. Later, when Strether is 'the most newly disembarked of the two men', we see how both elegant variation and the grammatical subordination of physical events are related to the general Jamesian tendency to present characters and actions on a plane of abstract categorisation; the mere statement, 'Mr. Waymarsh had already been in England for [so many] months', would itself go far to destroy the primarily mental continuum in which the paragraph as a whole exists.

The last general stylistic feature of the passage to be listed above was the use of negative forms. There are 6 'noes' or 'nots' in the first 4 sentences; four implied negatives—'postpone'; 'without disappointment'; 'at the worst'; 'there was little fear': and two qualifications that modify positiveness of affirmation—'not wholly', and 'to that extent'. This abundance of negatives has no doubt several functions: it enacts Strether's tendency to hesitation and qualification; it puts the reader into the right judicial frame of mind; and it has the further effect of subordinating concrete events to their mental reflection; 'Waymarsh was not to arrive', for example, is not a concrete statement of a physical event: it is subjective—because it implies an expectation in Strether's mind (which was not fulfilled); and it has an abstract quality—because while Waymarsh's arriving would be particular and physical, his *not* arriving is an idea, a non-action. More generally, James's great use of negatives or near-negatives may also, perhaps, be regarded as part of his subjective and abstractive tendency: there are no negatives in nature but only in the human consciousness.

II

The most obvious grammatical features of what Richard Chase has called Henry James's 'infinitely syntactical language' (*The American Novel and its Tradition*, New York, 1957), can, then, be shown to reflect the essential imperatives of his narrative point of view; and they could therefore lead into a discussion of the philosophical qualities of his mind, as they are discussed, for example, by Dorothea Krook in her notable article 'The Method of the Later Works of Henry James' (*London Magazine*, I [1954], 55–70); our passage surely exemplifies James's power 'to generalise to the limit the particulars of experience', and with it the characteristic way in which both his 'perceptions of the world itself, and his perceptions of the logic of the world . . . happen simultaneously, are part of a single comprehensive experience'. Another aspect of the connection between James's metaphysic and his method as a novelist has inspired a stimulating stylistic study—Carlo Izzo's 'Henry James, Scrittore Sintattico' (*Studi Americani*, II [1956], 127–142). The connection between thought and style finds its historical perspective in John Henry Raleigh's illuminating study 'Henry James: The Poetics of Empiricism' (*PMLA*, LXVI [1951], 107–123), which establishes connections between Lockean epistemology and James's extreme, almost anarchic, individualism; while this epistemological preoccupation, which is central to Quentin Anderson's view of how James worked out his father's cosmology in fictional terms (*The American Henry James*, New Brunswick, 1957), also leads towards another large general question, the concern with 'point of view', which became a crucial problem in the history and criticism of fiction under the influence of the sceptical relativism of the late nineteenth-century.

In James's case, the problem is fairly complicated. He may be classed as an 'Impressionist', concerned, that is, to show not so much the events themselves, but the impressions which they make on the characters. But James's continual need to generalise and place and order, combined with his absolute demand for a point of view that would be plastic enough to allow him freedom for the formal 'architectonics' of the novelists' craft, eventually involved him in a very idiosyncratic kind of multiple Impressionism: idiosyncratic because the dual presence of Strether's consciousness and of that of the narrator, who translates what he sees there into more general terms, makes the narrative point of view both intensely individual and yet ultimately social.

Another possible direction of investigation would be to show that the abstractness and indirection of James's style are essentially the result of this characteristic multiplicity of his vision. There is, for example, the story reported by Edith Wharton that after his first stroke James told Lady Prothero that 'in the very act of falling . . . he heard in the room a voice which was distinctly, it seemed, not his own, saying: "So here it is at last, the distinguished thing".' James, apparently, could not but see even his own most fateful personal experience, except as evoked by some other observer's voice in terms of the long historical and literary tradition of death. Carlo Izzo regards this tendency as typical of the Alexandrian style, where there is a marked disparity between the rich inheritance of the means of literary expression, and the meaner creative world which it is used to express; but the defence of the Jamesian habit of mind must surely be that what the human vision shares with that of animals is presumably the perception of concrete images, not the power to conceive universals: such was Aristotle's notion of man's distinguishing capacity. The universals in the present context are presumably the awareness that behind every petty individual circumstance there ramifies an endless network of general moral, social and historical relations. Henry James's style can therefore be seen as a supremely civilised effort to relate every event and every moment of life to the full complexity of its circumambient conditions.

Obviously James's multiple awareness can go too far; and in the later novels it often poses the special problem that we do not quite know whether the awareness implied in a given passage is the narrator's or that of his character. Most simply, a pronoun referring to the subject of a preceding clause is always liable to give trouble if one hasn't been very much aware of what the grammatical subject of that preceding clause was; in the last sentence of the paragraph, for example, 'the apprehension, already, on Strether's part, that . . . it would, at best, . . . prove the "note" of Europe,' 'it' refers to Waymarsh's countenance: but this isn't at first obvious; which is no doubt why, in his revision of the periodical version for the English edition James replaced 'it' by 'he'—simpler, grammatically, but losing some of the ironic visual precision of the original. More seriously, because the narrator's consciousness and Strether's are both present, we often don't know whose mental operations and evaluative judgments are involved in particular cases. We pass, for instance, from the objective analysis of sentence 3 where the analytic terminology of 'the same secret principle' must be the responsibility of the narrator, to what must be a verbatim quotation of Strether's mind in sentence 4: 'with all respect to dear old Waymarsh' is obviously Strether's licensed familiarity.

But although the various difficulties of tense, voice, and reference require a vigilance of attention in the reader which some have found too much to give, they are not in themselves very considerable: and what perhaps is much more in need of attention is how the difficulties arising from the multiplicity of points of view don't by any means prevent James from ordering all the elements of his narrative style into an amazingly precise means of expression: and it is this positive, and in the present case, as it seems to me, triumphant, mastery of the difficulties which I want next to consider.

Our passage is not, I think, James either at his most memorable or at his most idiosyncratic: *The Ambassadors* is written with considerable sobriety and has, for example, little of the vivid and direct style of the early part of *The Wings of the Dove*, or of the happy symbolic complexities of *The Golden Bowl*. Still, the passage is fairly typical of the later James; and I think it can be proved that all or at least nearly all the idiosyncrasies of diction or syntax in the present passage are fully justified by the particular emphases they create.

The most flagrant eccentricity of diction is presumably that where James writes 'the most newly disembarked of the two men' (lines 12–13). 'Most' may very well be a mere slip; and it must certainly seem indefensible to any one who takes it as an absolute rule that the comparative must always be used when only two items are involved.[5] But a defence is at least possible. 'Most

---

[5]Though consider *Rasselas*, ch. xviii: 'Both conditions may be bad, but they cannot both be worst'.

newly disembarked' means something rather different from 'more newly disembarked'. James, it may be surmised, did not want to compare the recency of the two men's arrival, but to inform us that Strether's arrival was 'very' or as we might say, 'most' recent; the use of the superlative also had the advantage of suggesting the long and fateful tradition of transatlantic disembarcations in general.

The reasons for the other main syntactical idiosyncrasies in the passage are much clearer. In the first part of the opening sentence, for example, the separation of subject—'question'—from verb—'was'—by the longish temporal clause 'when he reached the hotel', is no doubt a dislocation of normal sentence structure; but, of course, 'Strether' must be the first word of the novel: while, even more important, the delayed placing of the temporal clause forces a pause after 'question' and thus gives it a very significant resonance. Similarly with the last sentence; it has several peculiarities, of which the placing of 'throughout' seems the most obvious. The sentence has three parts: the first and last are comparatively straightforward, but the middle is a massed block of portentous qualifications: 'Mixed with everything was the apprehension—already, on Strether's part, that he would, at best, throughout,—prove the note of Europe in quite a sufficient degree.' The echoing doom started by the connotation of 'apprehension' reverberates through 'already' ('much more to come later') 'on Strether's part' ('even he knows') and 'at best' ('the worst has been envisaged, too'); but it is the final collapse of the terse rhythm of the parenthesis that isolates the rather awkwardly placed 'throughout', and thus enables James to sound the fine full fatal note; there is no limit to the poignant eloquence of 'throughout'. It was this effect, of course, which dictated the preceding inversion which places 'apprehension' not at the start of the sentence, but in the middle where, largely freed from its syntactical nexus, it may be directly exposed to its salvos of qualification.

The mockingly fateful emphasis on 'throughout' tells us, if nothing had before, that James's tone is in the last analysis ironic, comic, or better, as I shall try to suggest, humorous. The general reasons for this have already been suggested. To use Maynard Mack's distinction (in his Preface to *Joseph Andrews*, Rinehart Editions, New York, 1948), 'the comic artist subordinates the presentation of life as experience, where the relationship between ourselves and the characters experiencing it is a primary one, to the presentation of life as a spectacle, where the primary relation is between himself and us as onlookers'. In the James passage, the primacy of the relation between the narrator and the reader has already been noted, as has its connection with the abstraction of the diction, which brings home the distance between the narrator and Strether. Of course, the application of abstract diction to particular persons always tends towards irony,[6] because it imposes a dual way of

[6]As I have argued in 'The Ironic Tradition in Augustan Prose from Swift to Johnson', *Restoration and Augustan Prose* (Los Angeles, 1957).

looking at them: few of us can survive being presented as general representatives of humanity.

The paragraph, of course, is based on one of the classic contradictions in psychological comedy—Strether's reluctance to admit to himself that he has very mixed feelings about his friend: and James develops this with the narrative equivalent of *commedia dell'arte* technique: virtuoso feats of ironic balance, comic exaggeration, and deceptive hesitation conduct us on a complicated progress towards the foreordained illumination.

In structure, to begin with, the six sentences form three groups of two: each pair of them gives one aspect of Strether's delay; and they are arranged in an ascending order of complication so that the fifth sentence—72 words—is almost twice as long as any other, and is succeeded by the final sentence, the punch line, which is noticeably the shortest—26 words. The development of the ideas is as controlled as the sentence structure. Strether is obviously a man with an enormous sense of responsibility about personal relationships; so his first question is about his friend. That loyal *empressement*, however, is immediately checked by the balanced twin negatives that follow: 'on his learning that Waymarsh *was not* to arrive till evening, he *was not* wholly disconcerted': one of the diagnostic elements of irony, surely, is hyperbole qualified with mock-scrupulousness, such as we get in 'not wholly disconcerted'. Why there are limits to Lambert Strether's consternation is to transpire in the next sentence; Waymarsh's telegram bespeaking a room 'only if not noisy' is a laconic suggestion of that inarticulate worthy's habitually gloomy expectations—from his past experiences of the indignities of European hotel noise we adumbrate the notion that the cost of their friendly *rencontre* may be his sleeping in the street. In the second part of the sentence we have another similar, though more muted, hint: 'the understanding that they should meet in Chester rather than at Liverpool remained to that extent sound'; 'to that extent', no doubt, but to *any other?*—echo seems to answer 'No'.

In the second group of sentences we are getting into Strether's mind, and we have been prepared to relish the irony of its ambivalences. The negatived hyperbole of 'not absolutely to desire', turns out to mean 'postpone'; and, of course, a voluntarily postponed 'enjoyment' itself denotes a very modified rapture, although Strether's own consciousness of the problem is apparently no further advanced than that 'he could still wait without disappointment'. Comically loyal to what he would like to feel, therefore, we have him putting in the consoling reflection that 'they would dine together at the worst'; and the ambiguity of 'at the worst' is followed by the equally dubious thought: 'there was little fear that in the sequel they shouldn't see enough of each other'. That they should, in fact, see too much of each other; but social decorum and Strether's own loyalties demand that the outrage of the open statement be veiled in the obscurity of formal negation.

By the time we arrive at the climactic pair of sentences, we have been told enough for more ambitious effects to be possible. The twice-mentioned 'secret

principle', it appears, is actually wholly 'instinctive' (line 13); but in other ways Strether is almost ludicrously self-conscious. The qualified hyperbole of 'his business would be a trifle bungled', underlined as it is by the alliteration, prepares us for a half-realised image which amusingly defines Strether's sense of his role: he sees himself, it appears, as the stage-manager of an enterprise in which his solemn obligations as an implicated friend are counterbalanced by his equally ceremonious sense that due decorums must also be attended to when he comes face to face with another friend of long ago—no less a person than Europe. It is, of course, silly of him, as James makes him acknowledge in the characteristic italicising of 'the "note" of Europe';[7] but still, he does have a comically ponderous sense of protocol which leads him to feel that 'his business would be a trifle bungled' should he simply arrange for this countenance to present itself to the nearing steamer as the first 'note' of Europe. The steamer, one imagines, would not have turned hard astern at the proximity of Waymarsh's sacred rage; but Strether's fitness for ambassadorial functions is defined by his thinking in terms of 'arranging' for a certain countenance at the docks to give just the right symbolic greeting.

Strether's notion of what Europe demands also shows us the force of his aesthetic sense. But in the last sentence the metaphor, though it remains equally self-conscious, changes its mode of operation from the dramatic, aesthetic, and diplomatic, to something more scientific: for, although ten years ago I should not have failed to point out, and my readers would not, I suppose, have failed to applaud, the ambiguity of 'prove', it now seems to me that we must choose between its two possible meanings. James may be using 'prove' to mean that Waymarsh's face will 'turn out to be' the 'note of Europe' for Strether. But 'prove' in this sense is intransitive, and 'to be' would have to be supplied; it therefore seems more likely that James is using 'prove' in the older sense of 'to test': Waymarsh is indeed suited to the role of being the sourly acid test of the siren songs of Europe 'in quite a sufficient degree', as Strether puts it with solemn but arch understanding.

The basic development structure of the passage, then, is one of progressive and yet artfully delayed clarification; and this pattern is also typical of James's general novelistic method. The reasons for this are suggested in the Preface to *The Princess Casamassima*, where James deals with the problem of maintaining a balance between the intelligence a character must have to be interesting, and the bewilderment which is nevertheless an essential condition of the novel's having surprise, development, and tension: 'It seems probable that if we were never bewildered there would never be a story to tell about us.'

In the first paragraph of *The Ambassadors* James apprises us both of his hero's supreme qualities and of his associated limitations. Strether's delicate critical intelligence is often blinkered by a highly vulnerable mixture of moral generosity towards others combined with an obsessive sense of personal

[7]See George Knox, 'James's Rhetoric of Quotes,' *College English*, XVII (1956), 293–297.

inadequacy; we see the tension in relation to Waymarsh, as later we are to see it in relation to all his other friends; and we understand, long before Strether, how deeply it bewilders him; most poignantly about the true nature of Chad, Madame de Vionnet—and himself.

This counterpoint of intelligence and bewilderment is, of course, another reason for the split narrative point of view we've already noted: we and the narrator are inside Strether's mind, and yet we are also outside it, knowing more about Strether than he knows about himself. This is the classic posture of irony. Yet I think that to insist too exclusively on the ironic function of James's narrative point of view would be mistaken.

Irony has lately been enshrined as the supreme deity in the critical pantheon: but, I wonder, is there really anything so wonderful about being distant and objective? Who wants to see life only or mainly in intellectual terms? In art as in life we no doubt can have need of intellectual distance as well as of emotional commitment; but the uninvolvement of the artist surely doesn't go very far without the total involvement of the person; or, at least, without a deeper human involvement than irony customarily establishes. One could, I suppose, call the aesthetically perfect balance between distance and involvement, open or positive irony: but I'm not sure that humour isn't a better word, especially when the final balance is tipped in favour of involvement, of ultimate commitment to the characters; and I hope that our next critical movement will be the New Gelastics.

At all events, although the first paragraph alone doesn't allow the point to be established fully here, it seems to me that James's attitude to Strether is better described as humorous than ironical; we must learn like Maria Gostrey, to see him 'at last all comically, all tragically'. James's later novels in general are most intellectual; but they are also, surely, his most compassionate: and in this particular paragraph Strether's dilemma is developed in such a way that we feel for him even more than we smile at him. This balance of intention, I think, probably explains why James keeps his irony in such a low key: we must be aware of Strether's 'secret' ambivalence towards Waymarsh, but not to the point that his unawareness of it would verge on fatuity; and our controlling sympathy for the causes of Strether's ambivalence turns what might have been irony into something closer to what Constance Rourke characterises as James's typical 'low-keyed humor of defeat' (*American Humor*, 1931).

That James's final attitude is humorous rather than ironic is further suggested by the likeness of the basic structural technique of the paragraph to that of the funny story—the incremental involvement in an endemic human perplexity which can only be resolved by laughter's final acceptance of contradiction and absurdity. We don't, in the end, see Strether's probing hesitations mainly as an ironic indication by James of mankind's general muddlement; we find it, increasingly, a touching example of how, despite all their inevitable incongruities and shortcomings, human ties remain only, but still, human.

Here it is perhaps James's very slowness and deliberation throughout the narrative which gives us our best supporting evidence: greater love hath no man than hearing his friend out patiently.

III

The function of an introductory paragraph in a novel is presumably to introduce: and this paragraph surely has the distinction of being a supremely complex and inclusive introduction to a novel. It introduces the hero, of course, and one of his companions; also the time; the place; something of what's gone before. But James has carefully avoided giving us the usual retrospective beginning, that pile of details which he scornfully termed a 'mere seated mass of information'. All the details are scrupulously presented as reflections from the novel's essential centre—the narrator's patterning of the ideas going forwards and backwards in Strether's mind. Of course, this initially makes the novel more difficult, because what we probably think of as primary—event and its setting—is subordinated to what James thinks is—the mental drama of the hero's consciousness, which, of course, is not told but shown: scenically dramatised. At the same time, by selecting thoughts and events which are representative of the book as a whole, and narrating them with an abstractness which suggests their larger import, James introduces the most general themes of the novel.

James, we saw, carefully arranged to make 'Strether's first question', the first three words; and, of course, throughout the novel, Strether is to go on asking questions—and getting increasingly dusty answers. This, it may be added, is stressed by the apparent aposiopesis: for a 'first' question when no second is mentioned, is surely an intimation that more are—in a way unknown to us or to Strether—yet to come. The later dislocations of normal word-order already noted above emphasise other major themes; the 'secret principle' in Strether's mind, and the antithesis Waymarsh-Europe, for instance.

The extent to which these processes were conscious on James's part cannot, of course, be resolved; but it is significant that the meeting with Maria Gostrey was interposed before the meeting with Waymarsh, which James had originally planned as his beginning in the long (20,000) word scenario of the plot which he prepared for *Harper's*. The unexpected meeting had many advantages; not least that James could repeat the first paragraph's pattern of delayed clarification in the structure of the first chapter as a whole. On Strether's mind we get a momentously clear judgment at the end of the second paragraph: 'there was detachment in his zeal, and curiosity in his indifference'; but then the meeting with Maria Gostrey, and its gay opportunities for a much fuller presentation of Strether's mind, intervene before Waymarsh himself finally appears at the end of the chapter; only then is the joke behind Strether's uneasy hesitations in the first paragraph brought to its hilariously blunt climax: 'It was already upon him even at that distance—Mr. Waymarsh was for *his* part joyless'.

One way of evaluating James's achievement in this paragraph, I suppose, would be to compare the opening of James's other novels, and those of previous writers: but it would take too long to do more than sketch the possibilities of this approach. James's early openings certainly have some of the banality of the 'mere seated mass of information': in *Roderick Hudson* (1876), for example: 'Rowland Mallet had made his arrangements to sail for Europe on the 5th of September, and having in the interval a fortnight to spare, he determined to spend it with his cousin Cecilia, the widow of a nephew of his father. . . .' Later, James showed a much more comprehensive notion of what the introductory paragraph should attempt: even in the relatively simple and concrete opening of *The Wings of the Dove* (1902): 'She waited, Kate Croy, for her father to come in, but he kept her unconscionably, and there were moments at which she showed herself, in the glass over the mantle, a face positively pale with irritation that had brought her to the point of going away without sight of him. . . .' 'She waited, Kate Croy'—an odd parenthetic apposition artfully contrived to prefigure her role throughout the novel—to wait.

One could, I suppose, find this sort of symbolic prefiguring in the work of earlier novelists; but never, I imagine, in association with all the other levels of introductory function that James manages to combine in a single paragraph. Jane Austen has her famous thematic irony in the opening of *Pride and Prejudice* (1813): 'It is a truth universally acknowledged, that a single man in possession of a good fortune must be in want of a wife'; but pride and prejudice must come later. Dickens can hurl us overpoweringly into *Bleak House* (1852–3), into its time and place and general theme; but characters and opening action have to wait:

> London. Michaelmas Term lately over, and the Lord Chancellor sitting in Lincoln's Inn Hall. Implacable November weather. As much mud in the streets, as if the waters had but newly retired from the face of the earth, and it would not be wonderful to meet a Megalosaurus, forty feet long or so, waddling like an elephantine lizard up Holborn-Hill. Smoke lowering down from chimney-pots. . . .

In Dickens, characteristically, we get a loud note that sets the tone, rather than a polyphonic series of chords that contain all the later melodic developments, as in James. And either the Dickens method, or the 'mere seated mass of information' seem to be commonest kinds of opening in nineteenth-century novels. For openings that suggest something of James's ambitious attempt to achieve a prologue that is a synchronic introduction of all the main aspects of the narrative, I think that Conrad is his closest rival. But Conrad, whether in expository or dramatic vein, tends to an arresting initial vigour that has dangers which James's more muted tones avoid. In *An Outcast of the Islands* (1896), for example:

When he stepped off the straight and narrow path of his peculiar honesty, it was with an inward assertion of unflinching resolve to fall back again into the monotonous but safe stride of virtue as soon as his little excursion into the wayside quagmires had produced the desired effect. It was going to be a short episode—a sentence in brackets, so to speak, in the flowing tale of his life. . . .

Conrad's sardonic force has enormous immediate impact; but it surely gives too much away: the character, Willems, has been dissected so vigorously that it takes great effort for Conrad—and the reader—to revivify him later. The danger lurks even in the masterly combination of physical notation and symbolic evaluation at the beginning of *Lord Jim* (1900): 'He was an inch, perhaps two, under six feet . . .': the heroic proportion is for ever missed, by an inch, perhaps two; which is perhaps too much, to begin with.

It is not for me to assess how far I have succeeded in carrying out the general intentions with which I began, or how far similar methods of analysis would be applicable to other kinds of prose. As regards the explication of the passage itself, the main argument must by now be sufficiently clear, although a full demonstration would require a much wider sampling both of other novels and of other passages in *The Ambassadors*.[8] The most obvious and demonstrable features of James's prose style, its vocabulary and syntax, are direct reflections of his attitude to life and his conception of the novel; and these features, like the relation of the paragraph to the rest of the novel, and to other novels, make clear that the notorious idiosyncrasies of Jamesian prose are directly related to the imperatives which led him to develop a narrative texture as richly complicated and as highly organised as that of poetry.

No wonder James scorned translation and rejoiced, as he so engagingly confessed to his French translator, Auguste Monod, that his later works were 'locked fast in the golden cage of the *intraduisible*'. Translation could hardly do justice to a paragraph in which so many levels of meaning and implication are kept in continuous operation; in which the usual introductory exposition of time, place, character, and previous action, are rendered through an immediate immersion in the processes of the hero's mind as he's involved in perplexities which are characteristic of the novel as a whole and which are articulated in a mode of comic development which is essentially that, not only of the following chapter, but of the total structure. To have done all that is to have gone far towards demonstrating the contention which James announced at the end of the Preface to *The Ambassadors*, that, 'the Novel remains still, under the right persuasion, the most independent, most elastic, most prodigious of literary forms'; and the variety and complexity of the functions carried out in the book's quite short first paragraph also suggest that, contrary to some notions, the demonstration is, as James claimed, made with 'a splendid particular economy'.

[8]A similar analysis of eight other paragraphs selected at fifty page intervals revealed that, as would be expected, there is much variation: the tendency to use non-transitive verbs, and abstract nouns as subjects, for instance, seems to be strong throughout the novel, though especially so in analytic rather than narrative passages; but the frequent use of 'that' and of negative forms of statement does not recur significantly.

The Logic of Delegation in *The Ambassadors*

Julie Rivkin

In his interview with Maria Gostrey at the end of *The Ambassadors*, Lambert Strether justifies his rejection of her offer with a guiding principle: "That, you see, is my only logic. Not, out of the whole affair, to have got anything for myself."[1] Strether's claim—or disclaimer—sounds like a restatement of that all too familiar ethos of renunciation that shapes so many of James's terminations. And, in a sense, it is just that. But in *The Ambassadors*, the ethos of renunciation takes peculiar force from its link with what is both the novel's subject and its strategy of composition: ambassadorship. Employing Strether as ambassador for Mrs. Newsome, James invites us to see Strether's role as substitute or delegate for another absent authority, James himself; further, by having Strether invoke a "logic" of delegation that governs his own actions and permits him no direct profits from his mission, James implies the existence of a similar textual logic that regulates the novel's representational system, central to which is Strether's role as authorial stand-in or delegate.[2] Strether's final decision should be seen not as an act of personal preference but as part of a larger textual logic, and this revision requires a shift in the ground of critical discussion from questions of morality or character (the realm to which the term *renunciation* belongs) to questions of representation or delegation.[3] I argue that the ethical issues of the novel

From *PMLA* 101 (1986), 819–831. Copyright © 1986 by the Modern Language Association. Reprinted by permission of the author and the Modern Language Association of America. Notes have been slightly revised by the author.

[1] Henry James, *The Ambassadors* (New York: Scribner's, 1909), vol. 22, p. 326. Subsequent references to the novel are to this edition (vols. 21 and 22 of the New York Edition) and appear in parentheses in the text.

[2] Although the more common term is "centre of consciousness," in the preface to *The Golden Bowl* James calls this figure "the impersonal author's concrete deputy or delegate, a convenient substitute or apologist for the creative power otherwise so veiled and disembodied" (*The Art of the Novel: Critical Prefaces*, ed. Richard P. Blackmur [New York: Scribner's, 1934], p. 327). Subsequent references to the prefaces are to this edition and appear in parentheses in the text.

[3] "Character-centered" readings of this final scene range from Yvor Winters' view that Strether's renunciation is a slightly hypocritical act designed to preserve his good name at Woollett at the cost of Maria Gostrey's feelings ("Maule's Well, or Henry James and the Relation of Morals to Manners," in *In Defense of Reason* [Chicago: Swallow, 1947], pp. 300–43) to the conviction that it is the fullest expression of his idealism—whether a sacrifice to the ideal of transcendent love (Manfred Mackenzie, *Communities of Honor and Love in Henry James*

need to be reconsidered from the point of view of what Derrida calls the "logic of supplementarity," a logic that governs not only such textual concerns as authority, reference, and intention but also the novel's central thematic conflict between the New England ethos of propriety and property and the Parisian ethos of experience and expenditure.

Derrida works out his representational "logic of the supplement" in his reading of Rousseau in *Of Grammatology*. The supplement, like the ambassador, is a stand-in supposed to alter nothing of that which it stands in for; it is defined as an addition having no effect on the original to which it is being joined. Yet the existence of the addition implies that the original is incomplete and in need of supplementation; the paradoxical logic of supplementarity is that what adds onto also subtracts from, or reveals a lack in, the original. This logic emerges from Derrida's critique of the traditional theory of representation, according to which representation is a secondary copy added onto an original or primary presence, be it of an object or an idea. Writing, for example, is a supplement supposedly added onto an already intact and self-identical speech, which, in the traditional theory, is characterized as a token of pure presence. The supplement of writing is dangerous to speech because writing is not immediately attached to a living presence; it can always go astray, betraying the presence it supposedly communicates. In his critique of this theory, Derrida argues that the ostensible order of priority between speech and writing is in fact reversible, since speech can only function if it uses signs that share a characteristic of writing, detachability from their origin—the capacity to function in the absence of the speaker. The putative original, in other words, could not exist without its copy. Derrida generalizes from this example to all representation and argues that there is no original presence outside supplementation. The presence that is delegated into representation is in a curious way constituted by that representational delegation. The prerepresentational immediacy of the original is, according to Derrida, an

---

[Cambridge: Harvard UP, 1976], pp. 150–52) or that of civilization (Alwyn Berland, *Culture and Conduct in the Novels of Henry James* [Cambridge: Cambridge UP, 1981], pp. 224–27). Other readings emphasize Strether's mixed motives; see, for example, Christopher Wegelin, *The Image of Europe in Henry James* (Dallas: Southern Methodist UP, 1958), pp. 101–04; Ellen Douglass Leyburn, *Strange Alloy: The Relation of Comedy to Tragedy in the Fiction of Henry James* (Chapel Hill: U of North Carolina P, 1968), pp. 133–35; or, for a particularly thorough discussion, Oscar Cargill, *The Novels of Henry James* (New York: Macmillan, 1961), pp. 321–24. Sallie Sears, on the other hand, emphasizes the implications for plot design (*The Negative Imagination: Form and Perspective in the Novels of Henry James* [Ithaca: Cornell UP, 1968], pp. 114–51), while Laurence Holland, taking the representational implications further, stresses the analogy between Strether's sacrifice and the costs James incurs in the enactment of his own art (*The Expense of Vision: Essays in the Craft of Henry James* [Princeton: Princeton UP, 1964], pp. 279–82. Leo Bersani notes the derivation of the story itself from compositional necessity ("The Jamesian Lie," in *A Future for Astyanax* [Boston: Little, 1976], pp. 128–55), and Charles Feidelson works out the representational problem of the "centre of consciousness" technique in a reading of the preface ("James and the Man of Imagination," in *Literary Theory and Structure: Essays in Honor of William K. Wimsatt*, ed. Frank Brady, John Palmer, and Martin Price [Princeton: Princeton UP, 1964], pp. 331–52).

illusion, and the advent of the original will always be deferred along a chain of supplements.

> Through this sequence of supplements a necessity is announced: that of an infinite chain, ineluctably multiplying the supplementary mediations that produce the sense of the very thing they defer: the mirage of the thing itself, of immediate presence, of originary perception. Immediacy is derived. That all begins through the intermediary is what is indeed "inconceivable [to reason]."[4]

The logic of supplementarity undermines the authority and priority assigned to the original (the presence of the idea in the mind or of the thing itself) in the traditional theory of representation. If all representation resembles writing, then originals will always run the risk of being betrayed by the representations on which they depend for their own being, of seeing their delegates go astray, generating meanings and effects that are in no way proper to the original.[5]

The logic of supplementarity bears an uncanny resemblance to the "logic" traced in *The Ambassadors*; "all begins through the intermediary" could be the novel's own epigraph. The book literally begins with the intermediary or ambassador, and the effect of this beginning is to expose the absence of the very originating authority he is employed to represent—whether Mrs. Newsome or Henry James. But if the ambassador betrays his origin in representing it, his own use of representatives will be subject to the same law. And by the novel's end he testifies to his comprehension of that necessity when he speaks of a "logic." Far from invoking moral principle or personal desire, his explanation of his behavior invokes the representational: it is because he is serving as ambassador and working in the interests of another that he denies himself experience in his own person. But interestingly enough the "logic" that requires this sacrifice justifies all Strether's gains; while an ambassador is not free to derive profits when in the employ of another, the same law dictates that an ambassador make use of other ambassadors and appreciate the accumulations of their own experiences. Strether's attempt to live vicariously—to live through intermediaries like Gloriani, little Bilham, and Chad Newsome—simply transfers the role of ambassador to those around him, thus putting them in exactly the same bind that his mission for Mrs. Newsome has placed him in. The logic of delegation, then, is not a principle of renunciation so much as one of displacement; its effect is to replicate itself, compensating for sacrifices by creating a chain of ambassadors. What this representational logic leads us to, then, are the experiential difficulties that constitute the novel's central themes and action: the problem of missed and vicarious experience; the plot of substitution, deflection, and deferral; and the novel's dual econ-

---

[4]Jacques Derrida, *Of Grammatology*, trans. Gayatri Chakravorty Spivak (Baltimore: Johns Hopkins UP, 1976), p. 157.

[5]For a further account of the "logic of supplementarity" see Jonathan Culler, *On Deconstruction: Theory and Criticism after Structuralism* (Ithaca: Cornell UP, 1982), pp. 89–110.

omy. An economic theory of representation as the preservation of an original is replaced with a theory of representation as a potentially infinite dispersal of delegates without a guiding origin or authority. And a New England economy of experience as holding in reserve or saving is replaced with a Parisian economy of experience as necessitating an expenditure without reserve, loss without a guaranteed gain. This dual economy accounts for the singular plurality of the novel's title, a plurality dictated by the text's own logic of delegation—not *The Ambassador*, but, rather, *The Ambassadors*.

I

Before tracing this logic in the novel, I should like to discuss the preface, where James rewrites the novel's tale of deviation from authority and of mediation of experience as the story of the novel's own composition. More strikingly, the preface does not simply rewrite but reenacts the logic it describes, serving as ambassador for the authority of the text it introduces. Like all Jamesian prefaces, then, this one occupies the classic position of a supplement—purely additional and yet forever reminding us, in James's words, "that one's bag of adventures, conceived or conceivable, has been only half-emptied by the mere telling of one's story" (*Art*, p. 313). The preface ostensibly completes the project, telling the story that has not been told. But its effect is clearly the opposite: in telling us more, it reminds us of that which is absent; the preface reminds us of an incompleteness that the novel half disguises.[6] By supplementing the novel with the story of its composition, the preface also inevitably hints at the intended novel that never got written. When the author traces the path that moves from initial intention to final realization, he may be more conscious of what he misses than of what he sees:

> As always—since the charm never fails—the retracing of the process from point to point brings back the old illusion. The old intentions bloom again and flower—in spite of all the blossoms they were to have dropped by the way. (*Art*, p. 319)

As the process continues, the dropped blossoms become more important than those that flowered; what the writer sees is not what is there but what was to have been there: "Cherished intention too inevitably acts and operates, in the book, about fifty times as little as I had fondly dreamt it might." Like Spencer Brydon in *The Jolly Corner*, Henry James in the prefaces is searching for the ghost of the "might have been" and periodically has to remind himself of compensatory satisfactions; the sentence above continues, "but that scarce

---

[6]In the preface to *Roderick Hudson*, James stresses the novel's illusion of closure and completeness: "Really, universally, relations stop nowhere, and the exquisite problem of the artist is eternally but to draw, by a geometry of his own, the circle within which they shall happily *appear* to do so" (*Art*, p. 5).

spoils for me the pleasure of recognising the fifty ways in which I had sought to provide for it" (*Art*, p. 319).

If cherished intentions must be sacrificed, then James might at least incorporate that principle into his practice; the compositional law he arrives at in the last paragraph of the preface bears a significant relation to the "logic" Strether formulates at the end of his course:

> One would like, at such an hour as this, for critical license, to go into the matter of the noted inevitable deviation (from too fond an original vision) that the exquisite treachery even of the straightest execution may ever be trusted to inflict even on the most mature plan. (*Art*, p. 325)

"One would like" to do so, but even here, in the preface, one must defer such intentions, sacrificing matter of import and alluding only to the inevitability of such a postponement. James's sentence enacts the compositional law that it discovers, deferring, for perhaps another preface, a full exploration of that "original vision" sacrificed in the execution. Like the Derridean supplement, the Jamesian preface exposes that which is missing in its attempt to complete the story, inviting, in the failure of its own intentions, future prefaces, further supplements.

The preface is supplementary in yet another sense explored by Derrida: written after the novel and printed before it, following the novel's composition and yet providing an account of origins, supposedly extrinsic to the text and yet based on it; the preface confounds distinctions between earlier and later, inside and out, of the sort that Strether's ambassadorial voyage also undermines. When pointing out the metaphoric resemblances between preface and novel, one is, of course, tempted to show how the "houses of fiction" and "gardens of life" are "realized" in the tale or how the novel's exchanges enact an economy described in the prefaces. But the chronology of composition suggests a different derivation: the very account of origins that the prefaces provide can be derived from the novels themselves.[7]

The circular derivation of *The Ambassadors'* origins is particularly striking: James quotes a speech from the novel as the novel's own "germ" or source. As if wary of the compositional story revealed by such a paradigmatic *mise en abyme*, James then tells an alternative story, emphasizing how the speech was taken from real life. In this second account James claims that the germ was given him "bodily . . . by the spoken word" and adds that he took "the image over exactly as [he] happened to have met it" (*Art*, p. 308). But even in this account, the emphasis on physical presence, speech, and duplication is belied by the sentence that follows: "A friend had repeated to me, with great appreciation, a thing or two said to him by a man of distinction, much his

---

[7]For the Derridean account of the preface as supplement see Jacques Derrida, *Dissemination*, trans. Barbara Johnson (Chicago: U of Chicago P, 1981), pp. 3–59. See also Shoshana Felman, "Turning the Screw of Interpretation," *Yale French Studies* 55–56 (1977): 94–207.

senior, and to which a sense akin to that of Strether's melancholy eloquence might be imputed . . ." (*Art*, p. 308). In place of duplication, we have repetition with "appreciation" (a term that always carries economic resonances in James); in place of direct speech and bodily presence, we have quotation: these are the words of another, spoken in a different place by a man of a different age. The original moment is already at one remove from its origin; the young man who repeats the words of another is himself an ambassador or intermediary, and the original speech is itself a quotation. It is the final phrase, though, that puts before us the fictional status of origins: if a "sense akin to that of Strether's melancholy eloquence" must be "imputed" to these words, has not Strether's speech become the origin for this one, rather than the reverse?

What the preface, in fact, presents is a double story of the novel's composition. To the degree that it reveals the impossibility of fixing origins, it proclaims a sure foundation for the novel; in the words of the reviser, there was "never one of those alarms as for a suspected hollow beneath one's feet, a felt ingratitude in the scheme adopted, under which confidence fails and opportunity seems but to mock" (*Art*, p. 309). While at one point James laments "the exquisite treachery even of the straightest execution," he earlier insists, "Nothing resisted, nothing betrayed" (*Art*, pp. 325, 310). The preface opens, "Nothing is easier to state than the subject of *The Ambassadors*," but it goes on not to state but to locate the subject. The centrality of the location is striking—the subject can be found in the novel's formal center ("in the second chapter of Book Fifth . . . planted or 'sunk' . . . in the centre of the current"), in its geographical and by extension existential center ("in Gloriani's garden" in the center of Paris), and in the novel's own "germ"; however, the emphasis on centrality should not disguise for us this first act of displacement. The preface closes by acknowledging the inevitability of displacement and devia-tion, but in the beginning it insists on the directness of the novel's growth: "Never can a composition of this sort have sprung straighter from a dropped grain of suggestion, and never can that grain, developed, overgrown and smothered, have yet lurked more in the mass as an independent particle" (*Art*, p. 307). The rhetorical balance of this sentence suggests a correspon-dence not only between part and whole, "grain" and "mass," but also between composition and interpretation; the straight growth of the whole composition from the original part determines the direct perception of the original part in the mass. The compositional story coincident with this organic figure of "germ" and "growth" is as far from the logic of the intermediary as we can imagine; indeed, to suggest that the grain can be found in the mass as easily as the mass can grow from the grain is to deny both deviation from one's intentions and the inevitability of loss over time.

Not surprisingly, the contradictions of the compositional story are those of the novel; the preface puts itself in a "false position" much like the one in which it finds its protagonist. The compositional story and the protagonist's story intersect with particular intensity in the novel's "germ," where the contradictions noted above appear with full thematic resonance. Indeed, the germ directly challenges the assumptions implicit in its own organic metaphor. Far from suggesting that intentions can be realized in a process as natural and unimpeded as the "straight growth" of a plant, the germ itself conveys not only the deviant course taken in executing intentions but also the inevitability of a certain failure in the attempt. Instead of supporting that easy match between part and whole, composition and interpretation suggested by the natural analogy, the germ is presented as a mismatch, a "crisis." "The idea of the tale," James points out, "resides indeed in the very fact that an hour of such unprecedented ease should have been felt by him [Strether] *as* a crisis, and he is at pains to express it for us as neatly as we could desire" (*Art*, p. 307). The expression takes the form of the following speech:

> Live all you can; it's a mistake not to. It does n't so much matter what you do in particular so long as you have your life. If you have n't had that what *have* you had? I'm too old—too old at any rate for what I see. What one loses one loses; make no mistake about that. Still, we have the illusion of freedom; therefore don't, like me to-day, be without the memory of that illusion. I was either, at the right time, too stupid or too intelligent to have it, and now I'm a case of reaction against the mistake. Do what you like so long as you don't make it. For it *was* a mistake. Live, live! (*Art*, pp. 307–08)

This speech, appearing as it is quoted in the preface, sets in peculiar relief the compositional success story with which the preface opens. It does not promise an easy recovery of the past, or a neat correspondence between part and whole; rather, it presents a new version of the logic of delegation. This moment of retrospection, which constitutes the "germ," "essence," and "centre" of *The Ambassadors*, deconstructs the notions of origins and unmediated experience that it supposedly embodies. Its particular bad faith is that it confesses the impossibility of the very success it recommends for another. When the speech (in a somethat more expansive form) appears in the novel, delivered to the exquisitely sensitive little Bilham, this bad faith seems even more pronounced. The "freedom" to live that Strether urges for his young friend is knowingly presented as an illusion; in wishing he had "the memory of that illusion" himself, Strether denies the possibility of any such illusions to the young man who stands before him. The urgency of Strether's "Live, live!" is at odds with his conviction that the freedom to live is illusory. But if in the act of delegating this mission to "live," Strether both acknowledges and attempts to evade the logic of delegation, little Bilham is "too intelligent" to deceive himself. Little Bilham's response to the injunction to "live" demonstrates not only the inevitability of this logic of deflected intentions and mediated experience but also his acceptance of the stance of ambassador; if on the one hand little Bilham turns "quite solemn, and . . . this was a contradiction of the innocent gaiety the speaker had wished to promote," on the other hand he replies, "Oh but I don't know that I want to be, at your age, too different from you!" (21, pp. 218–19). While Strether's speech is supposedly designed to invite a course of development different from his own, it acknowledges the impossibility of that which it recommends, and acknowledges it to someone who in fact anticipates just such a course of necessary deviation— and just such an act of future retrospection.

Distinctive as the tone of this speech is, it should already sound familiar to us: Strether's tone on reexamining the course of his life sounds much like James's on reexamining the course of his novel—specifically in those moments when he links success to failure and exposes the fiction of origins. Just as Strether regrets not the freedom of youth but the *illusion* of freedom, James himself can only regret the intentions he had "fondly dreamt" might have been realized in the novel. In view of his claim that the novel is "frankly, quite the best, 'all round,' of my productions" (*Art*, p. 309), James's focus on its mistakes has a peculiar impact. For in *The Ambassadors* mistakes are intimately connected to successes. Not only does James make his story out of the deflection of Strether's original intentions, but the novel's subject and "germ" is a moment of retrospection that predicts the inevitability of such deflection. Of his novel, James says, "The book, . . . critically viewed, is touchingly full of these disguised and repaired losses, these insidious recoveries, these intensely redemptive consistencies" (*Art*, p. 326). If we substitute Strether for James and "my life" for "the book," we return to a statement very like Strether's speech to little Bilham. James's attitude, on rereading his most successful book, is reminiscent of Strether's on reviewing the less successful text of his life; the moment of retrospection that James quotes as the novel's origin predicts his own response in his moment of retrospection about the novel itself.

If James sounds like Strether in his general sense of the inevitability of deviation from design, he is even more closely linked to his ambassador in the particular deviation he chooses to mention in the preface. First, he emphasizes that his "law" of representation necessitates such compromises; that is, it is largely because he can present the world only as mediated by his authorial delegate that he is constrained to depart from his original design. The one compromise that he notes reveals even more compellingly the operation of this "law": "one of the suffered treacheries had consisted precisely, for Chad's whole figure and presence, of a direct presentability diminished and compromised" (*Art*, p. 325). James's selection of Chad as the locus of his own regret repeats the regret of his delegate, Strether; Chad figures for Strether as the person who, even more than little Bilham, is free to "live" without mediation, much as Chad figures for his author as one who could embody "presence," were he only seen directly. But "direct presentability," like unmediated experience, is illusory—even if the failure of the illusion is suffered as treachery. What James attempts and regrets with Chad is like what Strether attempts and regrets with both Chad and little Bilham; in confining his preface to the ostensibly formal problems of composition and representation, James finds himself at the heart of the experiential difficulties that plague his fictional representative. Moreover, James's response to this representational challenge—"the whole economy of his author's relation to him [Chad] has at important points to be redetermined" (*Art*, pp. 325–26)—suggests the revisions in the economy that governs the similarly mediated relation between the authority of Mrs. Newsome and her son Chad, revisions, that, after all, constitute the plot of *The Ambassadors*.

II

The ambassadorial logic that is inscribed in the preface and that links the story of the story inextricably to the story of the hero regulates all the novel's transactions, from the linguistic to the economic, from the familial to the cultural. Hired to mediate between mother and son, between American and European cultural and economic practices, Strether is asked to perform a mission that restores propriety as much as property, sexual as well as commercial fidelity. Returning the wayward son to his mother, the irresponsible heir to the family business, the illicit lover to the legally sanctioned marriage—all should follow from the literal communication of the message that the ambassador carries. Literality is the linguistic form of fidelity; if language could be kept from deviating into figuration, if messages could suffer no change in transmission, then the ambassador's errand of restoration might succeed. But the fate of the words that Strether carries—those "Boston 'really's'" and "virtuous attachments" that attempt to fix words to referents only to open up abysses of ambiguity—suggests both the infidelities of language toward the experience to which it supposedly corresponds and the possible promiscuities harbored in the novel's relationships themselves. What such linguistic aberrations demonstrate is that the fidelity Mrs. Newsome demands is at odds with the means she employs; the terms of the ambassador's engagement with Mrs. Newsome become the terms under which that engagement is betrayed. Instead of fixing New England categories on Parisian experience, then, Strether discovers that infidelities and deviations characterize his "straight" New England errand from the outset. The ambassador cannot come home to either proper behavior or literal meaning; rather, he remains the figure for the necessary figurative turns and errors that accompany all acts of exchange and representation. In his own about-face—as he shifts from representing the interests of Mrs. Newsome to representing those of Mme de Vionnet—he suggests the reversals to which all the novel's representational terms are subject; he deconstructs, rather than preserves, the novel's structuring oppositions of domestic and foreign, proper and improper, legal and illicit on which the New England values depend.

It is a necessary irony that Mrs. Newsome, the figure who sets this representational logic in motion, is the one least able to acknowledge its existence. As the absent authority who stands behind all the novel's ambassadors, she sends her delegates off with the express understanding that they alter nothing of that for which they stand in. She wants a representative who can fill in for her, maintain a likeness, without a difference, who can deliver the message she speaks "to the letter." Were she to enunciate her theory of representation, it would resemble those passages in the preface where James speaks of straight growth, direct speech, and exact replication. Although she makes use of ambassadors, she assumes that her business will be carried out as it would be in person; her fixity of purpose makes it impossible for her to imagine any shift or deviation. After taking the measure of his own deviation in the performance of his ambassadorial mission, Strether comments:

> That's just her difficulty—that she does n't admit surprises. It's a fact that, I think, describes and represents her; and it falls in with what I tell you—that she's all, as I've called it, fine cold thought. She had, to her own mind, worked the whole thing out in advance, and worked it out for me as well as for herself. Whenever she has done that, you see, there's no room left; no margin, as it were, for any alteration. (22, p. 222)

Given her assumptions and attitudes, it is particularly ironic that Mrs. Newsome must resort to using ambassadors to realize her conception. The ambassador is just the "margin for alteration" that she does not acknowledge.

But the absolutism of Mrs. Newsome's authority complements the deviations of her ambassadors; had she not "worked the whole thing out in advance . . . for [Strether] as well as for herself," she would not experience ambassadorial revision as a complete betrayal of her design. Were the fidelity she demanded less than complete, were the specific terms of her plan's execution left to the improvisations of her ambassador, she could accommodate the alterations incurred in the act of execution. In remaining outside the novel's sphere of ambassadorial representation and attempting to maintain complete control over it, she renders herself vulnerable to its logic, dependent on it, present only in the persons of her ambassadors, who by necessity differ from her and thereby misrepresent her.

If Mrs. Newsome can be seen as almost a parody of the absent author who "works the whole thing out in advance" only to find the scheme revised in the act of execution, then Maria Gostrey can be seen as the expert on the ambassadorial logic that will substitute for Mrs. Newsome's authority. The novel's first chapter serves as Strether's introduction to this logic of revision and substitution, and, appropriately enough, Maria Gostrey is herself not only a substitute for the figure that Strether expects—Waymarsh—but also what James calls a *ficelle*, a supplementary figure in the compositional story.[8] The

---

[8]The *ficelle* is a figure James takes from French drama, a confidant who is able to turn what would be "the seated mass of information after the fact" (*Art*, p. 321) into scene and dialogue. James is quite explicit about the supplementary status of the *ficelle*, who belongs not to the

novel opens, famously, with Strether's first question concerning the where-
abouts of his friend Waymarsh, and it is only because his friend is not there
that Strether finds himself in the company of this alternative acquaintance.
The wandering walk that they take through Chester suggests the deviant
course that results from any act of substitution, be it representational or
ambassadorial, and by the time Strether encounters Waymarsh at the end of
the chapter, he has traveled a path that leads far from Waymarsh's straight and
narrow way of propriety.

Maria Gostrey's revisionary impact on Strether's plans parallels her impact
on James's design in the compositional story; she is a substitute not only for
the figure Strether awaits but also for the one James had planned. In the
"project" for the novel, Strether was to meet Maria Gostrey only after he met
Waymarsh, and indeed only through Waymarsh's acquaintance. This revision
suggests the common representational logic that binds the compositional story
to the fictional one; the novel can only begin as a substitute for the design that
ostensibly serves as its origin, just as Strether's experience as a delegate can
only begin as a turn away from his plan. James's other revision of the novel's
"project" further stresses deviation as a principle of narrative development; in
changing "Way*mark*" to "Way*marsh*,"[9] James suggests not only the inevitable
changes that come in the course of execution but also the transformation of
severity into uncertainty and the breakdown of proper boundaries that is the
fate of New England in the novel. Maria Gostrey—her name falls one
consonant short of "go straight" and leaves us with the open-ended sound and
open path of "go stray"—comes between Strether and Waymarsh and in this
act of mediation opens up a way for Strether that is far from the course he
intended to travel.

What Maria Gostrey has to teach Strether about ambassadorial logic begins
as a response to the practical social problem they face as strangers desiring to
make each other's acquaintance and eventually leads into an exploration of the
premises on which Strether's mission is based. Though James's preface describes her function as eliciting "certain indispensable facts" about Strether in
a form that allows James to treat the otherwise "inserted block of merely
referential narrative" in entertainingly scenic form (*Art*, pp. 323, 321), she
exposes the "facts" as something other than factual and the "referential
narrative" as oddly detached from reference. This critique of the referential
begins with her first words. Echoing the hotel receptionist who has just

---

"subject" but to the "treatment" (*Art*, p. 53), and who therefore must have "the seams or joints of
[her] ostensible connectedness taken particular care of, duly smoothed over, that is, and anxiously
kept from showing as 'pieced on' " (*Art*, pp. 323–24). James adds that Maria Gostrey does achieve
"something of the dignity of a prime idea" (*Art*, p. 324); I would argue that this occurs because
the supplement itself is a "prime idea" in *The Ambassadors*. It seems no accident that the "logic"
of ambassadorship comes out most fully in the novel's closing scene, of which James says: "its
function is to give or to add nothing whatever" (*Art*, p. 324).
   [9]Henry James, *The Notebooks of Henry James*, ed. F. O. Matthiessen and Kenneth P.
Murdock (New York: Oxford UP, 1947), p. 376.

produced a telegram from Strether's absent friend Waymarsh, she is "moved to ask, by his leave, if it were possibly a question of Mr. Waymarsh of Milrose Connecticut—Mr. Waymarsh the American lawyer" (21, p. 6). Although she ostensibly seeks to attach Strether's friend's identity to a fixed point of geographical and professional reference, the name "Waymarsh" serves as a mere pretext for conversation, less important as a designation than as the vehicle of a certain effect. The unimportance of Maria Gostrey's reference emerges when she substitutes another name for that of Waymarsh. Asked whether he knows the Munsters, Strether is compelled to admit that he does not, but, interestingly enough, the name of someone he does not know serves just as well as the name of someone he does to provide a basis for this new connection. Under the guise of offering references, Maria Gostrey exposes the precariousness of such foundations; proper names, far from being the rigid designators Strether's New England sense of propriety would have trained him to expect, begin to operate instead as intermediaries loosened from reference.[10] In his absence "Waymarsh" legitimizes relations that he himself might not authorize in person, suggesting the fate of that other character who appears in the novel in name alone: "Mrs. Newsome."

The proper names that pose the greatest difficulties for Strether and Maria Gostrey are, of course, not "Waymarsh" and "Munster" but their own. Faced with the social problem of providing introductions when they have no basis for their new acquaintance, they find themselves relying on calling cards. But though Strether pockets Maria Gostrey's card as if it were the person it names (he finds it "positively droll . . . that he should already have Maria Gostrey, whoever she was—of which he had n't really the least idea—in a place of safe keeping" [21, pp. 12–13]), Maria Gostrey's mistaking of Strether's card for her own links the interchangeability of cards to the interchangeability of other representations. Like the cards they carry as tokens of their identity, these two ambassadors are, they discover, also detachable from a fixed ground of reference.

Maria Gostrey's continuing investigations into the background of her new friend only reveal further the precarious foundation on which his identity rests. His profession is no more fixed than his name. Strether speaks to Maria Gostrey of his position as editor of a journal:

> "Woollett has a Review—which Mrs. Newsome, for the most part, magnificently pays for and which I, not at all magnificently, edit. My name's on the cover"
> . . . "And what kind of Review is it?"
> . . . "Well, it's green."
> "Do you mean in political colour as they say here—in thought?"
> "No; I mean the cover's green—of the most lovely shade." (21, p. 64)

[10]For a discussion of the more commonly noticed ambiguities of pronoun reference in James, see Ralf Norrman, *The Insecure World of Henry James's Fiction: Intensity and Ambiguity* (New York: St. Martin's, 1982).

Strether's comic insistence on the literal in the face of Maria Gostrey's more convincing figurative interpretation of his words suggests that he fears such deviations into the metaphoric will lead him to stray from propriety. But in substituting cover for content, pigment for point of view, he exposes what he tries to conceal. Strether's joke of identifying the book by its cover is more serious than it might appear, for it bears directly on his identity: "He was Lambert Strether because he was on the cover, whereas it should have been, for anything like glory, that he was on the cover because he was Lambert Strether" (21, p. 84). The names printed on calling cards are like this name printed on the review; instead of being based on some preexisting and prerepresentational referent, Strether's identity derives from its publication. The text that advertises his public identity also creates it.

In principle, Woollett, Massachusetts, epitomizes proper identity and proper behavior, a literal world untouched by compromising metaphors. When Maria Gostrey asks, for example, "Who in the world's Jim Pocock?" Strether replies, "Why Sally's husband. That's the only way we distinguish people at Woollett" (21, p. 72). According to the "Woollett standard," as Strether will call it later, the Newsome family stands as an absolute, the source of all "distinction," both designation and value. Other residents are distinguished—both known and seen as worthy—by their relation to the Newsomes. But Maria Gostrey senses a "cover" even here. As she explores the origins of the Newsome clan, she comes on a foundation as dubious as any that she and Strether have just invented for their own connection. On Maria Gostrey's questioning, Strether divulges, "The source of [Chad's] grandfather's wealth—and thereby of his own share in it—was not particularly noble." Asked further about the source, Strether can only reply, "Well—practices . . . I shan't describe *him* nor narrate his exploits." Maria Gostrey remarks, "Lord, what abysses!" The "Woollett standard" turns out to be founded on an abyss, the source of all value to be something unspeakable. Strether says, "The men I speak of—they did as everyone does; and (besides being ancient history) it was all a matter of appreciation" (21, p. 63). In place of some grounded and morally proper origin for inherited wealth, Maria Gostrey discovers a supplementary process of accumulation or "appreciation." Through her questions about the figures—both personal and monetary—who stand behind Strether, Maria Gostrey deconstructs the literal system of designation Woollett supposedly embodies by tracing it back to the "unspeakable."

"Ancient history" is, in fact, no different from the present story. All parties stand to gain by Chad's return—the Newsomes in wealth, Strether in marriage. But these "appreciations" are also hidden by covers. When Maria Gostrey asks Strether, "Then how do they distinguish *you?*" he sidesteps the question that would have obliged him to confess that he stood to gain from his mission. "They *don't*—except, as I've told you, by the green cover." But clearly Strether's "distinction" in the world of Woollett is to inhere in being

Mrs. Newsome's husband. So Maria Gostrey is correct to sense that the "green cover" is a cover in another sense: "The green cover won't—nor will any cover—avail you with *me*. You're of a depth of duplicity" (21, p. 72). Again Maria Gostrey turns to the metaphoric in her critique of this New England "straight talk," which lays claim to disinterested moral probity and strict literality. What she draws out is the necessity of metaphors or figures to the supposedly prefigural, "virtuous," and uncompromised world of Woollett. Indeed, the town's propriety, like the identity behind proper names, seems to depend on representations, metaphors that create an effect of propriety but that designate no fixed literal referent.

As she explores the grounds of Strether's ambassadorship, then, Maria Gostrey begins to confound the simple distinctions between literal and figurative, proper and improper, America and Europe, on which his mission apparently rests. In questioning proper names, Maria Gostrey is also questioning the origins of property, and, by extension, of Mrs. Newsome's rights of ownership over both her ambassador, Strether, and her son, Chad. She exposes as problematic both the origin of the Newsome fortune and the mother's absolute authority, thereby questioning Mrs. Newsome's assumptions about representation as exact replication. She replaces the New England conservative economy and retentive theory of representation with an economy that encourages extravagance and a model of representation as deviation from a source. As a "general guide," "a sort of superior 'courier-maid,'" "a companion at large"—apart from being James's own *ficelle*—she not only stands for a principle of ambassadorial representation as "going astray"; she also knows the ambassadorial economy that offers no return on one's investment. In words that anticipate Strether's final recognition, she acknowledges, "I don't do it, you know, for any particular advantage. I don't do it, for instance—some people do, you know—for money" (21, p. 18). From the initial violations of propriety to the exposure of property, Maria Gostrey signals that the ambassador's fate is inevitably a straying from authority, as well as a departure from the logic of investment as personal gain.

III

When Strether arrives in Paris, his first impulse is to establish contact with Mrs. Newsome, as if to correct himself from the deviant explorations he has already embarked on with Maria Gostrey. But just as proper names led into an investigation of improprieties, so now the letters that Strether seeks as a link with authority will become the marks of his distance from the Woollett standard that is his source. Much like his effort to meet Waymarsh before embarking on European explorations, his attempt to take up his correspondence with Mrs. Newsome is also baffled by an absence—her letters have not yet arrived. And when the letters do come the next day, Strether has already displaced himself from his New England basis.

Literally, this displacement is traced in his restless wanderings from the bank at Rue Scribe, where the letters arrive, to the "penny chair" in the Luxembourg Gardens where he finally reads them; figuratively, he has enacted a shift from a New England economy of equal exchange (the bank) to a Parisian economy of expenditure (the penny chair). Moreover, this shift in economy is a shift in the concept of representation: while Mrs. Newsome's letters give him "chapter and verse for the moral that nothing would suffer" in his absence, telling him "who would take up this and who take up that exactly where he had left it" (21, p. 82), he has come to discover that his act of replacement and displacement makes such scriptural literalism no longer possible. He reflects, "It was the difference, the difference of being just where he was and *as* he was, that formed the escape—this difference was so much greater than he had dreamed it would be; and what he finally sat there turning over was the strange logic of his finding himself so free" (21, p. 81). What the letters from Mrs. Newsome trace in their journey from bank to garden is Strether's shift from the rigors of New England authority to the pleasures of Parisian experience. But what Strether has yet to discover is that the representational "logic" that governs his relation to authority will also govern his relation to Parisian experience. Though Strether rather comically wonders, "Was he to renounce all amusement for the sweet sake of that authority? . . . [A]lmost any acceptance of Paris might give one's authority away" (21, p. 89), neither "authority" nor "Paris" is his simply for the bartering.

Operative in Strether's reckoning is the American conception that Paris embodies "experience" in as unmediated and direct a fashion as Mrs. Newsome herself embodies authority. Though Strether, with his elaborate scruples about participation, might seem to escape such a simplification, the care with which he confines his indulgences to the vicarious confesses to his acceptance of the American myth of Paris. While the choice to live vicariously might seem to acknowledge a necessarily mediated relation to experience, it actually bases itself on just the opposite perception. Life or experience is there to be had, even if Strether cannot enjoy it in person. Strether's image of Paris confirms this conviction: behind the city's manifold appearances is a reality to which those in the know have access. Though he is compelled to admit that in this city "parts were not to be discriminated nor differences comfortably marked . . . what seemed all surface one moment seemed all depth the next" (21, p. 89), he still thinks of penetrating facades, touching bottom, and arriving at the "truth." Whether his emphasis is metaphysical (presence, life) or epistemological (the truth), he conceives of "experience" as a goal that can be reached, a prize that can be won—if not by himself, then by another.

The "other" who has been posited from the start as occupying a privileged relation to Parisian experience is Chad Newsome; and just as it is initially Chad whom Strether must rescue and protect from that experience, it will later be Chad through whom Strether will imagine his own vicarious access to that experience. These contradictory responses share an assumption: that

Chad is in "life" in a way that Strether can only imagine. Strether's first meeting with Chad is critical in establishing this privileged relation to Parisian experience, even as it marks Strether's separation from anything like a New England point of origin. In particular, Strether's peculiar response to the changes in Chad—what Strether calls "this sharp rupture of an identity" (21, p. 137)—and the immediacy with which this rupture translates into a disconnection between Chad and his "New England female parent" (21, p. 140) allow Strether to see the new Chad as the product of a different origin, the Parisian experience that Strether now sees as his own goal. Speculating to Maria Gostrey about the source of these changes, he says, "Well, the party responsible is, I suppose, the fate that waits for one, the dark doom that rides. . . . One wants, confound it, don't you see? . . . one wants to enjoy anything so rare. Call it then life . . . call it poor dear old life simply that springs the surprise" (21, pp. 167–68). In naming this source life, Strether suggests that, if the authority of Mrs. Newsome has been challenged, it has been supplanted by an equally absolute agency of experience.

Although Strether's new Parisian friends confirm his impression of Chad's improvements, they qualify Strether's sense that the change has been absolute. And in doing so, they challenge his conceptual model of experience. Maria Gostrey warns Strether, "He's not so good as you think!" (21, p. 171), and little Bilham echoes the doubt: Chad is "like the new edition of an old book that one has been fond of—revised and amended, brought up to date, but not quite the thing one knew and loved" (21, p. 177). Little Bilham's metaphor of the revised book substitutes for Strether's notion of experience as an absolute concealed behind its representative, Chad. Strether's attempt to find the "truth" about Chad, for example, has just this structure. "Are you engaged to be married—is that your secret?—to the young lady?" Strether asks Chad. The response—"I have no secret—though I may have secrets" (21, p. 235)—challenges Strether's model of a single explanatory reality behind all appearances. A later conversation with Mme de Vionnet makes this difference even more explicit; advised by Mme de Vionnet that he should simply tell Mrs. Newsome the truth, Strether is moved to inquire, "And what do you call the truth?" Again, Mme de Vionnet not only refuses to give the expected answer but also revises the assumptions of the question: "Well, any truth—about us all—that you see yourself" (21, p. 253).

If Maria Gostrey teaches Strether that ambassadorial representatives go astray in the absence of their guiding New England authority—thus teaching him something about all representation—the Parisians teach him that the experience, the truth of life, that he imagined stood behind representatives like Chad is also something detached from any fixed ground, something that, like Chad, might be revisable according to one's perspective and that, like Mme de Vionnet, might be multiple rather than unique, singular and distinct. But what Maria Gostrey could only tell Strether, suggesting that he was already participating in the phenomenon without knowing it, he learns for himself in Gloriani's garden. There, it becomes clear that the revisionary process he has already begun to experience, the process of substitution and deviation he has been embarked on from the novel's opening sentence, is in fact the life he has been seeking. Thinking he stands outside, like Mrs. Newsome, holding in reserve, he in fact is already in the middle of a new economy of representation and exchange, caught in the logic that requires multiple delegates and expenditure without return.

This revisionary process may have been evident from Strether's first steps in Chester, but the potential for change takes on climactic force in Gloriani's garden, a setting that promises Strether a vision not only of Parisian life at its most exclusive but also of the particular "life" behind Chad's miraculous transformation. Here, at the heart of the novel, in the heart of Paris, Strether stands off to one side, wondering as he watches those who belong to the "great world" whether "he himself, for the moment and thus related to them by his observation, [was] *in* it?" (21, p. 219). The vision in the garden shows experience to be the product or effect of a juxtaposition of representations, rather than the revelation of some truth of presence or experience that stands as a ground behind the world of appearances. Indeed, Strether—by juxtaposing and comparing himself to others he desires to be "like," by sending forth delegates like little Bilham to catch their naive notions of life, and by endlessly revising his own perceptions—shows himself to be already thoroughly in the middle (an intermediary without anchor, authority, or goal) of that which he seeks, its living embodiment or ambassador.

Standing in the garden with little Bilham, Strether says, "I know, if we talk of that—whom *I* should enjoy being like." Following Strether's line of vision, focused now on an encounter taking place in the center of the garden between his host Gloriani and a woman of the world, little Bilham guesses at his allusion: "Gloriani?" (21, p. 220). As the scene alters, though, so does Strether's desire, so that while he might have begun with Gloriani in mind, by the time he has finished speaking he finds that a different figure has been interposed. Between his initial wish and his final claim, or between little Bilham's guess—"Gloriani?"—and Strether's answer, this other vision grows:

> He had just made out, in the now full picture, something and somebody else; another impression had been superimposed. A young girl in a white dress and a softly plumed white hat had suddenly come into view, and what was presently clear was that her course was toward them. What was clearer still was that the handsome young man at her side was Chad Newsome, and what was clearest of all was that she was therefore Mademoiselle de Vionnet, that she was unmistakeably pretty— bright gentle shy happy wonderful—and that Chad now, with a consummate calculation of effect, was about to present her to his old friend's vision. What was clearest of all indeed was something much more than this, something at the single stroke of which—and was n't it simply juxtaposition?—all vagueness vanished. It was the click of a spring—he saw the truth. He had by this time also met Chad's look; there was more of it in that; and the truth, accordingly, so far as Bilham's enquiry was concerned, had thrust in the answer. "Oh Chad!"—it was that rare youth he should have enjoyed being "like." (21, p. 220)

Although Strether believes that he has found his ideal ambassador and his image of life incarnate at the heart of the Parisian garden, his conviction is countered by its status as a revision of his own intention, a revision that shifts the meaning of his words in the very moment of their utterance. Moreover, the picture itself—as fixed and complete as Strether might wish it to be—exposes its own revisionary potential in the very demonstration of its plenitude. He desires a New England literality, but he is given a Parisian process of substitution, deviation, and revision. Though the emphasis is on immediacy and presence—the picture is "now full"; the "truth" suddenly clear "before him" and "present" to "his vision"—there are symptoms of inadequacy, displacement, and supplementation. For example, in the very "now" of revelation (twice repeated), Strether sees something "more" in Chad's look, an invitation to supplements that Strether might prefer to ignore. Similarly, the sequence of adjectives that marks the process of clarification—"clear," "clearer still," "clearest of all," "clearest of all indeed"—adds something "more" at the moment it should be complete: the repetition of the superlative suggests that the ultimate can be superseded, that the superlative itself is simply a product of comparison. Indeed, comparison—or "juxtaposition"—turns out to be the source of Strether's vision of truth; in seeing Chad next to Gloriani, and Mlle de Vionnet next to Chad, Strether perceives an ideal "likeness" between himself and Chad. But if truth is a product of juxtaposition rather than a revelation of an absolute, there is no reason that truth should stop here, for different juxtapositions will give rise to different truths. And truth does not stop here: as convinced as Strether is that he has discovered in Jeanne de Vionnet the living source of Chad's mysterious enrichment (and thereby in the "rare youth" his own chosen delegate), this truth will quickly dissolve in the face of further juxtaposition. But the point is not that Strether gets it wrong in guessing Chad is involved with Jeanne de Vionnet when Chad is actually involved with Jeanne's mother; nor is it that Strether is wrong in guessing that Chad's attachment is "virtuous" in the New England sense of the word when it is actually adulterous. Rather, what Strether will discover as he replaces one truth about experience with another is that there is no stopping point in this logic of revision, no superlative that will stand beyond all comparison, no originating intention that can hold its meaning fixed to the ultimate referent. Just as authority will find intention revised in the act of representation, so too one representative will give way to another, one apparently "full picture" will be "superimposed" by another.

Gloriani's garden encourages Strether's myth of Parisian life as a fully present plenitude only to expose it as an effect of supplementarity, of possibly endless substitutions; instead of a presence that gives rise to delegational representations, life turns out to be an effect of the interplay or juxtaposition of representatives. Indeed, Chad is "life" in that he is associated with a "consummate calculation of effect," a product of representation rather than a ground standing behind it. Though Strether anxiously wonders whether things show "for what they really are" (21, p. 207), his New England conception of identity as a stable reality behind appearances is giving way to a Parisian conception of identity as a product and function of appearances.

The person who comes most to epitomize the life that Strether has been seeking through delegational representatives like Chad, the presence of experience that stands behind all those intersubstitutable and supplementary representatives as a stable referent, ground, or origin to which they point and from which they derive their meaning, as Strether does from Mrs. Newsome, is Mme de Vionnet. Yet what Strether discovers is that the life that seemed to stand outside the logic of supplementary delegation is itself subject to its laws. Mme de Vionnet turns out to represent life as something far more problematic, supplementary, and plural than Strether's New England categories anticipated. She is lacking but, by virtue of that, rich in supplementary possibilities: though on first meeting her he notes that "there was somehow not quite a wealth in her; and a wealth was all that, in his simplicity, he had definitely prefigured" (21, p. 211), he will later find her "like Cleopatra in the play, indeed various and multifold" (21, p. 271). As one of the Parisian cognoscenti will put it, "She's fifty women." Strether, anxious about the instability such excesses imply, insists, "Ah but only one . . . at a time." The response refuses to pacify: "Perhaps. But in fifty times—!" (21, p. 265).

Thus, what Mme de Vionnet comes to reveal is that behind representation there is no firm ground. The supplements that make up representation, delegation, ambassadorship are potentially infinite. Indeed, she confirms what Strether had already begun to learn from Maria Gostrey—that property (as the self of proper names, the wealth of family, the propriety of behavior, and the presence that stands behind representation) is itself an effect, a product of the interplay of likenesses and likelihoods, the intersubstitution of representations. In Mme de Vionnet's world, there are no final authorities of the sort Mrs. Newsome claims to be; there are only ambassadors. Moreover, by displacing the economy of representation that governed Strether's initial conception of experience, Mme de Vionnet also displaces the economy of commercial transaction that governed his initial conception of his mission. Though Mrs. Newsome would have her ambassador hold fast to a single identity as her representative—and receive his promised reward in fair exchange—Strether learns from Mme de Vionnet a freely disseminated selfhood that asks for no return. The new economy is not all celebratory: as Mme de Vionnet acknowledges about her relationship with Chad, loss is the only certainty. But it is her economy rather than Mrs. Newsome's that accounts for Strether's final gesture. In renouncing profit, he renounces a New England system of representation and a New England exchange rate. But the logic that requires that renunciation is the logic that gives him the freedom to deviate and revise, to become fifty ambassadors if need be, even if only one at a time.

The Beast in the Closet

Eve Kosofsky Sedgwick

Among Thackeray's progeny in the exploration of bourgeois bachelors in bohemia, the most self-conscious and important are Du Maurier, Barrie, and—in a book like *The Ambassadors*—James. The filiations of this tradition are multiple and heterogeneous. For instance, Du Maurier offered James the plot of *Trilby* years before he wrote the novel himself.[1] Or again, Little Bilham in *The Ambassadors* seems closely related to Little Billee, the hero of *Trilby*, a small girlish-looking Left Bank art student. Little Billee shares a studio with two older, bigger, more virile English artists, whom he loves deeply—a bond that seems to give erotic point to Du Maurier's use of the Thackeray naval ballad from which Du Maurier, in turn, had taken Little Billee's name.

> There was gorging Jack and guzzling Jimmy,
> And the youngest he was little Billee.
> Now when they got as far as the Equator
> They's nothing left but one split pea.
>
> Says gorging Jack to guzzling Jimmy,
> "I am extremely hungaree."
> To gorging Jack says guzzling Jimmy,
> "We've nothing left, us must eat we."
>
> Says gorging Jack to guzzling Jimmy,
> "With one another we shouldn't agree!
> There's little Bill, he's young and tender,
> We're old and tough, so let's eat he.
>
> "Oh! Billy, we're going to kill and eat you,
> So undo the button of your chemie. . . ."[2]

As one moves past Thackeray toward the turn of the century, toward the

From Eve Kosofsky Sedgwick, "The Beast in the Closet: Henry James and the Writing of Homosexual Panic," in *Sex, Politics, and Science in the Nineteenth-Century Novel*, ed. Ruth Bernard Yeazell (Baltimore and London: The Johns Hopkins University Press, 1986), 161–82, 184–86. Copyright © 1986 by The English Institute. Reprinted by permission of the author and the press.

[1] F. O. Matthiessen and Kenneth B. Murdock, eds., *The Notebooks of Henry James* (New York: Oxford University Press, 1947), pp. 97–98.

[2] "Ballads," in *Works of Thackeray* (New York: National Library, n.d.) 6:337.

ever greater visibility across class lines of a medicalized discourse of—and newly punitive assaults on—male homosexuality, however, the comfortably frigid campiness of Thackeray's bachelors gives way to something that sounds more inescapably like panic. Mr. Batchelor had played at falling in love with women, but felt no urgency about proving that he actually could. For the bachelor heroes of *Trilby* and *Tommy and Grizel*, though, even that renunciatory high ground of male sexlessness has been strewn with psychic landmines.

In fact, the most consistent keynote of this late literature is exactly the explicitly thematized sexual anesthesia of its heroes. In each of these fictions, moreover, the hero's agonistic and denied sexual anesthesia is treated as being *at the same time* an aspect of a particular, idiosyncratic personality type *and also* an expression of a great Universal. Little Billee, for instance, the hero of *Trilby*, attributes his sudden inability to desire a woman to "a pimple" inside his "bump of" "fondness"—"for that's what's the matter with me—a pimple—just a little clot of blood at the root of a nerve, and no bigger than a pin's point!"[3] In the same long monologue, however, he again attributes his lack of desire, not to the pimple, but on a far different scale to his status as Post-Darwinian Man, unable any longer to believe in God. "Sentimental" Tommy, similarly, the hero of Barrie's eponymous novel and also of *Tommy and Grizel*, is treated throughout each of these astonishingly acute and self-hating novels both as a man with a crippling moral and psychological defect and as the very type of the great creative artist.

Reading James Straight

James's "The Beast in the Jungle" (1902)[4] is one of the bachelor fictions of this period that seems to make a strong implicit claim of "universal" applicability through heterosexual symmetries, but that is most movingly subject to a change of Gestalt and of visible saliencies as soon as an assumed heterosexual male norm is at all interrogated. Like *Tommy and Grizel*, the story is of a man and a woman who have a decades-long intimacy. In both stories, the woman desires the man but the man fails to desire the woman. In fact—in each story—the man simply fails to desire at all. Sentimental Tommy desperately desires to feel desire; confusingly counterfeits a desire for Grizel; and, with all the best intentions, finally drives her mad. John Marcher, in James's story, does not even know that desire is absent from his life, nor that May Bartram desires him, until after she has died from his obtuseness.

To judge from the biographies of Barrie and James, each author seems to have made erotic choices that were complicated enough, shifting enough in the gender of their objects, and, at least for long periods, kept distant enough from *éclaircissement* or physical expression, to make each an emboldening

[3]George Du Maurier, *Trilby* (New York: Harper & Bros., 1922), p. 271
[4]Not published until 1903—Ed.

figure for a literary discussion of male homosexual panic.[5] Barrie had an almost unconsummated marriage, an unconsummated passion for a married woman (George Du Maurier's daughter!), and a lifelong uncategorizable passion for her family of sons. James had—well, exactly that which we now all know that we know not. Oddly, however, it is simpler to read the psychological plot of *Tommy and Grizel*—the horribly thorough and conscientious ravages on a woman of a man's compulsion to pretend he desires her—into the cryptic and tragic story of James's involvement with Constance Fenimore Woolson, than to read it directly into any incident of Barrie's life. It is hard to read Leon Edel's account of James's sustained (or repeated) and intense, but peculiarly furtive,[6] intimacies with this deaf, intelligent American woman author who clearly loved him, without coming to a grinding sense that James felt he had with her above all something, sexually, to prove. And it is hard to read about what seems to have been her suicide without wondering whether the expense of James's heterosexual self-probation—an expense, one envisions if one has Barrie in mind, of sudden "generous" "yielding" impulses in him and equally sudden revulsions—was not charged most intimately to this secreted-away companion of so many of his travels and residencies. If this is true, the working-out of his denied homosexual panic must have been only the more grueling for the woman in proportion to James's outrageous gift and his moral magnetism.

If something like the doubly destructive interaction I am sketching here did in fact occur between James and Constance Fenimore Woolson, then its structure has been resolutely reproduced by virtually all the critical discussion of James's writing. James's mistake here, biographically, seems to have been in moving blindly from a sense of the good, the desirability, of love and sexuality, to the automatic imposition on himself of a specifically *hetero*sexual

---

[5]The effect of emboldenment should be to some extent mistrusted—not, I think, because the attribution to these particular figures of a knowledge of male homosexual panic is likely to be wrong, but because it is so much easier to be so emboldened about men who are arguably homosexual in (if such a thing exists) "basic" sexual orientation; while what I am arguing is that panic is proportioned not to the homosexual but to the nonhomosexual-identified elements of these men's characters. Thus, if Barrie and James are obvious authors with whom to *begin* an analysis of male homosexual panic, the analysis I am offering here must be inadequate to the degree that it does not work just as well—even better—for Joyce, Milton, Faulkner, Lawrence, Yeats.

[6]Leon Edel, *Henry James: The Middle Years: 1882–1895*, vol. 3 of *The Life of Henry James* (New York: J. B. Lippincott, Co., 1962; repr., Avon Books, 1978), makes clear that these contacts—coinciding visits to some cities and shared trips to others (e.g., 3: 94), "a special rendezvous" in Geneva (3: 217), a period of actually living in the same house (3: 215–17)—were conducted with a consistent and most uncharacteristic extreme of secrecy. (James seems also to have taken extraordinary pains to destroy every vestige of his correspondence with Woolson.) Edel cannot, nevertheless, imagine the relationship except as "a continuing 'virtuous' attachment": "That this pleasant and *méticuleuse* old maid may have nourished fantasies of a closer tie does not seem to have occurred to him at this time. If it had, we might assume he would have speedily put distance between himself and her" (3: 217). Edel's hypothesis does nothing, of course, to explain the secrecy of these and other meetings.

compulsion. (I say "imposition on himself," but of course he did not invent the heterosexual specificity of this compulsion—he merely failed, at this point in his life, to resist it actively.) The easy assumption (by James, the society, and the critics) that sexuality and heterosexuality are always exactly translatable into one another is, obviously, homophobic. Importantly, too, it is deeply heterophobic: it denies the very possibility of *difference* in desires, in objects. One is no longer surprised, of course, at the repressive blankness on these issues of most literary criticism; but for James, in whose life the pattern of homosexual desire was brave enough and resilient enough to be at last biographically inobliterable, one might have hoped that in criticism of his work the possible differences of different erotic paths would not be so ravenously subsumed under a compulsorily—and hence, never a truly "hetero"—heterosexual model. With strikingly few exceptions, however, the criticism has actively repelled any inquiry into the asymmetries of gendered desire.

It is possible that critics have been motivated in this active incuriosity by a desire to protect James from homophobic misreadings in a perennially repressive sexual climate. It is possible that they fear that, because of the asymmetrically marked structure of heterosexual discourse, *any* discussion of homosexual desires or literary content will marginalize him (or them?) as, simply, *homosexual*. It is possible that they desire to protect him from what they imagine as anachronistically "gay" readings, based on a late twentieth-century vision of men's desire for men that is more stabilized and culturally compact than James's own. It is possible that they read James himself as, in his work, positively refusing or evaporating this element of his eros, translating lived homosexual desires, where he had them, into written heterosexual ones so thoroughly and so successfully that the difference *makes* no difference, the transmutation leaves no residue. Or it is possible that, believing—as I do—that James often, though not always, attempted such a disguise or transmutation, but reliably left a residue both of material that he did not attempt to transmute and of material that could be transmuted only rather violently and messily, some critics are reluctant to undertake the "attack" on James's candor or artistic unity that could be the next step of that argument. Any of these critical motives would be understandable, but their net effect is the usual repressive one of elision and subsumption of supposedly embarrassing material. In dealing with the multiple valences of sexuality, critics' choices should not be limited to crudities of disruption or silences of orthodox enforcement.

Even Leon Edel, who traced out *both* James's history with Constance Fenimore Woolson *and* some of the narrative of his erotic desires for men, connects "The Beast in the Jungle" to the history of Woolson,[7] but connects

[7] Edel, *Life of James*, vol 4, *The Master· 1910–1916*, pp. 132–40

neither of these to the specificity of James's—or of any—sexuality. The result of this hammeringly tendentious blur in virtually all the James criticism is, for the interpretation of "The Beast in the Jungle," seemingly in the interests of showing it as universally applicable (e.g., about "the artist"), to assume without any space for doubt that the moral point of the story is not only that May Bartram desired John Marcher but that John Marcher *should have desired* May Bartram.

Tommy and Grizel is clearer-sighted on what is essentially the same point. "*Should have desired*," that novel graphically shows, not only is nonsensical as a moral judgment but is the very mechanism that enforces and perpetuates the mutilating charade of heterosexual exploitation. (James's compulsive use of Woolson, for instance.) Grizel's tragedy is not that the man she desires fails to desire her—which would be sad, but, the book makes clear, endurable—but that he pretends to desire her, and intermittently even convinces himself that he desires her, when he does not.

Impressively, too, the clarity with which *Tommy and Grizel* conveys this process and its ravages seems *not* to be dependent on a given, naive, or monolithic idea of what it would mean for a man to "really" desire someone. On that issue the novel seems to remain agnostic—leaving open the possibility that there is some rather different quantity that is "real" male desire, or alternatively that it is only more and less intermittent infestations of the same murderous syndrome that fuel any male eros at all. That the worst violence of heterosexuality comes with the male *compulsion to desire* women and its attendant deceptions of self and other, however, Barrie says quite decisively.

Tommy and Grizel is an extraordinary, and an unjustly forgotten, novel. What has dated it and keeps it from being a great novel, in spite of the acuteness with which it treats male desire, is the—one can hardly help saying Victorian—mawkish opportunism with which it figures the desire of women. Permissibly, the novel's real imaginative and psychological energies focus entirely on the hero. Impermissibly—and here the structure of the novel itself exactly reproduces the depredations of its hero—there is a moralized pretense at an equal focus on a rounded, autonomous, imaginatively and psychologically invested female protagonist, who however—far from being novelistically "desired" in herself—is really, transparently, created in the precise negative image of the hero, created to be the single creature in the world who is most perfectly fashioned to be caused the most exquisite pain and intimate destruction by him and him only. The fit is excruciatingly seamless. Grizel is the daughter of a mad prostitute, whose legacies to her— aside from vitality, intelligence, imagination—have been a strong sensuality and a terror (which the novel highly valorizes) of having that sensuality stirred. It was acute of Barrie to see that this is the exact woman—were such a woman possible—who, appearing strong and autonomous, would be most unresistingly annihilable precisely by Tommy's two-phase rhythm of sexual come-on followed by repressive frigidity, and his emotional geology of pliant sweetness fundamented by unyielding compulsion. But the prurient exactitude of the female fit, as of a creature bred for sexual sacrifice without resistance or leftovers, drains the authority of the novel to make an uncomplicit judgment on Tommy's representative value.

Read in this context, "The Beast in the Jungle" looks—from the point of view of female desire—potentially revolutionary. Whoever May Bartram is and whatever she wants (I discuss this more later), clearly at least the story has the Jamesian negative virtue of not pretending to present her rounded and whole. She is an imposing character, but—*and*—a bracketed one. James's bravura in manipulating point of view lets him dissociate himself critically from John Marcher's selfishness—from the sense that there is no *possibility* of a subjectivity other than Marcher's own—but lets him leave himself in place of that selfishness finally an *askesis*, a particular humility of point of view as being *limited* to Marcher's. Of May Bartram's history, of her emotional determinants, of her erotic structures, the reader learns very little; we are permitted, if we pay attention at all, to *know* that we have learned very little. Just as, in Proust, it is always open to any minor or grotesque character to turn out at any time to have a major artistic talent with which, however, the novel does not happen to busy itself, so "The Beast in the Jungle" seems to give the reader permission to imagine some female needs and desires and gratifications that are not structured exactly in the image of Marcher's or of the story's own laws.

It is only the last scene of the story—Marcher's last visit to May Bartram's grave—that conceals or denies the humility, the incompleteness of the story's presentation of her subjectivity. This is the scene in which Marcher's sudden realization that *she* has felt and expressed desire for *him* is, as it seems, answered in an intensely symmetrical, "conclusive" rhetorical clinch by the narrative/authorial prescription: "The escape would have been to love her; then, *then* he would have lived."[8] The paragraph that follows, the last in the story, has the same climactic, authoritative (even authoritarian) rhythm of supplying Answers in the form of symmetrical supplementarities. For this single, this conclusive, this formally privileged moment in the story—this resolution over the dead body of May Bartram—James and Marcher are presented as coming together, Marcher's revelation underwritten by James's rhetorical authority, and James's epistemological askesis gorged, for once, beyond recognition, by Marcher's compulsive, ego-projective certainties. In the absence of May Bartram, the two men, author/narrator and hero, are reunited at last in the confident, shared, masculine knowledge of what she

---

[8]"The Beast in the Jungle," in *The Complete Tales of Henry James*, ed. Leon Edel (London: Rupert Hart-Davis, 1964), 11: 401. All subsequent references to this work are to this edition and are cited parenthetically in the text by page number.

Really Wanted and what she Really Needed. And what she Really Wanted and
Really Needed show, of course, an uncanny closeness to what Marcher Really
(should have) Wanted and Needed, himself.

Imagine "The Beast in the Jungle" without this enforcing symmetry.
Imagine (remember) the story with May Bartram alive.[9] Imagine a possible
alterity. And the name of alterity is not *always* "woman." What if Marcher
himself had other desires?

The Law of the Jungle

Names . . . Assingham—Padwick—Lutch—Marfle—Bross—Crapp—Didcock—
Wichells—*Putchin*—Brind—Coxeter—Coxster . . . Dickwinter . . . Jakes . . .
Marcher—

—James, *Notebook*, 1901

There has so far seemed no reason, or little reason, why what I have been
calling "male homosexual panic" could not just as descriptively have been
called "male heterosexual panic"—or, simply, "male sexual panic." Although I
began with a structural and historicizing narrative that emphasized the pre-
and proscriptively defining importance of men's bonds with men, potentially
including genital bonds, the books I have discussed have not, for the most
part, seemed to center emotionally or thematically on such bonds. In fact, it
is, explicitly, a male panic in the face of *hetero*sexuality that many of these
books most describe. It is all very well to insist, as I have done, that
homosexual panic is necessarily a problem only, but endemically, of
nonhomosexual-identified men; nevertheless the lack in these books of an
embodied male-homosexual thematics, however inevitable, has had a dissolu-
tive effect on the structure and texture of such an argument. Part, although
only part, of the reason for that lack was historical: it was only close to the end
of the nineteenth century that a cross-class homosexual role and a consistent,
ideologically full thematic discourse of male homosexuality became entirely
visible, in developments that were publicly dramatized in—though far from
confined to—the Wilde trials.

In "The Beast in the Jungle," written at the threshold of the new century,
the possibility of an embodied male-homosexual thematics has, I would like to

[9]Interestingly, in the 1895 germ of (what seems substantially to be) "The Beast in the Jungle,"
in James's *Notebooks*, p. 184, the woman outlives the man. "It's *the woman's sense of what might
[have been]* in him that arrives at the intensity. . . . *She is his Dead Self: he is alive in her and
dead in himself*—that is something like the little formula I seem to *entrevoir*. He himself, the
man, must, *in* the tale, also materially die—die in the flesh as he has died long ago in the spirit,
the *right* one. Then it is that his lost treasure revives most—no longer *contrarié* by his material
existence, existence in his false self, his wrong one."

argue, a precisely liminal presence. It is present as a—as a very particular, historicized—thematics of absence, and specifically of the absence of speech. The first (in some ways the only) thing we learn about John Marcher is that he has a "secret" (358), a destiny, a something unknown in his future. "You said," May Bartram reminds him, "you had from your earliest time, as the deepest thing within you, the sense of being kept for something rare and strange, possibly prodigious and terrible, that was sooner or later to happen" (359). I would argue that to the extent that Marcher's secret has *a* content, that content is homosexual.

Of course the extent to which Marcher's secret has anything that could be called a content is, not only dubious, but in the climactic last scene actively denied. "He had been the man of his time, *the* man, to whom nothing on earth was to have happened" (401). The denial that the secret has a content— the assertion that its content is precisely a lack—is a stylish and "satisfyingly" Jamesian formal gesture. The apparent gap of meaning that it points to is, however, far from being a genuinely empty one; it is no sooner asserted than filled to a plenitude with the most orthodox of ethical enforcements. To point rhetorically to the emptiness of the secret, "the nothing that is," is, in fact, oddly, *the same gesture* as the attribution to it of a compulsory content about heterosexuality—of the content specifically, "He should [have] desire[d] her."

> *She* was what he had missed. . . . The fate he had been marked for he had met with a vengeance—he had emptied the cup to the lees; he had been the man of his time, *the* man, to whom nothing on earth was to have happened. That was the rare stroke—that was his visitation. . . . This the companion of his vigil had at a given moment made out, and she had then offered him the chance to baffle his doom. One's doom, however, was never baffled, and on the day she told him his own had come down she had seen him but stupidly stare at the escape she offered him. The escape would have been to love her; then, *then* he would have lived. (401)

The "empty" meaning of Marcher's unspeakable doom is thus necessarily, specifically heterosexual; it refers to the perfectly specific absence of a prescribed heterosexual desire. If critics, eager to help James moralize this ending, persist in claiming to be able to translate freely and without residue from that (absent) heterosexual desire to an abstraction of all possibilities of human love, there are, I think, good reasons for trying to slow them down. The totalizing, insidiously symmetrical view that the "nothing" that is Marcher's unspeakable fate is necessarily a mirror image of the "everything" he could and should have had is, specifically, in an *oblique* relation to a very different history of meanings for assertions of the erotic negative.

The "full" meaning of that unspeakable fate, on the other hand, comes from the centuries-long historical chain of substantive uses of space-clearing nega- tives to void and at the same time to underline the possibility of male homosexual genitality. The rhetorical name for this figure is *preterition*. Unspeakable, Unmentionable, *nefandam libidinem*, "that sin which should be neither named nor committed,"[10] the "detestable and abominable sin, amongst Christians not to be named,"

> Whose vice in special, if I would declare,
> It were enough for to perturb the air,

"things fearful to name," "the obscene sound of the unbeseeming words,"

> A sin so odious that the fame of it
> Will fright the damned in the darksome pit,[11]

"the Love that dare not speak its name,"[12] such *were* the speakable nonmedical terms, in Christian tradition, of the homosexual possibility for men. The marginality of these terms' semantic and ontological status as substantive nouns reflected and shaped the exiguousness—but also, the potentially enabling secrecy—of that "possibility." And the newly specifying, reifying medical and penal public discourse of the male homosexual role, in the years around the Wilde trials, far from retiring or obsolescing these preteritive names, seems instead to have packed them more firmly and distinctively with homosexual meaning.[13]

John Marcher's "secret" (358), "his singularity" (366), "the thing she knew, which grew to be at last, with the consecration of the years, never mentioned between them save as 'the real truth' about him" (366), "the abyss" (375), "his queer consciousness" (378), "the great vagueness" (379), "the secret of the gods" (379), "what ignominy or what monstrosity" (379), "dreadful things . . . I couldn't name" (381): the ways in which the story refers to Marcher's secret fate have the same quasi-nominative, quasi-obliterative structure.

There are, as well, some "fuller," though still highly equivocal, lexical pointers to a homosexual meaning: "The rest of the world of course thought him *queer*, but she, she only, knew how, and above all why, queer; which was precisely what enabled her to dispose the concealing veil in the right folds. She took his *gaiety* from him—since it had to pass with them for gaiety—as she took everything else. . . . She traced his unhappy *perversion* through reaches of its course into which he could scarce follow it" (367; emphasis added). Still, it is mostly in the reifying grammar of periphrasis and

[10]Quoted in John Boswell, *Christianity, Social Tolerance, and Homosexuality: Gay People in Western Europe from the Beginning of the Christian Era to the Fourteenth Century* (Chicago: University of Chicago Press, 1980), p. 349 (from a legal document dated 533) and p. 380 (from a 1227 letter from Pope Honorious III).

[11]Quoted in Alan Bray, *Homosexuality in Renaissance England* (London: Gay Men's Press, 1982)—the first two from p. 61 (from Edward Coke's *Institutes* and Sir David Lindsay's *Works*), the next two from p. 62 (from William Bradford's *Plimouth Plantation* and Guillaume Du Bartas's *Divine Weeks*), and the last from p. 22, also from Du Bartas.

[12]Lord Alfred Douglas, "Two Loves," from *The Chameleon*, quoted in Byron R. S. Fone, *Hidden Heritage: History and the Gay Imagination* (New York: Irvington Publishers, 1981), p. 196.

[13]For a striking anecdotal example of the mechanism of this, see Beverley Nichols, *Father Figure* (New York: Simon & Schuster, 1972), pp. 92–99.

preterition—"such a cataclysm" (360), "the great affair" (360), "the catastrophe" (361), "his predicament" (364), "their real truth" (368), "his inevitable topic" (371), "all that they had thought, first and last" (372), "horrors" (382), something "more monstrous than all the monstrosities we've named" (383), "all the loss and all the shame that are thinkable" (384)—that a homosexual meaning becomes, to the degree that it does become, legible. "I don't focus it. I can't name it. I only know I'm exposed" (372).

I am convinced, however, that part of the point of the story is that the reifying effect of periphrasis and preterition on this particular meaning is, if anything, *more* damaging than (though not separable from) its obliterative effect. To have succeeded—which was not to be taken for granted—in cracking the centuries-old code by which the-articulated-denial-of-articulability always had the possibility of meaning two things, of meaning either (heterosexual) "nothing" or "homosexual meaning," would also always have been to assume one's place in a discourse in which there was *a* homosexual meaning, in which all homosexual meaning meant a single thing. To crack a code and enjoy the reassuring exhilarations of knowingness is to buy into the specific formula, "We Know What That Means." (I assume it is this mechanism that makes even critics who know about the male-erotic pathways of James's personal desires appear to be so untroubled about leaving them out of accounts of his writing.[14] As if this form of desire were the most calculable, the simplest to add or subtract or allow for in moving between life and art!) But if, as I suggested [earlier], men's accession to heterosexual entitlement has, for these modern centuries, always been on the ground of a cultivated and compulsory denial of the *un*knowability, of the arbitrariness and self-contradictoriness, of homosexual/heterosexual definition, then the fearful or triumphant interpretive formula "We Know What That Means" seems to take on an odd centrality. First, it is a lie. But second, it is the particular lie that animates and perpetuates the mechanism of homophobic male self-ignorance and violence and manipulability.

It is worth, then, trying to discriminate the possible plurality of meanings behind the unspeakables of "The Beast in the Jungle." To point, as I argue that the narrative itself points and as we have so far pointed, simply to *a* possibility of "homosexual meaning," is to say worse than nothing—it is to pretend to say one thing. But even on the surface of the story, the secret, "*the* thing," "the thing she knew," is discriminated, first of all discriminated temporally. There are at least two secrets: Marcher feels that he knows, but has never told anyone but May Bartram, (secret number one) that he is reserved for some

---

14Exceptions that I know of include Georges-Michel Sarotte's discussions of James in *Like a Brother, Like a Lover: Male Homosexuality in the American Novel and Theater from Herman Melville to James Baldwin*, trans. Richard Miller (New York: Doubleday & Co./Anchor, 1978); Richard Hall, "Henry James: Interpreting an Obsessive Memory," *Journal of Homosexuality* 8, no. 3/4 (Spring/Summer 1983): 83–97; and Robert K. Martin, "The 'High Felicity' of Comradeship: A New Reading of *Roderick Hudson*," *American Literary Realism* 11 (Spring 1978): 100–108.

very particular, uniquely rending fate in the future, whose nature is (secret number two) unknown to himself. Over the temporal extent of the story, both the balance, between the two characters, of cognitive mastery over the secrets' meanings, and the temporal placement, between future and past, of the second secret, shift; it is possible, in addition, that the actual content (if any) of the secrets changes with these temporal and cognitive changes, if time and intersubjectivity are of the essence of the secrets.

Let me baldly, then, spell out my hypothesis of what a series of "full"—that is, homosexually tinged—meanings for the Unspeakable might look like for this story, differing both over time and according to character.

For John Marcher, let us hypothesize, the future secret—the secret of his hidden fate—importantly includes, though it is not necessarily limited to, the possibility of something homosexual. *For Marcher*, the presence or possibility of a homosexual meaning attached to the inner, the future secret, has exactly the reifying, totalizing, and blinding effect we described earlier in regard to the phenomenon of the Unspeakable. Whatever (Marcher feels) may be to be discovered along those lines, it is, in the view of his panic, *one* thing, and the worst thing, "the superstition of the Beast" (394). His readiness to organize the whole course of his life around the preparation for it—the defense against it—remakes his life monolithically in the image of *its* monolith of, in his view, the inseparability of homosexual desire, yielding, discovery, scandal, shame, annihilation. Finally, he has "but one desire left": that it be "decently proportional to the posture he had kept, all his life, in the threatened presence of it" (379).

This is how it happens that the outer secret, the secret of having a secret, functions, in Marcher's life, precisely as *the closet*. It is not a closet in which there is a homosexual man, for Marcher is not a homosexual man. Instead, however, it is the closet of, simply, the homosexual secret—the closet of imagining *a* homosexual secret. Yet it is unmistakable that Marcher lives as one who is *in the closet*. His angle on daily existence and intercourse is that of the closeted person,

> the secret of the difference between the forms he went through—those of his little office under government, those of caring for his modest patrimony, for his library, for his garden in the country, for the people in London whose invitations he accepted and repaid—and the detachment that reigned beneath them and that made of all behaviour, all that could in the least be called behaviour, a long act of dissimulation. What it had come to was that he wore a mask painted with the social simper, out of the eye-holes of which there looked eyes of an expression not in the least matching the other features. This the stupid world, even after years, had never more than half-discovered. (367–68)

Whatever the content of the inner secret, too, it is one whose protection requires, for him, a playacting of heterosexuality that is conscious of being only window dressing. "You help me," he tells May Bartram, "to pass for a man like another" (375). And "what saves us, you know," she explains, "is that we answer so completely to so usual an appearance: that of the man and woman whose friendship has become such a daily habit—or almost—as to be at last indispensable" (368–69). Oddly, they not only appear to be but are such a man and woman. The element of deceiving the world, of window dressing, comes into their relationship *only* because of the compulsion he feels to invest it with the legitimating stamp of visible, institutionalized genitality: "The real form it should have taken on the basis that stood out large was the form of their marrying. But the devil in this was that the very basis itself put marrying out of the question. His conviction, his apprehension, his obsession, in short, wasn't a privilege he could invite a woman to share; and that consequence of it was precisely what was the matter with him" (365).

Because of the terrified stultification of his fantasy about the inner or future secret, Marcher has, until the story's very last scene, an essentially static relation to and sense of both these secrets. Even the discovery that the outer secret is already shared with someone else, and the admission of May Bartram to the community it creates, "the dim day constituted by their discretions and privacies" (363), does nothing to his closet but furnish it—camouflage it to the eyes of outsiders, and soften its inner cushioning for his own comfort. In fact, the admission of May Bartram importantly *consolidates and fortifies* the closet for John Marcher.

In my hypothesis, however, May Bartram's view of Marcher's secrets is different from his and more fluid. I want to suggest that—while it is true that she feels desire for him—her involvement with him occurs originally on the ground of her understanding that he is imprisoned by homosexual panic; and her interest in his closet is not at all in helping him fortify it but in helping him dissolve it.

In this reading, May Bartram from the first sees, correctly, that the possibility of Marcher's achieving a genuine ability to attend to a woman— sexually or in any other way—depends as an absolute precondition on the dispersion of his totalizing, basilisk fascination with and terror of homosexual possibility. It is only through his coming out of the closet—whether as *a homosexual man,* or as a man with a less exclusively defined sexuality that nevertheless admits the possibility of desires for other men—that Marcher could even begin to perceive the attention of a woman as anything other than a terrifying demand or a devaluing complicity. The truth of this is already evident at the beginning of the story, in the surmises with which Marcher first meets May Bartram's allusion to something (he cannot remember what) he said to her years before: "The great thing was that he saw in this no vulgar reminder of any 'sweet' speech. The vanity of women had long memories, but she was making no claim on him of a compliment or a mistake. With another woman, a totally different one, he might have feared the recall possibly even of some imbecile 'offer' " (356). The alternative to this, however, in his eyes, is a different kind of "sweetness," that of a willingly shared confinement: "her knowledge . . . began, even if rather strangely, to taste sweet to him" (358). "Somehow the whole question was a new luxury to him—that is from the moment she was in possession. If she didn't take the sarcastic view she clearly took the sympathetic, and that was what he had had, in all the long time, from no one whomsoever. What he felt was that he couldn't at present have begun to tell her, and yet could profit perhaps exquisitely by the accident of having done so of old" (358). So begins the imprisonment of May Bartram in John Marcher's closet—an imprisonment that, the story makes explicit, is founded on his inability to perceive or value her as a person beyond her complicity in his view of his own predicament.

The conventional view of the story, emphasizing May Bartram's interest in liberating, unmediatedly, Marcher's heterosexual possibilities, would see her as unsuccessful in doing so until too late—until the true revelation that comes, however, only after her death. If what needs to be liberated is in the first place Marcher's potential for homosexual desire, however, the trajectory of the story must be seen as far bleaker. I hypothesize that what May Bartram would have liked for Marcher, the narrative she wished to nurture for him, would have been a progress from a vexed and gaping self-ignorance around his homosexual possibilities to a self-knowledge of them that would have freed him to find and enjoy a sexuality of whatever sort emerged. What she sees happen to Marcher, instead, is the "progress" that the culture more insistently enforces: the progress from a vexed and gaping self-ignorance around his homosexual possibilities, to a completed and rationalized and wholly con-cealed and accepted one. The moment of Marcher's full incorporation of his erotic self-ignorance is the moment at which the imperatives of the culture cease to enforce him, and he becomes instead the enforcer of the culture.

Section 4 of the story marks the moment at which May Bartram realizes that, far from helping dissolve Marcher's closet, she has instead and irremedi-ably been permitting him to reinforce it. It is in this section and the next, too, that it becomes explicit in the story that Marcher's fate, what was to have happened to him and did happen, involves a change in him from being the suffering object of a Law or judgment (of a doom in the original sense of the word) to being the embodiment of that Law.

If the transition I am describing is, in certain respects, familiarly Oedipal, the structuring metaphor behind its description here seems to be oddly alimentative. The question that haunts Marcher in these sections is whether what he has thought of as the secret of his future may not be, after all, in the past; and the question of passing, of who is passing through what or what is passing through whom, of what residue remains to *be* passed, is the form in which he compulsively poses his riddle. Is the beast eating him, or is he eating the beast? "It hasn't passed you by," May Bartram tells him. "It has done its office. It has made you its own" (389). "It's past. It's behind," she finally tells him, to which he replies, "*Nothing*, for me, is past; nothing *will* pass till I pass myself, which I pray my stars may be as soon as possible. Say, however, . . . that I've eaten my cake, as you contend, to the last crumb—how can the thing I've never felt at all be the thing I was marked out to feel?"

(391). What May Bartram sees, that Marcher does not, is that the process of incorporating—of embodying—the Law of masculine self-ignorance is the one that has the least in the world to do with feeling.[15] To gape at and, rebelliously, be forced to swallow the Law is to feel; but to have it finally stick to one's ribs, become however incongruously a part of one's own organism, is then to perfect at the same moment a new hard-won insentience of it and an assumption of (or subsumption by) an identification with it. May Bartram answers Marcher's question, "You take your 'feelings' for granted. You were to suffer your fate. That was not necessarily to know it" (391). Marcher's fate is to cease to suffer fate, and, instead, to become it. May Bartram's fate, with the "slow fine shudder" that climaxes her ultimate appeal to Marcher, is herself to swallow this huge, bitter bolus with which *she* can have *no* deep identification, and to die of it—of what is, to her, knowledge, not power. "So on her lips would the law itself have sounded" (389). Or, tasted.

To end a reading of May Bartram with her death, to end with her silenced forever in that ultimate closet, "her" tomb that represents (to Marcher) *his fate,* would be to do to her feminine desire the same thing I have already argued that James M. Barrie, unforgivably, did to Grizel's. That is to say, it leaves us in danger of figuring May Bartram, or more generally the woman in heterosexuality, as only the exact, heroic supplement to the murderous enforcements of male homophobic/homosocial self-ignorance. "The Fox," Emily Dickinson wrote, "fits the Hound."[16] It would be only too easy to describe May Bartram as the fox that most irreducibly fits this particular hound. She seems the woman (don't we all know them?) who has not only the most delicate nose for but the most potent attraction toward men who are at crises of homosexual panic . . .—Though for that matter, won't most women admit

---

[15]A fascinating passage in James's *Notebooks,* p. 318, written in 1905 in California, shows how a greater self-knowledge in James, and a greater acceptance and *specificity* of homosexual desire, transform this half-conscious enforcing rhetoric of anality, numbness, and silence into a much richer, pregnant address to James's male muse, an invocation of fishing-as-*écriture:*

> I sit here, after long weeks, at any rate, in front of my arrears, with an inward accumulation of material of which I feel the wealth, and as to which I can only invoke my familiar demon of patience, who always comes, doesn't he?, when I call. He is here with me in front of this cool green Pacific—he sits close and I feel his soft breath, which cools and steadies and inspires, on my cheek. Everything sinks in: nothing is lost; everything abides and fertilizes and renews its golden promise, making me think with closed eyes of deep and grateful longing when, in the full summer days of L[amb] H[ouse], my long dusty adventure over, I shall be able to [plunge] my hand, my arm, *in,* deep and far, and up to the shoulder—into the heavy bag of remembrance—of suggestion—of imagination—of art—and fish out every little figure and felicity, every little fact and fancy that can be to my purpose. These things are all packed away, now, thicker than I can penetrate, deeper than I can fathom, and there let them rest for the present, in their sacred cool darkness, till I shall let in upon them the mild still light of dear old L[amb] H[ouse]—in which they will begin to gleam and glitter and take form like the gold and jewels of a mine.

[16]*Collected Poems of Emily Dickinson,* ed. Thomas H. Johnson (Boston: Little, Brown & Co., 1960), p. 406.

that an arousing nimbus, an excessively refluent and dangerous maelstrom of eroticism, somehow attends men in general at such moments, even otherwise boring men?

If one is to avoid the Barrie-ism of describing May Bartram in terms that reduce her perfectly to the residue-less sacrifice John Marcher makes to his Beast, it might be by inquiring into the difference of the paths of her own desire. What does she want—not for him, but for herself—from their relationship? What does she actually get? To speak less equivocally from my own eros and experience, there is a particular relation to truth and authority that a mapping of male homosexual panic offers to a woman in the emotional vicinity. The fact that male heterosexual entitlement in (at least modern Anglo-American) culture depends on a perfected but always friable self-ignorance in men as to the significance of their desire for other men, means that it is always open to women to know something that it is much more dangerous for any nonhomosexual-identified man to know. The ground of May Bartram's and John Marcher's relationship from the first is that she has the advantage of him, cognitively: she remembers, as he does not, where and when and with whom they have met before, and most of all she remembers his "secret" from a decade ago while he forgets having told it to her. This differential of knowledge affords her a "slight irony," an "advantage" (353)—but one that he can at the same time use to his own profit as "the buried treasure of her knowledge," "this little hoard" (363). As their relationship continues, the sense of power and of a marked, rather free-floating irony about May Bartram becomes stronger and stronger, even in proportion to Marcher's accelerating progress toward self-ignorance and toward a blindly selfish expropriation of her emotional labor. Both the care and the creativity of her investment in him, the imaginative reach of her fostering his homosexual potential as a route back to his truer perception of herself, are forms of gender-political resilience in her as well as of love. They are forms of excitement, too, of real though insufficient power, and of pleasure.

In the last scene of "The Beast in the Jungle," John Marcher becomes, in this reading, not the finally self-knowing man who is capable of heterosexual love, but the irredeemably self-ignorant man who embodies and enforces heterosexual compulsion. In this reading, that is to say, May Bartram's prophecy to Marcher that "You'll never know now" (390) is *a true one.*

Importantly for the homosexual plot, too, the final scene is also the only one in the entire story that reveals or tests the affective quality of Marcher's perception of another man. "The shock of the face" (399)—this is, in the last scene, the beginning of what Marcher ultimately considers "the most extraordinary thing that had happened to him" (400). At the beginning of Marcher's confrontation with this male figure at the cemetery, the erotic possibilities of the connection between the men appear to be all open. The man, whose "mute assault" Marcher feels "so deep down that he winced at the steady thrust," is mourning profoundly over "a grave apparently fresh," but (perhaps

only to Marcher's closet-sharpened suspicions?) a slightest potential of Whit-
manian cruisiness seems at first to tinge the air, as well.

> His pace was slow, so that—and all the more as there was a kind of hunger in his
> look—the two men were for a minute directly confronted. Marcher knew him at
> once for one of the deeply stricken . . . nothing lived but the deep ravage of the
> features he showed. He *showed* them—that was the point; he was moved, as he
> passed, by some impulse that was either a signal for sympathy or, more possibly, a
> challenge to an opposed sorrow. He might already have been aware of our
> friend. . . . What Marcher was at all events conscious of was in the first place that
> the image of scarred passion presented to him was conscious too—of something
> that profaned the air; and in the second that, roused, startled, shocked, he was yet
> the next moment looking after it, as it went, with envy. (400–401)

The path traveled by Marcher's desire in this brief and cryptic non-encounter
reenacts a classic trajectory of male entitlement. Marcher begins with the
possibility of *desire for* the man, in response to the man's open "hunger"
("which," afterward, "still flared for him like a smoky torch" [401]). Deflecting
that desire under a fear of profanation, he then replaces it with envy, with an
identification with the man in that man's (baffled) desire for some other,
female, dead object. "The stranger passed, but the raw glare of his grief
remained, making our friend wonder in pity what wrong, what wound it
expressed, what injury not to be healed. What had the man *had,* to make him
by the loss of it so bleed and yet live?" (401).

What had the man *had*? The loss by which a man *so bleeds and yet lives* is,
is it not, supposed to be the castratory one of the phallus figured as mother,
the inevitability of whose sacrifice ushers sons into the status of fathers and
into the control (read both ways) of the Law. What is strikingly open in the
ending of "The Beast in the Jungle" is how central to that process is man's
desire for man—and the denial of that desire. The imperative that there *be* a
male figure to take this place is the clearer in that, at an earlier climactic
moment, in a female "shock of the face," May Bartram has presented to
Marcher her own face, in a conscious revelation that was far more clearly of
desire.

> It had become suddenly, from her movement and attitude, beautiful and vivid to
> him that she had something more to give him; her wasted face delicately shone
> with it—it glittered almost as with the white lustre of silver in her expression. She
> was right, incontestably, for what he saw in her face was the truth, and strangely,
> without consequence, while their talk of it as dreadful was still in the air, she
> appeared to present it as inordinately soft. This, prompting bewilderment, made
> him but gape the more gratefully for her revelation, so that they continued for
> some minutes silent, her face shining at him, her contact imponderably pressing,
> and his stare all kind but all expectant. The end, none the less, was that what he
> had expected failed to come to him. (386)

To the shock of the female face, Marcher is not phobic but simply numb. It is
only by turning his desire for the male face into an envious identification with

male loss that Marcher finally comes into *any* relation to a woman—and then it is a relation through one dead woman (the other man's) to another dead woman of his own. That is to say, it is the relation of *compulsory* heterosexuality.

When Lytton Strachey's claim to be a conscientious objector was being examined, he was asked what he would do if a German were to try to rape his sister. "I should," he is said to have replied, "try and interpose my own body."[17] Not the gay self-knowledge but the heterosexual, self-ignorant acting out of just this fantasy ends "The Beast in the Jungle." To face the gaze of the Beast would have been, for Marcher, to dissolve it.[18] To face the "kind of hunger in the look" of the grieving man—to explore at all into the sharper lambencies of that encounter—would have been to dissolve the closet. Marcher, instead, to the very end, turns his back—re-creating a double scenario of homosexual compulsion and heterosexual compulsion. "He saw the Jungle of his life and saw the lurking Beast; then, while he looked, perceived it, as by a stir of the air, rise, huge and hideous, for the leap that was to settle him. His eyes darkened—it was close; and, instinctively turning, in his hallucination, to avoid it, he flung himself, face down, on the tomb" (402).

[17]Lytton Strachey, quoted in Michael Holroyd, *Lytton Strachey: A Critical Biography* (London: W. H. Heinemann, 1968), 2: 179.
[18]Ruth Bernard Yeazell makes clear the oddity of having Marcher turn his back on the Beast that is supposed, at this late moment, to represent his self-recognition (in *Language and Knowledge in the Late Novels of Henry James* [Chicago: University of Chicago Press, 1976], pp. 37–38).

The Imagination of Metaphor

Ruth Bernard Yeazell

In *The Beast in the Jungle,* that late *nouvelle* whose theme tragically
mirrors that of *The Ambassadors,* James creates a man obsessed with a
metaphor. John Marcher, the tale's antihero, is convinced that "something or
other . . . [lies] in wait for him, amid the twists and turns of the months and
years, like a crouching beast in the jungle" (17, ii, p. 79).[1] Living in anxious
expectation, he awaits the "inevitable spring" of the metaphoric beast—the
moment at which his long-awaited destiny will manifest itself, and "*the* thing"
(i, p. 73) at last come upon him. Beneath the outwardly dull surface of his
existence, Marcher stalks his beast like a man on a "tiger hunt." At least, "such
was the image under which he had ended by figuring his life" (ii, p. 79).

But Marcher the tiger-hunter is in reality Marcher the terrified. The image
which haunts him implies a readiness to confront exotic horrors, but all the
while that he pursues his beast, Marcher flees in terror from ordinary human
contact and from love. On a late April afternoon in a quiet London town
house, May Bartram offers herself to him; but Marcher, obsessed with
metaphors of distant jungles and mysterious beasts, utterly fails to understand
what is happening. Through the metaphor of the beast in the jungle, apparently a talisman of hidden knowledge, Marcher actually retreats from
knowledge—both sexual knowledge of May and conscious knowledge of
himself. Metaphoric thinking allows him to evade immediate reality and its
demands, to avoid the risk of passionate confrontation.

Yet even the frustratingly obtuse Marcher at last comes to perceive the
pattern of his life, to understand the meaning of his escape and his loss. After
May Bartram has died, Marcher haunts her grave, and it is during one such
autumn vigil that the truth finally dawns. Shocked into awareness by the
grief-stricken face of a fellow visitor to the graveyard, by "the deep ravage of
the features he showed" (vi, p. 123), Marcher asks himself, "What had the

[1]All references to the fiction of Henry James are to *The Novels and Tales of Henry James* (New
York: Charles Scribner's Sons, 1907–9). The first number is that of the volume in the New York
Edition. For the convenience of readers with other editions, I also give (where relevant) by large
roman numerals for book numbers and small roman numerals for chapter numbers.

man *had*, to make him by the loss of it so bleed and yet live?" (p. 124). In typically Jamesian fashion, the very form of the question calls forth the answer: "Something—and this reached him with a pang—that *he*, John Marcher, hadn't; the proof of which was precisely John Marcher's arid end. No passion had ever touched him, for this was what passion meant; he had survived and maundered and pined, but where had been *his* deep ravage?" Too late comes "the truth, vivid and monstrous" (p. 125); in this long-delayed moment of illumination Marcher finally grasps the missing tenor of his metaphor:

> The Beast had lurked indeed, and the Beast, at its hour, had sprung; it had sprung in that twilight of the cold April when, pale, ill, wasted, but all beautiful, and perhaps even then recoverable, she had risen from her chair to stand before him and let him imaginably guess. It had sprung as he didn't guess; it had sprung as she hopelessly turned from him, and the mark, by the time he left her, had fallen where it *was* to fall. He had justified his fear and achieved his fate; he had failed, with the last exactitude, of all he was to fail of; and a moan now rose to his lips as he remembered she had prayed he mightn't know. This horror of waking—*this* was knowledge, knowledge under the breath of which the very tears in his eyes seemed to freeze. (vi, p. 126)

The exotic is brought home, and in this painful moment of awakening Marcher recognizes that May's offer of love and his own failure to respond marked the true spring of the beast. Paradoxically, the metaphor through which Marcher has escaped comes in the end to signify both the experience which he fled and the very flight itself. The beast sprang when May made her humble gesture of love; it sprang again when the self-absorbed Marcher failed to comprehend her gesture. And it springs once more, most horrifyingly, at this final moment of full awareness: "He saw the Jungle of his life and saw the lurking Beast; then, while he looked, perceived it, as by a stir of the air, rise, huge and hideous, for the leap that was to settle him. His eyes darkened—it was close; and instinctively turning, in his hallucination, to avoid it, he flung himself, face down, on the tomb" (vi, pp. 126–27). Marcher's beast—a distant cousin of that tiger with the gleaming eyes which in *Death in Venice* crouches in Aschenbach's hallucinatory jungle[2]—is at once sensual love, the failure of self-knowledge, and the pain of that knowledge come too late.

Marcher clings to his metaphor in order to distance reality, to postpone the anguish of knowledge, but when knowledge at last overwhelms him, the metaphor turns sickeningly real; the beast which leaps in the final lines of James's tale may be hallucinatory, but for Marcher the effect of its last spring is a condition virtually indistinguishable from death. So too does discovery come in *The Wings of the Dove*, where Milly Theale's enlightenment proves

    [2]Thomas Mann, "Death in Venice" (1911), in *Stories of Three Decades*, trans. H. T. Lowe-Porter (1930; rpt. New York: Knopf, 1941), pp. 380, 427.

even more unmistakably fatal: while the disease from which the American heiress suffers remains mysterious, the revelation about Kate and Densher nonetheless kills. In the late novels knowledge comes, even to the apparently healthy, with a terrible fatality. And metaphors, as ways of mediating that dangerous knowledge, assume a new and crucial power. Unlike James's early novels, whose titles point to literal people (*Roderick Hudson*), places (*Washington Square*), or cultures (*The American, The Europeans, The Bostonians*), the late novels are identified not by character or location, but by image and symbol (*The Sacred Fount, The Wings of the Dove, The Golden Bowl, The Ivory Tower*).[3] Experience itself now has—indeed for James's characters, it must have—a metaphoric name.[4]

Of course the unsuspecting reader who came across *The Beast in the Jungle* and, easily misled by metaphor, expected to find a dramatic tale of tiger-hunting in the African jungle—or at least a narrative with the outward adventure of Marlow's in *Heart of Darkness*—would suffer sharp disappointment. For *The Beast in the Jungle* is the story of a man who, as he himself comes too late to realize, has been "*the* man, to whom nothing on earth was to have happened" (vi, 125). As such, it is almost a parody of the classic Jamesian plot, and Marcher, that sensitive, passive, and deeply reserved gentleman, is the quintessential Jamesian hero—both plot and character unfortunately apt to make the impatient reader of James cringe. But even essentially responsive readers are likely to find the gross disproportion between Marcher and his metaphor obscurely disquieting, to sense beneath the surface a tension and a strain not easily accounted for. Like so many late Jamesian metaphors, Marcher's obsessive imagery arouses in us a persistent unease.

Indeed at their most characteristic, James's metaphors provoke a feeling of arbitrariness and extravagance, a sense of an uncomfortable break in the organic connection of things, that can be deeply disturbing. To F. R. Leavis, for example, this strain in the late imagery betrays the decline of James's art, signals the Master's final loss of poetic power: "We are conscious in these figures more of analysis, demonstration and comment than of the realizing imagination and the play of poetic perception. Between any original perception or feeling there may have been and what we're given there has come a process of judicial stock-taking; the imagery is not immediate and inevitable but synthetic. It is diagrammatic rather than poetic."[5] And even one of James's

---

3Others have noted this shift in James's titles. See Alexander Holder-Barrell, *The Development of Imagery and Its Functional Significance in Henry James's Novels* (Bern: Francke Verlag, 1959), p. 148; and Naomi Lebowitz, *The Imagination of Loving: Henry James's Legacy to the Novel* (Detroit: Wayne State University Press, 1965), p. 14.

4*The Ambassadors*, whose title has a relatively literal meaning but is rich in metaphoric overtones, is something of an exception. But *The Ambassadors* is a borderline case in several senses, as I argue below.

5F. R. Leavis, *The Great Tradition: George Eliot, Henry James, Joseph Conrad* (1948; rpt. Harmondsworth: Penguin, 1972), p. 193.

most sympathetic critics finds herself forced to condemn the more extreme images in *The Golden Bowl* as "arbitrary" and "heavy-handed."[6] Others, simply ignoring the problem, content themselves with explicating individual metaphors as they arise, or with classifying them by vehicle—informing us, for example, that one can count more than thirteen hundred water images in James's fiction.[7] But no matter how much water imagery we can find flooding James's pages, our sense of disquietude remains: the tension generated by many of James's later metaphors does not so easily wash away. And if the strange connections between jungle beasts and civil servants continue to puzzle and disturb, they continue to haunt us as well—to exert on us their own fearful fascinations.

Some of our unease—Leavis's sense that the imagery is not "immediate and inevitable"—stems from the fact that James's metaphors seem almost invariably responses of the brain, not of the senses. The Jamesian universe is not one of material resemblances; though the vehicles of his metaphors are themselves sensuously imagined, conceptual relationships govern the terms of comparison. The Venetian weather in *The Wings of the Dove* is "a bath of warm air" (20, IX, iv, p. 304), Paris has "a cool full studio-light" in *The Ambassadors* (22, VIII, ii, p. 76), and little Bilham shakes his ears "in the manner of a terrier who has got wet" (22, X, i, p. 173), but such physical comparisons are only occasional and incidental. Perception of sensuous correspondences is direct and immediate, but the world of the late novels does not allow of such easy connections among its parts. Even for Strether, whose education in Paris is so much an affair of the senses, perception is primarily cognition, and—perhaps especially for Strether—the correspondences between things take considerable working out.

In *The Golden Bowl*, Maggie Verver, like little Bilham, is compared to a wet dog shaking itself out; but unlike little Bilham's, her resemblance to the dog is not a physical one:

> Moving for the first time in her life as in the darkening shadow of a false position, she reflected that she should either not have ceased to be right—that is to be confident—or have recognised that she was wrong; though she tried to deal with herself for a space only as a silken-coated spaniel who has scrambled out of a pond and who rattles the water from his ears. Her shake of her head, again and again, as she went, was much of that order, and she had the resource to which, save for the rude equivalent of his generalising bark, the spaniel would have been a stranger, of humming to herself hard as a sign that nothing had happened to her.

---

[6]Dorothea Krook, *The Ordeal of Consciousness in Henry James* (1962; rpt. Cambridge: Cambridge University Press, 1967), p. 391.

[7]Robert Gale, *The Caught Image: Figurative Language in the Fiction of Henry James* (Chapel Hill, N.C.: University of North Carolina Press, 1964), pp. 18–21, 59–60. For another study which primarily involves classification by vehicle, see Holder-Barrell, *The Development of Imagery.*

She hadn't, so to speak, fallen in; she had had no accident nor got wet; this at any rate was her pretension until after she began a little to wonder if she mightn't, with or without exposure, have taken cold. (24, IV, i, pp. 6–7)

This metaphoric spaniel makes its appearance near the opening of the novel's second volume, as Maggie Verver, slowly awakening from her dream of innocence, begins to sense that all is not well with her world. No inherent resemblance links a wet spaniel and a young woman awakening to a knowledge of evil; the connection is not apparent until it is made, until dog and girl are brought in conjunction and their resemblances defined. Maggie is said to give a "shake of her head"—a shake itself ambiguously metaphoric or literal—but it is not physical gesture or appearance which makes her spaniel-like: there is no question here of puppy-dog eyes or barking voices, although the young princess perhaps shares with the spaniel a "silken coat." It is Maggie's whole state of consciousness which is likened to the shaking dog.

At this point in her history, Maggie knows nothing—consciously at least—about her husband's adultery with Charlotte, or about her own responsibility for the evil which has entered her world. She knows only that she has begun to feel distinctly uneasy; she is as yet far from knowing why. And she is frightened—frightened both of the feeling itself and of inquiring too closely into its causes. Suspecting unpleasant truths, like falling into the water, is a discomforting experience, and in metaphorically shaking herself dry, Maggie tries to reject that experience, to deny that she is in any way afraid. The desire to suppress her agitating suspicions runs deep: "She hadn't, so to speak, fallen in; she had had no accident nor got wet." But even more crucial than this metaphoric gesture is the fact of the metaphor itself—Maggie thinks not of painful human relationships but of a spaniel which has tumbled into a pond. The image of the wet dog allows her to avoid direct confrontation with the truth and to postpone the anguish which that truth may bring. Though it is a far less sinister creature, Maggie's spaniel is of the same species as Marcher's jungle beast.

Unlike Marcher, however, Maggie begins to face reality, not to flee from it. And her metaphoric thinking, though it is a means of evasion, is also a mode of discovery. Although she postpones full knowledge, wishing simply to shake off her uneasiness as if it were water, the process of image-making has a momentum of its own. One association suggests another; to juxtapose in the mind a wet spaniel and an apprehensive young princess is apparently to see more resemblances between them than one had originally bargained for. Thus even as Maggie denies her likeness to the dog, she does so in the metaphor's own terms: "She hadn't, so to speak, fallen in; she had had no accident nor got wet." And "so to speak" is to carry out the metaphor to its natural conclusion: like the spaniel, Maggie realizes, she too may have "taken cold." Falling into water can precipitate a cold—it is as though the common-sense associations of the metaphor had forced Maggie to acknowledge that she cannot completely suppress the psychic chills she has begun to feel.

But if Maggie begins "a little to wonder" whether she has "taken cold," she is not yet ready to translate the implications of her metaphor into a direct comment on her situation. She thinks in terms of taking cold, not in terms of psychic threats; the language which defines her new awareness remains in the context of metaphor rather than of fact. And the metaphor itself suggests meanings which Maggie at this point cannot consciously articulate. It is not fortuitous that she sees herself as a spaniel and not some other wet animal, for example; unconsciously, at least, she presumably senses a resemblance between the pliable, fawning nature of a spaniel and her own susceptibility to use and deception. Maggie knows more than she knows she knows, and her metaphor mediates between conscious knowledge and deeper modes of awareness.

For the Princess to approach the tangle of her husband's unfaithfulness, Charlotte's treachery, and her own reprehensible innocence by means of a wet spaniel is to take a devious route indeed. That her metaphoric vehicle nevertheless carries her in the direction of the truth comes to both Maggie and the reader with something of a metaphysical shock;[8] like Dr. Johnson confronted with the imagery of the seventeenth-century poets, we may well wonder at the "violence" with which these heterogeneous ideas are yoked together. Maggie's situation bears no more immediate resemblance to that of a wet dog than do Donne's two lovers to a pair of compasses.

Of course in "A Valediction: Forbidding Mourning," that paradigm of all metaphysical poems, the speaker's self-conscious wit is the violently yoking force; he takes an active delight in his imaginative exercise, wittily uncovering multiple resemblances where none would at first seem to exist. And as the language of a departing lover, trying to assure both himself and his beloved of the permanence of their union, this play with metaphor serves an urgent rhetorical function. The compasses image does not merely illustrate the lover's argument: rather, it *is* his argument—an imagistic proof that physical separation will not destroy his connection with the beloved. The more analogies he can draw between compasses and lovers, the more convincing his case. The elaboration of his metaphor becomes an assertion of control over a potentially threatening experience, a means of shaping language and love affair alike.

When Maggie makes the metaphysical leap between herself and the spaniel, she is not, like Donne's persona, engaged in a direct rhetorical argument. She has no need to prove anything or to persuade anyone— anyone, that is, except herself. Maggie's meditation is not even spoken aloud, but beneath its surface an argument nevertheless takes place, although the

---

[8]Several commentators have remarked in passing on the "metaphysical" quality of James's conceits; the resemblance has been sensed, but its significance unexplored. See especially the early Desmond MacCarthy review, "Mr. Henry James and His Public," *Independent Review* 6 (May 1905): 109; and Austin Warren, "Myth and Dialectic in the Later Novels of Henry James," *Kenyon Review* 5 (1943): 556–57.

parties to the conflict do not exist as separate persons at all and are not in fact easily distinguishable from one another. Self argues with self within Maggie Verver, as her deep fear of the truth contends with her strong need to know where she stands, as her uneasy suspicions arise, are suppressed, and irresistibly surface once again. And in this struggle, each side claims the metaphor for its own and uses it rhetorically, if the parts of the self can be said to engage in a kind of subconscious rhetoric. "I have not, so to speak, fallen in; I have had no accident nor got wet," insists the fearful self, extending the metaphor negatively, and thus "proving" that Maggie has no reason to be afraid. "Ah, but do you not feel as if you had in fact taken cold?" returns the other self, triumphantly reasserting the sinister possibilities inherent in the original image and forcing Maggie to acknowledge, at least metaphorically, the pain which she has begun to feel.

No such dialogue takes place, of course. Nor does Maggie's psyche so neatly divide into two equal and opposing parts. We read the passage as one continuous meditation and recognize only one consciousness at work (to ignore, for the moment, the hovering consciousness of the narrator himself). But the conflict which such a dialogue would overtly dramatize is genuine and accounts for much of the tension which we experience as we read. Though Maggie at this point knows so little of the actual facts of the case, her struggle is already intense—finally all the more intense for us as readers because we are not allowed the relief of direct statement. Like so much in late James, her conflict makes itself felt only obliquely, exerting its pressure through the indirection of style.

The sense of shock with which Dr. Johnson would have greeted Maggie and her incongruous spaniel is a feeling which all readers of the late James can appreciate, even if, F. R. Leavis apart, most of us are no longer prepared to condemn such incongruity as a stylistic flaw. The disparity between vehicle and tenor which makes so many of James's late images metaphysically surprising suggests a world in which connections are not easily made, one in which the imagination must strain to see the resemblances of things. In some instances (such as the comparison of Maggie to the spaniel or the Prince's extended contrast between himself as a *crème de volaille* and Adam Verver as "the natural fowl running about the *bassecour*" [23, 1, i, p. 8]) the vehicles of such metaphors startle by their very homeliness; at other points they shock by the melodramatic and even violent situations which they conjure up (Maggie as a victim of the French Revolution, awaiting execution [24, VI, ii, pp. 341–42]; or Milly Theale's clinging to the Rockies for dear life [19, V, vii, p. 302]), or simply by their air of exotic mystery (Maggie's pagoda or Milly Theale's eastern carpet [19, V, i, p. 216]). The strangeness of these vehicles resembles the strangeness of dreams—at once distant and bizarre, seemingly far removed from ordinary life, and startlingly immediate in their implications. Denied the ordinary dreams of sleep, James's characters appear to find in their waking imagery an equivalent release.

Yet the uneasiness which James's late images may evoke does not arise simply from the shock of heterogeneity but from the elaboration and extension of the original metaphor—what Dr. Leavis, that latter-day Dr. Johnson, calls "analysis, demonstration and comment" as opposed to "the realizing imagination and the play of poetic perception." The famous image of the pagoda which opens the second volume of *The Golden Bowl* is a troublesome case in point. Even Dorothea Krook, usually so responsive to the late James, has objected to this oriental oddity, and to the lengthy mental journeys by which Maggie approaches it: ". . . the oddness of the image is felt to be in excess of the originality of the experience, making it in this sense arbitrary; and its disproportionate and rather heavy-handed protraction noticeably slackens the dramatic pace at the point at which it occurs."[9] But the very oddness of this protracted image is crucial, forcing to our attention emotional strains which a more comfortable metaphor would fail to convey. To discover that one's husband is an adulterer may not, unfortunately, be a particularly original experience, although Maggie is far from realizing that adultery is even in question. But the originality of the image makes of the experience something rich and strange, tells us that for Maggie what is at stake here is indeed profoundly unusual and disturbing:

> This situation had been occupying for months and months the very centre of the garden of her life, but it had reared itself there like some strange tall tower of ivory, or perhaps rather some wonderful beautiful but outlandish pagoda, a structure plated with hard bright porcelain, coloured and figured and adorned at the overhanging eaves with silver bells that tinkled ever so charmingly when stirred by chance airs. She had walked round and round it—that was what she felt; she had carried on her existence in the space left her for circulation, a space that sometimes seemed ample and sometimes narrow: looking up all the while at the fair structure that spread itself so amply and rose so high, but never quite making out as yet where she might have entered had she wished. She hadn't wished till now—such was the odd case. . . . The thing might have been, by the distance at which it kept her, a Mahometan mosque, with which no base heretic could take a liberty; there so hung about it the vision of one's putting off one's shoes to enter and even verily of one's paying with one's life if found there as an interloper. She hadn't certainly arrived at the conception of paying with her life for anything she might do; but it was nevertheless quite as if she had sounded with a tap or two one of the rare porcelain plates. (24, IV, i, pp. 3–4)

The "outlandish" pagoda which sits in Maggie's Eden-like garden is an emblem of the bizarre social "arrangement" which has heretofore governed her life, but for us it might figure as well the entire world of James's late novels—a world of bright and intricate surfaces, extraordinarily beautiful and yet ominously "hard," concealing mysterious and possibly sinister depths. To Maggie the tower seems to have "reared itself," with a power that architectural

[9]*The Ordeal of Consciousness*, p. 391

monuments possess solely in dreams; knowing herself simply as passive and innocent, she cannot yet perceive her own complicity in the architecture of her past, nor assume active responsibility for the future design of her life. The peculiar arbitrariness and artifice of the pagoda image reflect her estrangement from the reality of her situation, the fact that for the innocent Princess the truths of her own life have all the mystery of the inscrutable Orient.[10]

Yet for the first time Maggie has become aware of a desire, however hesitant, to penetrate that mystery. At once fascinated and terrified, she anxiously circles around the pagoda, venturing at last to administer a tentative "tap or two" on its hard and unyielding surface. "She had knocked, in short— though she could scarce have said whether for admission or for what . . ." (p. 4). Even as she circles around the tower, so she circles around the metaphor itself—tentatively exploring each of its implications in turn, only to shrink back in fear when that exploration leads her in directions more dangerous than she is yet prepared to move. The pagoda may suggest a Mahometan mosque, threatening death to all interlopers, but "she hadn't certainly arrived at the conception of paying with her life for anything she might do." To argue that the prolongation of the metaphor "slackens the dramatic pace" is thus to measure the speed of Maggie's mind by a completely alien clock, for the dramatic pace at this point is precisely one of hesitant and fearful groping for knowledge rather than of sudden and blinding revelation. Eve may have acquired knowledge with a single bite of the apple, but for Maggie Verver—as for so many of James's late characters—the fall from innocence has become a painfully drawn-out process. Though Maggie will seem to awaken, in Fanny Assingham's words, "to what's called Evil—with a very big E" (23, III, xi, p. 385), she will really discover a world to which the clear-cut terms of good and evil no longer apply—a world of ambiguities and fearful mysteries, one in which knowledge itself must remain finally tentative and uncertain. And only through metaphoric indirection can such knowledge even be approached.

If the metaphysical extension of this exotic metaphor recalls the lyric poetry of the seventeenth century rather than the novelistic tradition of the nineteenth, the resemblance is not purely fortuitous. For the world of James's late fiction is an intensely private one—a world in which the individual consciousness must struggle, alone, to articulate the connections of things. To restrict point of view as radically as James does is to create characters who must perforce suffer a certain isolation, and the private elaboration of metaphor confirms that isolation. Like her nineteenth-century predecessor,

---

10Austin Warren has pointed out that James's oriental images usually "betoken the strangeness of that East which is East and hence incommunicable to the West" ("Myth and Dialectic," p. 559). The contrast between this mysterious pagoda and the comparable image of the Palladian Church—Adam Verver's architectural metaphor for the Prince (23, II, i, pp. 135-37)—is revealing. The Church, with its more rational and familiar architecture, conveys Adam's sense of the Prince's value and his slight strangeness, but it does not have the ominous and forbidding mystery of the pagoda.

George Eliot's Dorothea Brooke, Maggie Verver must awaken from a state of innocence to discover a deeply flawed marriage, and to acknowledge her own responsibility for its failure. But the metaphysical imagery which surrounds Maggie's awakening suggests that James's heroine must confront more than a failed marriage: she must puzzle out the very terms of her world anew.

In *Middlemarch*, when Dorothea Brooke begins to sense the truth about the aging, desiccated scholar whom she has married, she sees herself as entrapped in the narrow and oppressive labyrinths of his mind: "How was it that in the weeks since her marriage, Dorothea had not distinctly observed but felt with a stifling depression, that the large vistas and wide fresh air which she had dreamed of finding in her husband's mind were replaced by anterooms and winding passages which seemed to lead nowither?" Nothing more comes of these anterooms and winding passages at this particular point; the metaphor, like the passages themselves, leads nowhere. Instead, the omnipresent voice of the narrator immediately intrudes with analogous metaphors of her own:

> I suppose it was that in courtship everything is regarded as provisional and preliminary, and the smallest sample of virtue or accomplishment is taken to guarantee delightful stores which the broad leisure of marriage will reveal. But the door-sill of marriage once crossed, expectation is concentrated on the present. Having once embarked on your marital voyage, it is impossible not to be aware that you make no way and that the sea is not within sight—that, in fact, you are exploring an enclosed basin.[11]

Blocked passageways, door-sills, enclosed basins—Eliot's metaphors in *Middlemarch* proceed by analogy, and Dorothea's image gains in resonance from the larger pattern of labyrinths and enclosures of which it forms a part. Even so does Dorothea herself fit into the larger design of Middlemarch society—here reminding us strongly of Lydgate or even of Fred Vincy, there contrasting sharply with Rosamond or with Mary Garth. In *Middlemarch* the individual metaphor, like the individual character, derives much of its significance from its relation to others of its kind. Unlike Maggie Verver, Dorothea Brooke does not stand alone in the world of her novel: Lydgate, Fred, Rosamond, Bulstrode, and a host of minor characters all mirror her experience of frustrated expectation, and even the narrator clearly echoes and confirms her metaphors.

One imagines that if *Middlemarch* were a late James novel, Dorothea would have entered the anterooms of Casaubon's mind and explored its dark and winding passages—only to find herself, apparently trapped, searching desperately for an exit, some glimmer of light to suggest that not all her husband's mental passageways had dead ends. Even as early as *The Portrait of*

---

[11]George Eliot, *Middlemarch*, Riverside Edition (1871–72; rpt. Cambridge, Mass.: Houghton Mifflin, 1956), p. 145.

a Lady, in fact, James sends his heroine on just such an extended metaphorical journey.[12] Like Dorothea Brooke, Isabel Archer confronts the disappointing truth of her marriage, and like Dorothea, she finds not the vast expanses she had imagined, but only narrow alleys and dead walls:

> She had taken all the first steps in the purest confidence, and then she had suddenly found the infinite vista of a multiplied life to be a dark, narrow alley with a dead wall at the end. Instead of leading to the high places of happiness, from which the world would seem to lie below one, so that one could look down with a sense of exaltation and advantage, and judge and choose and pity, it led rather downward and earthward, into realms of restriction and depression where the sound of other lives, easier and freer, was heard as from above, and where it served to deepen the feeling of failure. (4, xlii, p. 189)

Both Isabel and Dorothea come to metaphoric dead ends, but in James's novel the metaphor itself continues to expand. In *Middlemarch* metaphors, like people, exist in analogical relationship to one another, bound by a common pattern, but in the second half of her novel Isabel Archer stands very much alone. Her metaphor extends itself vertically, not horizontally: in private meditation its meanings unfold.

The world of James's cosmopolites and expatriates is far from the provincial town of Middlemarch, with its closely knit web of relationships and metaphoric resemblances. But James's characters, though deeply lonely, live in a world inhabited by others, and when they come into contact with one another, they talk. Strether's falling in love with Paris or Kate's and Densher's with each other, for example, is partly a question of good conversation, of the satisfying exchange of thoughts ("It had come to be definite between them [Kate and Densher] at a primary stage that, if they could have no other straight way, the realm of thought at least was open to them. They could think whatever they liked about whatever they would—in other words they could say it. Saying it for each other, for each other alone, only of course added to the taste" [19, II, i, p. 65]). And much Jamesian conversation is the mutual creation of metaphor:

> "Mrs. Pocock's built in, or built out—whichever you call it; she's packed so tight she can't move. She's in splendid isolation"—Miss Barrace embroidered the theme.
> Strether followed, but scrupulous of justice. "Yet with every one in the place successively introduced to her."
> "Wonderfully—but just so that it does build her out. She's bricked up, she's buried alive!"
> Strether seemed for a moment to look at it; but it brought him to a sigh. "Oh but she's not dead! It will take more than this to kill her."
> His companion had a pause that might have been for pity. "No, I can't pretend I

---

[12]Barbara Hardy has previously called attention to the resemblance between this image and those in *Middlemarch*. See *The Novels of George Eliot: A Study in Form* (London: Athlone Press, 1959), p. 222.

think she's finished—or that it's for more than to-night." She remained pensive as if with the same compunction. "It's only up to her chin." Then again for the fun of it: "She can breathe."

"She can breathe!"—he echoed it in the same spirit. "And do you know," he went on, "what's really all this time happening to me?—through the beauty of music, the gaiety of voices, the uproar in short of our revel and the felicity of your wit? The sound of Mrs. Pocock's respiration drowns for me, I assure you, every other. It's literally all I hear."

She focussed him with her clink of chains. "Well—!" she breathed ever so kindly.

"Well, what?"

"She *is* free from her chin up," she mused; "and that *will* be enough for her."

"It will be enough for me!" Strether ruefully laughed. (*The Ambassadors*, 22, X, i, pp. 176–77)

Strether and Miss Barrace join in this verbal game-playing partly "for the fun of it"; Miss Barrace, in fact, with her cigarette-smoking and her ironic banter, incarnates that spirit of frivolous wit which both charms and frightens Strether in his Parisian friends. And certainly there is much here both to charm and to frighten, for if the tone of the exchange is lighthearted, ominous implications lurk beneath its surface. Sarah Pocock, outwardly presiding at a festive party given in her honor, is in metaphorical fact being "buried alive." And despite the "uproar" of music and party chatter, Strether can hear only the imagined sound of her breathing—so alarming a force does Mrs. Pocock represent for him that the mere fact of her presence obliterates all else.

In this joint image-making, Strether and Miss Barrace act both as friendly collaborators and as conspirators. For speaking in metaphors, like thinking in metaphors, is a way at once of confronting and of avoiding unpleasant facts; by inventing this grotesque image of Sarah "packed so tight she can't move," they manage to acknowledge Strether's hidden anxiety and yet to hold it at a safely comic distance. The incongruity of the metaphor itself is matched by the incongruity between the gay social surface of this conversation and the tensions it only partly conceals. And the very elaboration of the image intensifies the disparity, for in playfully extending their metaphor, Strether and his companion assert a kind of witty verbal control over the entire uneasy situation, even while they call heightened attention to it: by the end of the exchange the ominous breathing of Mrs. Pocock is very much in the air. At a Jamesian party, to play with metaphors is to risk being surprised into uncomfortable truths.

But Strether's uncomfortable truths, troubling as they often are, are only metaphorically questions of life and death. Given what we know of the redoubtable Mrs. Pocock, we need have little fear that she will literally be buried alive. Unlike *The Wings of the Dove*, *The Ambassadors* has no Milly Theale, who dies a quite literal, though intensely symbolic death. And unlike Maggie Verver in *The Golden Bowl*, Strether is not the immediate victim of the adultery which he uncovers. Like his feminine counterparts, he is betrayed by a pair of lovers, but unlike Milly and Maggie, Strether remains something of a detached observer of events, rather than an anguished participant in them. Although his journey to Paris deprives him of his innocence and radically transforms his way of seeing things, the facts which Strether must confront are not as directly threatening or as powerfully disturbing as those with which Milly Theale or Maggie Verver must finally come to terms. *The Ambassadors*, with its detached and frequently ironic tone, is, in fact, the most comic of the three late novels—and the least metaphoric.[13] For in James's late fiction, the metaphoric imagination works with its most feverish intensity when faced with knowledge that is both deeply desired and profoundly terrifying.

In *The Wings of the Dove*, the love affair between Merton Densher and Kate Croy calls forth precisely such desires and such terrors, as even their seemingly innocent metaphors may reveal: "You keep the key of the cupboard, and I foresee that when we're married you'll dole me out my sugar by lumps," says Densher to Kate in an early, relatively untroubled moment. Indeed, we are told that this sweetly domestic image has sprung to Densher's lips "more than once" in their brief acquaintance (20, VI, ii, p. 17)—an assertion which may strain our credulity in realistic terms but which suggests that the metaphoric key to the cupboard is a key to the nature of their relationship as well. Characteristically, Kate chooses to make explicit only the sweetness of the image: "she rejoiced in his assumption that sugar would be his diet." But for Densher, the reader suspects, the sweet overtones of the metaphor mask a taste of bitterness. Listening to Kate's confident pronouncements on the problem of their finding a satisfactory place to meet one another, he has tentatively admitted to himself a certain misgiving: "what Kate embraced altogether was indeed wonderful . . . though he perhaps struck himself rather as getting it out of her piece by piece than as receiving it in a steady light" (20, VI, ii, p. 16). Despite all the sweetness and light with which he associates her, and despite the hesitant "perhaps" and "rather," a spot of ambivalence creeps into Densher's picture of the "bright and handsome" Kate.

But like Maggie Verver at the opening of the second volume of *The Golden Bowl*, Densher at this point can only approach his own anxieties with timid indirection—extending the metaphor of the locked cupboard and the sugar lumps no further than a cautious negative will allow: "the supply from the cupboard at this hour was doubtless, of a truth, not altogether cloyingly sweet; but it met in a manner his immediate requirements" (20, VI, ii, p. 17). The image's more sinister implications—of Kate's arbitrary power and Den-

[13]Frederick C. Crews notes this distinction between the style of *The Ambassadors* and that of the two later novels. See *The Tragedy of Manners: Moral Drama in the Later Novels of Henry James* (New Haven: Yale University Press, 1957), p. 57. For a perceptive account of the comic tone of *The Ambassadors*, see Ian Watt, "The First Paragraph of *The Ambassadors*: An Explication," *Essays in Criticism* 10 (1960): 250–74. [Above, 118 ff].

sher's willful ignorance—go unexplored. It remains for the reader himself to pursue the logic of the metaphor and to wonder what else lies behind the locked doors of Kate's cupboard.

That closed cupboard might stand in fact as an emblem of the entire history of this passionate conspiracy. Until the final scenes of the novel, when Milly's death forces him to confront the full significance of what they have done, Densher will prefer to keep many of his mental cupboards locked, passively allowing Kate to assume charge of the keys. And she will respond by doling him out his lumps of sugar—offering him, bit by bit, only palatable interpretations of their acts, interpretations which he can pleasantly swallow, and holding back anything which might strike his moral palate as bitter. If Strether and Maggie Verver often act as their own censors, Densher frequently surrenders the role to Kate, allowing her to suppress the darker implications of a metaphor, and thus to save him from the terror of conscious self-knowledge.

Shaping metaphors, then, becomes a means of control; Kate avoids any overt disharmony in her relationship with Densher by acknowledging only the sweeter implications of his images. But in *The Wings of the Dove*, at least, a strange shift of power takes place: by the end of the novel, the living woman, Kate Croy, must step aside for the dead Milly Theale. And Milly triumphs not so much by inventing metaphors of her own as by adopting and transforming the metaphors of others. When Kate, with characteristic ambiguity, pronounces her a "dove," Milly welcomes the image as if it were a divine revelation, immediately adopting it as her own:

> It was moreover, for the girl, like an inspiration: she found herself accepting as the right one, while she caught her breath with relief, the name so given her. She met it on the instant as she would have met revealed truth; it lighted up the strange dusk in which she lately had walked. *That* was what was the matter with her. She was a dove. Oh *wasn't* she?—it echoed within her as she became aware of the sound, outside, of the return of their friends. (19, V, vi, p. 283)

The very next moment Milly finds herself acting out her new role, offering to Maud Lowder's question about whether Densher has returned the answer "most dovelike" (p. 284). That answer is of course technically a lie ("I don't *think*, dear lady, he's here," says Milly, although simply looking at Kate has already convinced her that Densher has indeed come back); but as a lie that graciously protects Kate, it sounds the dovelike note.

Milly consciously chooses to enact Kate's metaphor, and her decision is at once a gesture of self-acceptance and a radical re-creation of that self. For what is literally "the matter" with Milly Theale is not that she is a dove, but that she is dying. And if the unnamed disease that finally kills her is as much a figurative illness as a literal one, it is a figure which is open to a wide range of readings: one might easily argue that Milly dies because she is too passive, too timid, or like Daisy Miller, her Jamesian prototype, too foolishly innocent to survive in the world of the living. But if Milly is indeed a "dove," her death demands to be read in a different spirit—it becomes an act of supreme self-sacrifice, an affirmative gesture of grace and of love. The metaphor transforms Milly's death, bestows on it a significance that Daisy Miller's pathetic collapse never fully achieves. Although Milly's acceptance of Kate's metaphor is characteristically passive, she finally triumphs by inspiring just such a redefinition of what her life and death have meant:

> ". . . she died for you then that you might understand her. From that hour you *did*." With which Kate slowly rose. "And I do now. She did it *for* us." Densher rose to face her, and she went on with her thought. "I used to call her, in my stupidity—for want of anything better—a dove. Well she stretched out her wings, and it was to *that* they reached. They cover us."
> "They cover us," Densher said. (20, X, vi, pp. 403–4)

Although the dove image originated in Kate's "stupidity"—her condescending and superficial labeling of the innocent American girl—the manner of Milly's death compels Kate to reinterpret her metaphor, to acknowledge in it resonances far deeper than she had anticipated. Kate admits defeat, paradoxically, by asserting that she once spoke more truly than she knew.

But the cost of Milly's power is life itself; only through her sacrificial death does she fully become both a "princess" (Susan Stringham's favorite image of her companion) and a "dove." Unlike Maggie Verver, she does not survive to enjoy the consequences of her triumph. Nor does she actively invent new self-images: the princess and the dove are originally others' metaphors, not her own. And while Maggie defines herself anew toward the end of *The Golden Bowl* with metaphors of energetic creation—the dancer, the actress, the playwright, the images which Milly adopts evoke states of being, not action. For if Maggie Verver artfully redesigns the patterns of her life and the lives of those around her, Milly allows herself to assume the shapes imposed by others' needs. Indeed her death itself is, in one sense, the supreme example of her compliant shape-changing. When she "turns her face to the wall," Milly makes the ultimately passive gesture—removing herself from the picture altogether, apparently so that Kate and Densher, united, may form the only figures in its design. Milly's dying is in this sense the final, most extreme act of renunciation in James's fiction. But if Milly does not assume Maggie Verver's outward control over events, through her death she nonetheless anticipates Maggie's own artistry in human arrangements. As the closing words of the novel tell us, Kate and Densher will "never be again as they were." The pattern of their relationship to one another and to Milly has been permanently recomposed.

By adopting Kate's metaphor and making it truth, Milly releases a powerful subterranean force—a pressure which reveals the hidden stresses in the lovers' bond and ends by shattering that bond entirely. In calling Milly a dove, Kate had presumably meant to gloss over the sinister facts about that young American and the uses to which her innocence might be put, and in so doing to turn possible pain to the uses of compliment and social harmony. In

The Wings of the Dove, as in all the late fiction, such metaphoric speaking has great force: as the impulse magically to transform and redeem human suffering, it tempts us as the mark of the highest civilization. But by the ironic dialectic of James's world, Kate's metaphor finally acts not to conceal tensions but to reveal them. And at the center of that fine civilization, with its elaborate images and carefully preserved taboos, is a superstitious and terrible awe, akin to that felt by the most primitive of men:

> In his search for the origin of the metaphor a psychologist recently discovered to his surprise that one of its roots lies in the spirit of the taboo. There was an age when fear formed the strongest incentive of man, an age ruled by cosmic terror. At that time a compulsion was felt to keep clear of certain realities which, on the other hand, could not be entirely avoided. . . . Since to primitive man a word is somehow identical with the thing it stands for, he finds it impossible to name the awful object on which a taboo has fallen. Such an object has to be alluded to by a word denoting something else and thus appears in speech vicariously and surreptitiously. When a Polynesian, who must not call by name anything belonging to the king, sees the torches lighted in the royal hut, he will say, "The lightning shines in the clouds of heaven." Here again we have metaphorical elusion.[14]

The sophisticated men and women of James's late fiction are ruled by a "cosmic terror" as powerful as any felt by Ortega's awe-struck Polynesians. Their world is filled with unnamable facts:

> He [Densher] hadn't only never been near the facts of her condition—which counted so as a blessing for him; he hadn't only, with all the world, hovered outside an impenetrable ring fence, within which there reigned a kind of expensive vagueness, made up of smiles and silences and beautiful fictions and priceless arrangements, all strained to breaking; but he had also, with every one else, as he now felt, actively fostered suppressions which were in the direct interest of every one's good manners, every one's pity, every one's really quite generous ideal. It was a conspiracy of silence, as the *cliché* went, to which no one had made an exception, the great smudge of mortality across the picture, the shadow of pain and horror, finding in no quarter a surface of spirit or of speech that consented to reflect it. "The mere aesthetic instinct of mankind—!" our young man had more than once, in the connexion, said to himself. (20, IX, iv, pp. 298–99)

In *The Wings of the Dove* "the great smudge of mortality" hovers continually over events as an unspoken presence, yet the conspiracy of silence extends far beyond the simple fact of Milly's impending death. Taboo breeds further taboo: Kate's intentions toward the dying girl and Densher's deeply ambivalent feelings about those intentions are matters equally "impossible to name." Similarly, in both *The Ambassadors* and *The Golden Bowl* a taboo falls most obviously on the subject of adulterous liaisons, but the fear of naming is not limited to the fact of illicit sex. James's characters act as if they shared with

---

[14]Ortega y Gasset, "Taboo and Metaphor," in *The Dehumanization of Art and Notes on the Novel*, trans. Helene Weyl (1925; rpt. New York: Peter Smith, 1951), pp. 33–34

Ortega's primitives the belief that "a word is somehow identical with the thing it stands for," yet unlike those primitives, their fear is inspired not by sacred objects, but by the deepest and most complex regions of their own psyches. And the "beautiful fictions" which that fear generates are correspondingly intricate; if James's people dwell in a radically metaphoric world, it is at least in part because they find the reality of fact and feeling so terrifying.

The elaboration of metaphor in which James's characters delight conveys an impression of tremendous energy—an energy suppressed and diverted, but all the more intense for being thus indirect. Even at its most lighthearted, the extension of metaphor is not simply verbal game-playing, nor is it, as Leavis would have it, "a process of judicial stock-taking."[15] The strain which the reader senses in a Jamesian metaphor has as its deepest source this intense struggle between the pressure of feeling and the need to contain that pressure. If we follow such expanded metaphors with our own fearful fascination, we do so because our intellectual delight in their patterns is matched by an unconscious response to the emotions which those patterns both channel and release. Anxious as he is to avoid confrontation, even Strether is continually betrayed by his metaphors:

> Strether, watching, after his habit, and overscoring with thought, positively had moments of his own in which he found himself sorry for her—occasions on which she affected him as a person seated in a runaway vehicle and turning over the question of a possible jump. *Would* she jump, could she, would *that* be a safe place?—this question, at such instants, sat for him in her lapse into pallor, her tight lips, her conscious eyes. It came back to the main point at issue: would she be, after all, to be squared? He believed on the whole she would jump; yet his alternations on this subject were the more especial stuff of his suspense. One thing remained well before him—a conviction that was in fact to gain sharpness from the impressions of this evening: that if she *should* gather in her skirts, close her eyes and quit the carriage while in motion, he would promptly enough become aware. She would alight from her headlong course more or less directly upon him; it would be appointed to him, unquestionably, to receive her entire weight. (22, X, i, p. 162)

With this image of a runaway carriage and its terrified occupant, Strether captures the helplessness he imagines Sarah to feel, as she is carried along by the social whirl of Chad and his Parisian friends. But the suspense felt here is Strether's own; will Sarah decide to repudiate Chad and thus, inevitably, Strether himself? Though Strether begins by feeling sorry for her, he ends by imagining a grotesque scene with himself as comic victim—crushed beneath the full weight of the rather portly Mrs. Pocock. By a kind of emotional syntax, the picture of Sarah in a carriage meditating a jump leads Strether to a vision of the jump performed, and thence to an image of himself as the helpless object jumped upon. Like the runaway carriage, the vehicle of the

---

[15]*The Great Tradition*, p. 193.

metaphor seems propelled by an energy of its own—an energy which proves stronger than Strether's conscious reluctance, and which carries him ineluctably toward a vision of the confrontation he so dreads.

If James's characters seek to escape themselves through metaphors, they thus risk eventual defeat—for by a Newtonian emotional law, the fears and desires they so energetically suppress emerge with an equal and opposite force through those very same metaphors. Milly Theale leaves Susan Stringham to face Sir Luke and his medical report alone, but the painful knowledge she tries to avoid catches up with her: "What had been at the top of her mind about it and then been violently pushed down—this quantity was again working up" (19, V, vii, p. 301). In James's world, knowledge does "work up," and the paths it takes are often those of metaphorical elaboration; passion finds its release precisely in that which seems a Jesuitical attempt to dodge the realities of fact and feeling.

In its comic violence, Sarah's wild carriage ride oddly resembles Strether's earlier vision of his own inevitable "smash": "the sense that the situation was running away with him," at once his constant terror and his delight, is here projected onto the unfortunate Mrs. Pocock. Of course the carriages in which James's people actually ride do not go riotously out of control; in the late novels, the surface of human lives is formed of quiet walks about the city, visits paid and received, frequent dinners and endless conversation. When the Pococks arrive, Strether and Jim share a cab from the station and manage to "take a further turn round before going to the hotel" (22, VIII, ii, p. 84) without the slightest mishap. But though readers often complain that nothing ever "happens" in James's late fiction, metaphorically the novels bristle with daring adventures and melodramatic confrontations.[16] Densher after Milly's death, struggling to choose among painful alternatives, is Densher face to face with "a pair of monsters of whom he might have felt on either cheek the hot breath and the huge eyes" (20, X, iii, pp. 351–52); Kate Croy living at her Aunt Maud's is at once the victim of a siege, trapped in her citadel, and a young kid, trembling before a hungry lioness (19, I, ii, pp. 29–30; II, ii, p. 77); proposing to Charlotte, Adam Verver burns his ships—applies a flaming torch and watches "the fine pink glow . . . definitely blazing and crackling" (23, II, vi, pp. 215–21). Expanded metaphor becomes dramatic narrative—an entire small tale of adventure and escape: visiting Chad, the Pococks travel breathlessly down what seems a pleasant passageway, only to find themselves trapped in "a brave blind alley" (22, X, i, p. 160); seated in her "great gilded Venetian chair," Fanny Assingham makes a perilous voyage over "deep waters," while the Colonel watches anxiously on the opposite shore until he hears the reassuring bump of her boat (23, III, x, pp. 364–66).

16For a thorough discussion of the imagery of adventure in *The Ambassadors*, see John Paterson, "The Language of 'Adventure' in Henry James," *American Literature* 32 (1960): 291–301.

Fanny's spiritual "paddling" is at once mock-heroic and genuinely so; for all the charming incongruity of Bob's fear lest his firmly seated wife suddenly vanish into the depths of an imaginary lake, we cannot help sharing something of his suspense. Indeed the excitement of even the most playful of these metaphoric adventures is partly a matter of their incongruous origins—of the sharp disparity between the drawing rooms of London or Paris and the hazardous jungles of the imagination. In "A Tragedy of Error" (1864), James's first published story, a man literally drowns at sea; in *Roderick Hudson* (1875), the hero falls to his death in an Alpine storm; but by the late novels such perils have moved inward and become the stuff of metaphor. Elaborating these images, telling themselves stories, James's characters dramatize the human need to make such fictions—to channel intense feeling by giving it narrative form. The invention of metaphor becomes for them a means to escape, even to transcend the limits which their world imposes. And their fictions have both charm and power: in all his many tales of painters and writers, James's people are never so truly images of the artist himself as they thus become in his last novels. But the art that frees may simultaneously betray them: in the imagination of metaphor the desire for escape and the impulse toward uncomfortable discovery are strangely entwined. What excites us most deeply in the end is less the thought of beasts and burning ships than of just such strange entanglements.

The Consuming Vision

Jean-Christophe Agnew

Henry James . . . does not at first glance offer historians much more than a grudging acknowledgment of the tawdry spectacle of consumer culture. Indeed his revulsion from it is celebrated. Like his brother William, Henry displayed a seemingly "instinctive repugnance" toward the strident entreaties of the Age of Barnum—a repugnance so lively as to have stirred him eventually to flight.[1] Something akin to a note of embarrassment runs through those rare passages in James's writings that explicitly take up the question of the commodity world: the world of goods, newspapers, and advertisements. That note in turn reverberates upon an even more deeply felt sense of violation, one that James consistently associates with the shamelessly intrusive appeals of the market. What James sees violated in almost every case is "privacy," a term he uses quite broadly to refer to the indispensable conditions of familiarity upon which the fragile structure of human communities is formed. What dissolves the foundation of this familiarity is almost invariably "publicity," a word he uses with equal expansiveness to refer to the values and instrumentalities of a market society: the traffic in commodities, the habit of display, the inclination to theatricality, the worship of novelty and quantity.

Given the prominence of these themes, James's fiction appears as an ingeniously contrived and meticulously sealed shelter thrown up against the loud and discordant appeals of a commodity culture. The "house of fiction"— James's celebrated metaphor for the achieved literary form—figuratively expresses what James's English home—the isolated and tranquil Lamb House—materially represented: a sanctuary built by and for the creative imagination. A venture outside this enclave was always for James a calculated risk, yet it is only in such ventures that we find him confronting in a more or less direct fashion what he labeled as "the unredeemed commercialism" of his homeland's "vast crude democracy of trade."[2] *The American Scene* (1907)—

Excerpted from Jean-Christophe Agnew, "The Consuming Vision of Henry James," in *The Culture of Consumption: Critical Essays in American History, 1880–1980*, ed. Richard Wightman Fox and T. J. Jackson Lears (New York: Pantheon Books, 1983), 75–84, 91–99. Copyright © 1983 by Richard Wightman Fox and T. J. Jackson Lears. Reprinted by permission of the author and of Pantheon Books, a division of Random House, Inc.

[1]R. W. Perry, *The Thought and Character of William James* (Boston, 1935), 1:203.
[2]Henry James, *The American Scene* (Bloomington, Ind., 1968), pp. 66, 67.

James's memoir of his visit to America of 1904–5—provides the single most explicit judgment on his encounters with consumer culture. As such, it serves as a point of entry into the more complex relation between the writer and the world of goods.

In the opening section of *The American Scene* James recalls his first tremor of apprehension about his "new" world when, upon stepping off the boat, he inhaled "the air of unmitigated publicity, publicity as a condition, as a doom, from which there could be no appeal." On land, he feels himself at sea. Steeped in this all too public medium of trade, James can find no model, no inward projection, "no image, no presumption of constituted relations, possibilities, amenities" in the American social order. It is, he concludes, "as if the projection had been so completely outward that one could but find oneself almost uneasy about the mere perspective required for the common acts of the personal life." Here James's sharp and sudden sense of disorientation appears to grow from an impression that the symbolic constituents of personal relations have acquired an impersonal, public currency. This impression, in turn, adds to his quickening conviction that in America the wage relation (and what it fetches) has altogether replaced the more familiar and established reciprocities of manners. Public and private spheres have collapsed; "the market and home therefore look alike dazzling, at first, in this reflected, many-coloured lustre" of a life constructed out of commodities.[3] And nowhere is this feeling of bedazzlement more insistent than in the institution where home and market have been effectively merged: the hotel.

"One is thrown upon it," James writes of the Waldorf-Astoria, "as straight upon the general painted scene over which the footlights of publicity play with their large crudity, and against the freely-brushed texture and grain of which you thus rub your nose more directly, and with less ceremony, than elsewhere." The violence of James's language is unusual in itself, yet at the same time entirely consonant with the intimations of violation he has elsewhere associated with the effects of "publicity." The New York hotel is for him a monstrous incarnation of self-promotion and self-aggrandizement and, as such, embodies the "American spirit most seeking and most finding itself." It is the stationary Pullman of a "hotel civilization," an extraordinary maze of seemingly random encounters and exchanges whose totality threatens to engulf the single "visionary tourist." The Waldorf is for James nothing less than the "conception of publicity" organized as "the vital medium" of human relations.[4]

Feeling himself stirred about within this fluid medium of hotel life, James nonetheless suspects a hand or hands behind the movement. "Master-spirits of management" he calls them, powers whom he imagines in the form of "some high-stationed orchestral leader . . . keeping the whole effect together

3Ibid., pp. 9, 10, 197.
4Ibid., pp. 406, 102, 408, 438, 105.

and making it what it is." James sees the American scene, then, "in its crude plasticity, almost in the likeness of an army of puppets whose strings the wealth of his [the conductor's] technical imagination teaches him innumerable ways of pulling, and yet whose innocent, whose always ingenuous agitation of their members he has found means to make them think of themselves as delightfully free and easy."[5] It is for James both an appealing and an appalling image.

It is at the same time an extraordinarily prophetic image of the managed freedom of consumer societies. The passage, indeed the whole of *The American Scene*, foreshadows the modern critique of the consumer culture industry as "mass deception."[6] And like that critique, the book seems to look backward as well to the romantic tradition within which Marx first ventured his views on the human impoverishment of possessive individualism. For just as James discovers a new form of mobile, consumable wealth in midtown Manhattan, so he finds a new form of mobile, consumable poverty on the Lower East Side. There "the wants, the gratifications, the aspirations of the 'poor,' as expressed in the shops" signify for him "a new style of poverty," a shop-bought and shop-worn poverty thrusting itself "out of the possible purchasers" he encounters on the street and making them, "to every man and woman, individual throbs in the larger harmony." James recapitulates his orchestral metaphor, to which he adds the contrapuntal relation between the properties available in the ghetto shops and "the living unit's paying property in himself"—the relation, in short, between goods and labor. The Hester Street laborer's "property in himself"—his new and alien form of self-possession—has for James a defiant and abrasive side: the insolent liberties taken by free workers. But it has its pitiable side as well, since whatever deference or manners the wage has displaced, its earner still bows before the power "of the new remorseless monopolies." The laborer's property in himself now stands in relation to "properties overwhelmingly greater . . . that allow the asking of no questions and the making, for coexistence with them, of no conditions." The conclusion seems inescapable to James: "There is such a thing, in the United States, as freedom to grow up to be blighted, and it may be the only freedom in store for the smaller fry of future generations."[7]

Taken together, these observations constitute for the historian one of Henry James's grimmest and most pointed forays upon the terrain of social and cultural criticism; also one of his rarest. Whether out of revulsion or pity, James kept the forms of consumer culture he found in America's hotels and ghettos firmly confined to the outskirts of his fictive settings, muffling the

[5]Ibid., pp. 106–7.
[6]See, for example, Max Horkheimer and Theodor W. Adorno, "The Culture Industry: Enlightenment as Mass Deception," in *Dialectic of Enlightenment*, John Cumming, tr. (New York, 1972), pp. 120–67.
[7]James, *American Scene*, pp. 136, 137.

cries of the market behind the ancient walls and hedges of private villa and country house. This aloofness saps the analytical force of his reportage upon consumer culture. His prescience becomes for us altogether facile, and thus suspect. For if his observations do anticipate the critique of mass culture imported to America three decades later, they also open themselves to the charge of elitism. Revulsion and pity, after all, are alike forms of condescension, and despite James's misgivings upon the corruptions of Europe, he was never loath to use the heritage of the Old World to touch the raw nerve of the New. However promising his judgments of America's market world may appear to the historian, they nonetheless assert themselves as the judgments of an outsider.

No one did more to sustain this image of remoteness than James himself. Reflecting on his own sense of disorientation in *The American Scene*, he attributed it less to departures from a scale of life he had grown up with as a "small boy" in America than to departures from a scale of life he had embraced as a young man in Europe. "Importances," he found, "are all strikingly shifted and reconstituted, in the United States, for the visitor attuned, from far back, to 'European' importances."[8] The image is true to the letter of his experience but not to the substance. James had indeed been "attuned" to European importances from far back, but the manner in which he had thus acclimated himself had been eminently American and preeminently consumerist. The "hotel civilization" that he found so unsettling in turn-of-the-century America was the same medium through which he had first become acquainted with mid-century Europe. James's celebrated posture of detachment—his conjoined attitudes of icy aloofness and intense scrutiny—may have had as much to do, in the end, with the emotional and intellectual proximity he once felt to a burgeoning mass-market society as with the distance he eventually adopted.

The possibility is worth exploring. For if we treat James's detachment as something more than a convenient ground for accepting or dismissing his particular assessments of the Age of Barnum; if, in fact, we treat it as a part of an age that requires explaining, then we may find ourselves better able to unpack the historical significance of that literary baggage of James's late style, which has remained for so long within the particular jurisdiction of formalist critics. We may be able to break the seal of historical solipsism and idiosyncracy surrounding James and treat the record of his sensibility as the remarkable document it is. And we may trace through that sensibility a route of access to the very culture of consumption from which it is assumed to have recoiled in dismay.

We may see this route toward the commodity world first figuratively inscribed within James's consciousness as the great avenue leading out of the

[8]Ibid., p. 136.

"small and compact and ingenuous society" of his youth, the society of New York's Washington Square. "Broadway was the feature and the artery, the joy and the adventure of one's childhood," James recalls in one of his autobiographies, "and it stretched, and prodigiously, from Union Square to Barnum's great American Museum by the City Hall." His is if anything an affectionate memory of a boulevard crowded with theaters, confectioners, and "vast, marmorean, plate-glassy" department stores—a peripheral world "bristling" with goods "heaped up for our fond consumption." A prodigiousness of avenue was matched by a prodigiousness of childlike appetite, the two of which are joined retrospectively in James's autobiography as expressions of a bucolic America's "Edenlike consciousness." "We ate everything in those days," James confesses, "as from stores that were infinite."[9]

But if it is innocence that James wishes to conjure up as the theme of his (and by extension America's) childhood, it is a characteristically mindful innocence. His child's consciousness selected and weighed even as it prepared to consume. And more than any other feature of the Broadway experience, it was Barnum's Museum that evoked in the young James this market-wise balance of hedonism and detachment, of psychic investment and psychic withholding. Would he scatter his allowance "in the dusty halls of humbug, amid bottled mermaids, 'bearded ladies' and chill dioramas," he asked himself, or would he hold out for the drama of the lecture room? "The impression appears to have been mixed," he remembers; "the drinking deep and the holding out, holding out in particular against failure of food and of stage-fares, provision for transport to and fro, being questions equally intense."[10] Such rudimentary appreciations of his own consumer preferences—his own demand schedule—were but one aspect, however, of a detachment he felt in the midst of his intense attraction to the "Barnum association." Indeed, it was this detached perception that was at bottom the source of James's enchantment with a carnivalesque setting he otherwise regarded as sordid and impoverished.

For James does remember the "Barnum picture" as "above all ignoble and awful, its blatant face or frame studded with innumerable flags that waved, poor vulgar-sized ensigns, over spurious relics and catchpenny monsters in effigy." He remembers as well the "audible creak of carpentry" and properties upon the stage of Barnum's theater and envies "the simple faith of an age beguiled by arts so rude." Such makeshift arts failed to work their fascination upon the youthful James because *his* fascination lay entirely with the workings of the illusion. As he puts it in *A Small Boy and Others* (1913), "The point exactly was that we attended the spectacle just in order *not* to be beguiled, just in order to enjoy with ironic detachment and, at the very most, to be amused ourselves at our sensibility should it prove to have been trapped and

---

[9]Henry James, *Autobiography*, Frederick W. Dupee, ed. (New York, 1956), pp. 38, 39–42.
[10]Ibid., pp. 89–90.

caught." The small boy found himself absorbed not so much by Barnum's theater as by Barnum's theatricality; if he identified himself with any of the figures in *Uncle Tom's Cabin*, it was not with the characters but with the actors, perhaps even with the producer-director.[11] Thoroughly absorbed, James's mind was at the same time thoroughly divided. Thus divided, he found a doubled appreciation of the scene. He had been sold a (play) bill of goods—the crude scenic contextualizations of Barnum's drama—only to have restored its value by recontextualizing the play as an exercise in theatricality, a hoax in cheap clothing. He had, in his words, enjoyed an "aesthetic adventure" at the painless price of intellectual condescension.

James's condescension, however, was as misplaced as his mock envy for the "simple faith" of Barnum's audience. For as Neil Harris has noted, Barnum had built his success less upon the credulity of his public than upon its suspicion.[12] His wild promotional schemes tested the limits of plausibility in order to goad his audience into discovering (for a price) the mechanics of his deceptions and into measuring their sense of the "trick" against that of their companions. Barnum thus doubled his fortune by doubling his public's curiosity, or, more accurately, by importing the manipulations and suspicions of Yankee peddling into the sphere of entertainment. This lesson of the master imprinted itself deeply, if obliquely, upon James's mind, upon a "consciousness," as he puts it, "that was to be nothing if not mixed and a curiosity that was to be nothing if not restless." The sordid commodity world of Barnum's museum became for James "a brave beginning," a "great initiation" into the "possibility of a free play of mind" over its objects.[13] The battle of wits of the country store, translated by Barnum into the cognitive game of the popular museum, was recast once more by James into the leitmotif of his life and work: his concern with the play or presence of mind, with the struggle of sensibilities that could be "trapped and caught."

To locate the cultural and historical sources of this agonistic strain within James's early aesthetic awakenings is to understand the peculiarly active and powerful inflection James gives to the word "spectatorship." His is a vision that, in an almost physical sense, "takes in" the world; takes it in so as not to be taken in by it. He describes his youthful hunger for impressions as "a visionary ache," and speaks of this ache as a "dark difficulty at which one could but secretly stare—secretly because one was somehow ashamed of its being there and would have quickly removed one's eyes, or tried to clear them, if caught in the act of watching." He remembers his state of mind as a consciousness "positively disfurnished" of business sense—a want of knowledge that he experienced as a form of exposure. He sees himself as having drawn upon others' experience, upon his brother's in particular, filling himself

11Ibid., pp. 94–95.
12Neil Harris, *Humbug: The Art of P. T. Barnum* (Boston, 1973), pp. 77–79.
13James, *Autobiography*, pp. 94–95.

on "the crumbs of his feast and the echoes of his life." In *A Small Boy and Others* he compares himself to William as "some commercial traveller who has lost the key to his packed case of samples and can but pass for a fool while other exhibitions go forward." In sum, Henry James portrays himself as a vicarious, voyeuristic consumer always living near "the constant hum of borrowed experience."[14]

Obeying his father's injunction to "convert" his impressions into more "soluble stuff," the small boy window-shopped his way through Europe during the 1850s as his nomadic family—"housed and disconnected"—moved from one lodging to another. His visual appropriations of the European scene accumulated at every step until, as he recalls, his "small uneasy mind" felt like "a little jacket ill cut or ill sewn," a garment "bulging and tightening in the wrong, or at least in unnatural and unexpected places." The natural cornucopia of the New World soon paled in comparison to the accumulations of the Old. Europe was for the young James a "thick" rather than a "thin" wilderness, and he gloried in the power of converting any residual thinness into thickness, into density.[15]

"Housed and disconnected," James's active mind sought to embody itself by attaching its "gaping view" to "things and persons, objects and aspects." He became for all intents and purposes an entrepreneur of observation. "I take possession of the Old World," he exclaimed upon his arrival in England in 1875. "I inhale it—I appropriate it." Later he reported himself able "to carry all England in my breeches pocket." The images are arresting, suggesting as they do the almost visceral sense in which James felt himself to have incorporated the world he had "taken in" through his vision. And having thus incorporated this world, he was correspondingly reluctant to leave it. Nearly four decades after his arrival in England, James refused an invitation to return once again to America. "You see," he wrote his friend William Dean Howells, "my capital—yielding all my income, intellectual, social, associational, on the old investment of so many years—my capital is *here*, and to let it all slide would be simply to become bankrupt."[16]

James was hardly the first American capitalist, figurative or real, to acknowledge his dependence on British accumulations, but the lesson of their conversion into more "soluble stuff" had been learned at home. The story of James's life, as of his art, is the story of relentless commitment to acquisition, an unceasing *furnishing* of his "inward life" with objects whose properties—personal, material, theatrical—formed the capital of his imagination.[17] His

---

14Ibid., pp. 253–54, 246, 8, 481.

15Ibid., pp. 133–44, 122–23, 256, 337–38, 273, 280.

16Ibid., pp. 337–38; Letter, Henry James to his family, November 1, 1875, in *Henry James Letters*, Leon Edel, ed. (Cambridge, Mass., 1964), vol. 1, p. 484; James quoted in Leon Edel, *Henry James, The Conquest of London: 1870–1881* (New York, 1962), p. 279; James quoted in Leon Edel, *Henry James, The Master: 1901–1916* (New York, 1972), p. 504.

17See Daniel J. Schneider, "The Divided Self in the Fiction of Henry James," *PMLA* 90 (May 1975): 449; *The Crystal Cage: Adventures of the Imagination in the Fiction of Henry James* (Lawrence, Kan., 1978), chaps. 4, 5.

envy of those more active than himself, such as his "soldier-brothers" of the Civil War, was not directed at the celebrated benefits of the strenuous life. What he envied above all was their "wondrous opportunity of vision"; not their stand at one or another battle, but their standpoint. Vision, he concluded, would do "half the work" of carrying him through life, so much so that the moment one ceased "to live in large measure by one's eyes (with the imagination of course all the while waiting on this) one would have taken the longest step towards not living at all."[18] No more poignant expression of James's own consuming vision of life may be found, outside his novels.

By hinging his own sense of survival upon the power of his possessive outlook, James may have been expressing—perhaps more than he knew—the anxieties of a middle class accustomed to affluence yet no longer secure in its proprietary powers; a class seeking to replace an older set of resources (ownership of the means of production and distribution) with another (control over the means of communication and service).[19] Born into a wealthy family at odds with the thought of its own material possessions—a home intensely familial yet intensely defamiliarizing—James felt himself painfully exposed from an early age. Urged "to be something, something unconnected with specific doing, something free and uncommitted," James turned his own apprehensions about the world into apprehensions of it.[20] Spectatorship, understood as an appropriative gesture of the mind, belies its outward semblance of passivity; it is rather a vision armed to meet a wilderness, thick or thin, where sensibilities may be "trapped and caught." James's reminiscences reveal what we might call the social construction of a motive: an overwhelming desire to possess as knowledge springing out of the experience of an idiosyncratic childhood, a transitional class formation, and an embryonic consumer culture.

James would never have seen himself in this way, of course. The image he had selected for himself was in his eyes unique and unshareable. "I had not found him in the market as an exhibited or *offered* value. I had in a word to draw him forth from within rather than meet him in the world before me, the more convenient sphere of the objective, and to make him objective, in short, had to turn nothing less than myself inside out." In a sense, this reading is quite true. Threatened by a sense of his precarious position in a market society, James had fallen back upon his own resources. But those resources and the method of their acquisition had had everything to do with the market he otherwise found so empty and sterile. He had learned the lessons of his

18James, *Autobiography*, pp. 460, 443.

19For discussions of the emergence of a "new middle class" and of the role of the mass media, see Robert H. Wiebe, *The Search for Order, 1877–1920* (New York, 1967), chap. 5; Burton J. Bledstein, *The Culture of Professionalism* (New York, 1976), chaps. 2, 3; Magali Sarfatti Larson, *The Rise of Professionalism* (Berkeley, 1977); Pat Walker, ed., *Between Labor and Capital: The Professional-Managerial Class* (Boston, 1979); Raymond Williams, "Means of Communication as Means of Production," in *Problems in Materialism and Culture* (London, 1980), pp. 50–63.

20James, *Autobiography*, p. 268.

peculiar upbringing all too well, too well indeed to accept any crudeness in their expression. So deeply and finely had he internalized the social world of goods as the foundation of his own psyche that any material expression of it loomed before him as a horrifying yet fascinating extraction of himself, a fragment of an encompassing alter ego.[21] Publicity affronted him because it confronted him with a reflected image, albeit gross and deformed, of the "densities" he had accumulated within himself, accumulated in order to turn them, once again, inside out.

The critique James developed against America's burgeoning consumer culture was thus an immanent critique, a critique from within rather than from without. He may have detested the Age of Barnum, but from it he drew the rules of humbug to which he subjected his characters and, at times, his readers. Popular romancers might see their novels as requiring the creaking paraphernalia "of boats, or of caravans, or of tigers, or of 'historical characters,' or of ghosts, or of forgers, or of beautiful wicked women," but not James. Though each of these devices did enter into his fiction at one time or another, they did so largely as metaphors for more "common and covert" dangers that to the unarmed eye "look like nothing" but which "can be but inwardly and occultly dealt with."[22] In the dense and bristling "forest of symbols" that was Phineas T. Barnum's and Henry James's preserve, the impresario and impressionist alike appointed themselves as scouts of the mind, as Pathfinders for an inquisitive, acquisitive cognition. If the setting was deceptive and confusing, so much the better; for James, like Barnum, was prepared to use his peculiarly doubled vision—personal and fictive—to point the way to the egress. . . .

If James's "visionary ache" was not exhausted in his "phantasmagorical" works of the late nineteenth century, it was in many ways assuaged in the magisterial works of the following decade. But it was only in *The Golden Bowl* that James achieved a kind of peace with his "consuming passion." There, in what Edel terms "the richest of all his creations," James drew together his creative powers and his major themes to produce what is, in effect, a deliberate and consummate reply to the manic and fragmentary fantasy of *The Sacred Fount*. The general visual avidity that threatens to disrupt the fragile and glittering world of Newmarch is transformed into an energy that both shapes and animates the equally precarious and lustrous world of Eaton Square and Portland Place, the world of *The Golden Bowl*. The very cognitive drive that from the outset is the problem of the earlier work is made to grow and flower into the solution of the later work. In this, *The Golden Bowl* offers itself as the first fully achieved literary expression of an American culture of consumption.

---

[21]Ibid., p. 455; James gave form to this alter ego in his short story "The Jolly Corner" of 1908.
[22]Henry James, *The Art of the Novel*, R. P. Blackmur, ed. (New York, 1934), pp. 32–33.

At first glance, the novel seems dense and massive. Yet the massiveness of the form conceals what is an altogether simple, almost slender, narrative scheme. A wealthy, expatriated American widower and his daughter (Adam and Maggie Verver) "acquire" spouses—a charming American woman and an equally charming Italian prince—who, unbeknownst to them, are former lovers. Encouraged by their renewed proximity and by the seeming complacency of both father and daughter, the two lovers resume their relationship. When the liaison is eventually discovered by Maggie, the widower's daughter, she uses her newfound knowledge to isolate the lovers from one another and to restore the forms, if not the substance, of her and her father's marriages. Each character is ultimately required to give up one relation in order to preserve another: The informal and "unnatural" attachments of implicit incest and explicit adultery are sacrificed to the formal and "natural" attachments of marriage. Here, *The Golden Bowl* is a work of almost perfect symmetry, a work in which the social and moral resolutions of the narrative blend imperceptibly with the aesthetic resolutions of the form; it is, in its own way, James's fulfillment of Flaubert's aspiration to write a formally exquisite novel about nothing.

There is of course much ado about this "nothing." The novel teems with "common and covert" dangers, dangers that the choric character, Fanny Assingham, delightedly and obsessively ponders. "One can never be ideally sure of anything," she observes at one point. "There are always possibilities." Against the skeptical attitude of her laconic husband, Fanny upholds the ideal of an exquisite presence of mind. Her eye for propriety is one with her proprietary eye, and it is through her eyes that the novel's four main characters initially seek to take hold of their situation. "I can do pretty well anything I *see*," the anxious Prince tells Fanny on the eve of his marriage to Maggie. "Therefore it is that I want, that I shall always want, your eyes. Through *them* I wish to look—even at any risk of their showing me what I mayn't like."[23] Fanny operates as the Prince's (and the reader's) scout, scanning the terrain so as to anticipate and forestall any misstep he or others might make. The ground of the novel is treacherous because it is invariably owned by someone; it exists only as a visual or cognitive possession of the characters, and, as such, it endows their movements across its landscape with intimations of trespass and piracy.

The novel, in fact, opens and closes amid images of gold and booty. Maggie likens herself and her father to a pair of "stage pirates" and her prospective husband, the Prince, to their treasure. "You're a rarity, an object of beauty, an object of price," she tells the Prince. "You're what they call a *morceau de musée*." The Prince takes the point, but James makes it the point on which the central triangle of his tale—the relation between Maggie, the Prince, and his lover, Charlotte—balances. The novel is, in this respect, one long speculation

[23] Henry James, *The Golden Bowl* (Harmondsworth, 1966), pp. 86, 47–48.

on the felt exchange value of the Prince, one that begins with the Prince's own ruminations:

> It was as if he had been some old embossed coin, of a purity of gold no longer used, stamped with glorious arms, medieval, wonderful, of which the "worth" in mere modern change, sovereigns and half-crowns, would be great enough, but as to which, since there were finer ways of using it, such taking to pieces was superfluous. That was the image for the security in which it was open to him to rest; he was to constitute a possession, yet was to escape being reduced to his component parts. What would this mean but that, practically, he was never to be tried or tested? What would it mean but that, if they didn't "change" him, they really wouldn't know—he wouldn't know himself—how many pounds, shillings and pence he had to give?[24]

The Prince feels himself "invested with attributes" by Maggie and her father, Adam, but is unable to fathom the price they put upon them. He is not to *do* anything for the Ververs; he is to *be* something for them: an exquisite "cluster of attributes." He is to be an object not of utility but of appreciation.

Appreciation—always an emotionally charged word for James—regains some of its earliest historical connotations in *The Golden Bowl*. Its Victorian associations with taste and esteem are continually subverted by James's use of the word to suggest appraisal or assessment: the setting, though not necessarily the naming, of a price. This at least is how the Prince experiences the appreciation of "the decent family eyes"—the eyes of Adam and Maggie—he encounters at Eaton Square.

> This directed regard rested at its ease, but it neither lingered nor penetrated, and was, to the Prince's fancy, much of the same order as any glance directed, for due attention, from the same quarter, to the figure of a cheque received in the course of business and about to be enclosed to a banker. It made sure of the amount—and just so, from time to time, the amount of the Prince was made sure. He was being thus, in renewed instalments, perpetually paid in; he already reposed in the bank as a value, but subject, in this comfortable way to repeated, to infinite endorsement.[25]

But if he is purchased or consumed in relation to his wife and her father, he is in turn purchaser and consumer in relation to Charlotte Stant, the woman whom Maggie takes as a friend, Adam as a wife, and the Prince as a lover. In one of the earliest and most extraordinary episodes of the novel—the pre-nuptial scene at Fanny Assingham's in which the Prince is unexpectedly reunited with his former lover—James has Charlotte offer herself up to the Prince's vision "for his benefit and pleasure." The Prince's appreciative response amounts to a mental inventory of Charlotte's features.

[24]Ibid., pp. 35–36, 43.
[25]Ibid., pp. 245–46.

But it was, strangely, as a cluster of possessions of his own that these things, in Charlotte Stant, now affected him; items in a full list, items recognized, each of them, as if, for the long interval, they had been "stored"—wrapped up, numbered, put away in a cabinet. While she faced Mrs. Assingham the door of the cabinet had, opened of itself; he took the relics out, one by one, and it was more and more, each instant, as if she were giving him time. . . . He knew her narrow hands, he knew her long fingers and the shape and colour of her finger-nails, he knew her special beauty of movement and line when she turned her back, and the perfect working of all her main attachments, that of some wonderful finished instrument, something intently made for exhibition, for a prize. He knew above all the extraordinary fineness of her flexible waist, the stem of an expanded flower which gave her a likeness also to some long, loose silk purse, well filled with gold pieces, but having been passed, empty, through a finger-ring that held it together. It was as if, before she turned to him, he had weighed the whole thing in his open palm and even heard a little the chink of the metal.[26]

The passage evokes the memory of the predatory Gilbert Osmond, but with this difference: The proprietary vision is no longer the distinctive feature of one character but rather the distinctive and constitutive relation among *all* the characters. Even Adam, the "consummate collector" of art, cannot forbear from seeing in Maggie "the appearance of some slight, slim draped 'antique' of Vatican or Capitoline halls." He acknowledges this perception as a "trick" of his mind that comes "from his caring for precious vases only less than for precious daughters."[27] But such tricks are just the stuff out of which the novel (and its title) is made. Adam's authority comes not from his wealth alone—the creature comforts and security it affords—but from the power of that wealth to fulfill the appropriative habits of mind that collectively form the second nature, the social medium within which the characters have for so long operated. The world of Portland Place and Eaton Square cannot be more distantly removed from the crude and callous transactions of the marketplace (the place where Adam made his millions), yet it is nonetheless a world saturated with the imagery of the market, a world constructed and deconstructed by the appreciative vision.

Consequently, when the rare material transaction does enter James's narrative, it does not so much disrupt as fulfill the logical possibilities of a deeply internalized commodity world. Charlotte's and the Prince's sortie to Bloomsbury in search of a wedding gift for Maggie, Adam's and Charlotte's shopping trip to Brighton, and Maggie's solitary return to the Bloomsbury shop (all reminiscent of James's childhood journeys up Broadway), are instances of the quickening or heightening function of material exchange in *The Golden Bowl.* Charlotte uses the occasion of the Bloomsbury excursion—the occasion on which the flawed bowl is first proffered and rejected—to bind the Prince to

[26]Ibid., pp. 58–59.
[27]Ibid., pp. 484, 153–54.

her in a prefigurative act of collusion on the eve of his marriage. At the very moment of renouncing her earlier claim upon him, she plants the seed of their eventual adultery. Passion, in the conventional sense, is scarcely at issue; it is not sensual or affectional desire that prompts their secrecy, but secrecy that sets their desire in motion, in particular, the desire to *know*. In a fictive world of what economists concede as "imperfect knowledge," a shared lie becomes a shared tie. Deprived of its ordinary yet rich emotional meanings, intimacy reduces itself in *The Golden Bowl* to a conspiratorial community—in Laurence Holland's phrase—of "knowledge and possession."[28]

The Prince himself muses on this peculiar sense of community in the solitary moments before Charlotte arrives to consummate their own affair. He has, for his part, quietly prepared himself for this possibility by treating it as the logical fulfillment of the tacit understandings by which the Ververs— father and daughter—have so good-naturedly arranged for the group's comfort and convenience. "This understanding had wonderfully," the Prince reflects, "the same deep intimacy as the commercial, the financial association founded, far down, on a community of interest." Commercial affairs thus acquire the same furtive and illicit undertones as love affairs; indeed the two sorts of relations are collapsed together in the novel as productive of the same sorts of satisfactions and the same sorts of shame. Adam's scheme to marry Charlotte—that is, to possess her as a "human acquisition" and a "domestic resource"—is a "thing of less joy than a passion." His drive to acquire, to collect, to consume must serve in place of love and lust; the result is that James has Adam propose to Charlotte only after an exceptionally lurid scene (for James) in which she is forced to watch as Adam transacts business with a Brighton art broker.

> She had listened to the name of the sum he was capable of looking in the face. Given the relation of intimacy with him she had already, beyond all retractation, accepted, the stir of the air produced at the other place by that high figure struck him as a thing, that, from the moment she had exclaimed or protested as little as he himself had apologized, left him, but one thing more to do. A man of decent feeling didn't thrust his money, a huge lump of it, in such a way, under a poor girl's nose— a girl whose poverty was, after a fashion, the very basis of her enjoyment of his hospitality—without seeing, logically, a responsibility attached.[29]

The restraints of delicacy and tact usually reserved for sexual misadventures are here transferred to the marketplace. And once again a material transaction prompts and figures a social one.

Maggie's purchase of the golden bowl—its hidden crack the symbol and "document" of all the flawed relationships—is the third example of the quickening effect of material exchange in the novel. With its acquisition, she

    [28]Laurence B. Holland, *The Expense of Vision: Essays on the Craft of Henry James* (Princeton, 1964), p. 391.
    [29]James, *Golden Bowl*, pp. 223, 160, 169, 173.

is at last put into possession of "real knowledge." The disclosure of the object's curious history allows her to piece together the extent of her (and her father's) betrayal at the hands of Charlotte and the Prince. And when her discovery is challenged by Fanny (much like the narrator's confrontation with Mrs. Briss in *The Sacred Fount*) and the bowl is dashed to pieces, Maggie does not flee the scene. Instead, she uses the episode to impress the Prince with the extent of her knowledge and of his vulnerability. She begins, in a sense, where the narrator of *The Sacred Fount* leaves off. What was once the occasional "throb" of Maggie's curiosity now yields to "the perpetual throb" of her new "sense of possession," a pulse "almost too violent either to recognize or to hide." She no longer sees herself as an understudy thrust unexpectedly upon the stage with only a "humbugging smile" to mask her uncertainty; she is now the director, looking through the windows of the country house of *her* fiction, looking in to see the "figures rehearsing some play of which she herself was the author."[30]

Prices are finally named. Charlotte "bargains" with Maggie to assure her silence, but the standoff becomes in Maggie's hands a trade-off: Maggie gives up her father to Charlotte in return for her full possession of the Prince; Charlotte gives up her lover in order to remain Adam's "domestic resource." The delicate balance of marginal utilities is recalibrated; the decision to part couples is made; and Maggie and Adam take a final inventory of their possessions:

> . . . the other objects in the room, the other pictures, the sofas, the chairs, the tables, the cabinets, the "important" pieces, supreme in their way, stood out, round them, consciously, for recognition and applause. Their eyes moved together from piece to piece, taking in the whole nobleness—quite as if for him to measure the wisdom of old ideas. The two noble persons seated, in conversation, at tea, fell thus into the splendid effect and the general harmony: Mrs. Verver and the Prince fairly "placed" themselves, however unwittingly, as high expressions of the kind of human furniture required, aesthetically, by such a scene. The fusion of their presence with the decorative elements, their contribution to the triumph of selection, was complete and admirable; though, to a lingering view, a view more penetrating than the occasion really demanded, they also might have figured as concrete attestations of a rare power of purchase. There was much indeed in the tone in which Adam Verver spoke again, and who shall say where his thought stopped? *"Le compte y est.* You've got some good things."[31]

With exquisite grace and tact, Maggie brokers the concluding transactions of the novel; her appreciative vision rearranges the fragments of a shattered world and, in so doing, redeems the magic power of the commodity form. James's rare intrusion into the narrative—his "lingering" and "penetrating" view—indicates how deeply indebted he feels to a "power of purchase" that has restored the symmetry not only of Maggie's world but of his own. The

[30]Ibid., pp. 436, 353, 439, 458.
[31]Ibid., p. 541.

manipulative treatment of persons as so much "human furniture" that was once a source of concern in *The Sacred Fount* is now a source of celebration. Maggie, like James, uses the characters as her "compositional resources" and, by her skill, makes of herself and the novel a "value intrinsic."[32] James, of course, is never to be wholly identified with his characters, but it is fair to say that he never gives more fully of himself to any character than he does to the triumphant Maggie Verver of the closing pages of *The Golden Bowl*.

But James's complicity in the commodity vision of his supersensible characters is more than a matter of his (and our) emotional identification with the unconquerable Maggie. For emotion itself takes on a peculiarly restricted form in James's later works: It becomes wholly submerged and exhausted in the act of seeing. The emotional intensity of the fictive relationships is raised to its highest pitch in *The Golden Bowl*, but the gain in affective power is achieved only at the loss of variety and richness of feeling. Emotions in the novel, like those in *The Sacred Fount*, are almost invariably cognitive or epistemic; they have entirely to do with a character's impulse to possess as knowledge. James's characters are alternately conscious and surprised, enlightened and benighted, engrossed and amused, aware and bewildered, bemused and interested, but they are seldom anything else. And the emotional nuance varies proportionately with the possessive status each term suggests. As Seymour Chatman puts it, "It is hard to think of an occasion in a novel of James when a real taste is tasted or a real smell smelled."[33] "All the physical and spiritual senses," to recur to Marx, are replaced by "the sense of *having*," a sense James implants deeply within the cognitive act itself.

The distinctive density and detachment of *The Golden Bowl* reveal the extent of James's immersion in the novel's projected commodity world. The density is itself the outcome of a consuming vision's merciless power to detach not only itself, but its objects: alienating them quite literally from their conventional associations and context and accumulating them as resources, as capital. The market metaphors that so infuse his later writings are more than mere conceits or occasional tropes. They define the very medium—the fluid medium or solvent—in which the characters and their relations dissolve. For it is not just that the *characters* feel themselves "invested with attributes." The reader is made to feel the same sensation by means of a language that transforms active verbs into passive participles and participles, in turn, into nouns. In place of human actors engaging one another in a material environment, James substitutes their properties or characteristics—fully materialized, fully animated, and fully prepared to take on a life of their own. "Thoughts and perceptions in James's world are entities more than actions, things more than movements," Chatman writes in his study of James's later style. "They occupy a space—the mind; though intangible, they are 'things' *in*

---

[32]James, preface to *The Golden Bowl*, in *Art of Novel*, p. 329.
[33]Seymour Chatman, *The Later Style of Henry James* (Oxford, 1972), p. 30.

the mind. Further, there is established between them and the characters a relation not unlike the relation which characters bear to each other, indeed, one which may be livelier." In short, the world of *The Golden Bowl* is a reified world. James represents the relation between characters as a relation between things, luxurious and rarefied things to be sure, but things nonetheless. The result, to paraphrase him, is a "rich little spectacle of objects embalmed in his wonder."[34]

A universe in which the "properties" of goods and people imperceptibly mingle is a world of precarious substantiality. It is, to say the least, unsettling, defamiliarizing. It induces the same uncertainty and anxiety as that occasioned by "some bad-faced stranger surprised in one of the thick-carpeted corridors of a house of quiet on a Sunday afternoon." To read *The Golden Bowl*, as Ruth Yeazell observes, "is to suffer a kind of epistemological vertigo," not simply, I would add, because of the shocks that lie concealed within its plot but because of the incongruities that lie embedded within its form—the commodity form.[35]

For the world projected in *The Golden Bowl* is, in the final analysis, virtually identical with the world disclosed in contemporary market research, that is, a world constructed by and for a consuming vision. It is an imagined world, of course, but one in which imagination itself strives to gild, glaze, and ultimately commodify its objects. Here the psychological novel and the psychographic study meet. James's celebrated "balloon of experience," it turns out, contains the same "clusters of attributes," the same freestanding and free-moving commodity characteristics as the trial balloons launched by modern marketers. Whether taken as art or artifact, these two forms of inquiry into social relationships indicate the presence, in Raymond Williams's terms, of a "common conventional mode" or rule in which needs, satisfactions, and anxieties are understood as mediated through the commodity form. Indeed, as Williams points out, it is only when the commodity form has become the "dominant mode of human perception and interaction" that a basis develops for a culture (films, magazines, novels, programs, etc.) "which present[s] human beings and their detachable characteristics as commodities, either for purchase or, more generally and more discreetly, for window-shopping."[36]

To be sure, more than a half-century separates James's last complete novel from the marketing wisdom it so eerily prefigures. And while it is possible to adduce the presence of the commodity form as the dominant cultural form of our own time, it is quite another matter to take it as such in the year of *The Golden Bowl*. The lag is not unlike that between Einstein's special theory of relativity, published at roughly the same time as James's final work, and our

[34]Ibid., p. 22; Henry James, preface to *What Maisie Knew*, in *Art of Novel*, p. 146.
[35]James, *Golden Bowl*, p. 459; Ruth Bernard Yeazell, *Language and Knowledge in the Late Novels of Henry James* (Chicago and London, 1976), p. 71.
[36]Raymond Williams, *Television: Technology and Cultural Form* (New York, 1974), pp. 70–71.

own cultural accommodations to the theory's operative principles. The scientific analogy is not altogether farfetched. There was, after all, more of the ruthless, dissecting, microscopic reflex in Henry James than in his brother, whatever the former's disclaimers. And the peculiar events of his life do suggest the way in which James's own mind might have served as a laboratory in which the embryonic possibilities of a consumer culture could be incubated.

But if James was a scientist, he was a strange one, preferring as he did a parsimony of instances and a plenitude of explanations. Such science is more oracular than anything else, and it was as prophet that James ultimately preferred to think of himself. His preface to *The Golden Bowl* portrays him as a "seer," a self-conscious play on his own consuming vision. For his was, if anything, an acquiring as well as inquiring mind. "To criticise," he wrote, "is to appreciate, to appropriate, to take intellectual possession, to establish in fine a relation with the criticised thing and make it one's own. The large intellectual appetite projects itself thus on many things, while the small—not better advised, but unconscious of need for advice—projects on few."[37] By allowing his imagination to play the market, by allowing his deepest desires and fears to take their shape and course within an aestheticized commodity form, in sum, by allowing the culture of consumption to enter into the very form and substance of his discourse, James has given us perhaps the most complex portrait of the lived experience—the phenomenology—of American consumer culture. His work is more than a grace note on Marx's score for the "fetishism of commodities"—it is a masterwork in its own right.

[37]James, preface to *What Maisie Knew*, in *Art of Novel*, p. 155.

Chronology of Important Dates

1843	Born (April 15) to Mary Robertson Walsh and Henry James, Sr., 21 Washington Place, New York City.
1843–45	Taken to Europe by parents.
1845–55	Childhood in Albany and New York City.
1855–58	Travels with family and attends school in Europe.
1858–60	Father moves family to Newport, R. I., then to Geneva, before returning to Newport in 1860. HJ attends various schools in U.S. and Europe; briefly studies art in Newport.
1861	Suffers "obscure hurt" while fighting fire.
1862–63	Attends Harvard Law School.
1864	Family moves to Boston. First story published anonymously; begins book reviewing.
1865	First signed short story published in *Atlantic Monthly*; begins reviewing for *Nation*.
1866	Family settles in Cambridge, Mass.
1869–70	First adult travels in Europe. Death of cousin, Minny Temple.
1870–71	Returns to Cambridge. Publishes (serially) first novel, *Watch and Ward*.
1872–74	Travels in Europe.
1875	First books published: *Roderick Hudson, A Passionate Pilgrim, Transatlantic Sketches*.
1875–76	Spends year in Paris, fraternizing with Turgenev, Flaubert, Zola, Daudet, Edmund de Goncourt. Settles permanently in London.
1877	*The American.*
1878	International success of "Daisy Miller." Also publishes *The Europeans, French Poets and Novelists*.
1879	*Hawthorne, Confidence.*
1880–81	*Washington Square, The Portrait of a Lady.* Revisits United States.
1882–83	Death of parents; revisits United States.
1884	"The Art of Fiction."
1886	*The Bostonians, The Princess Casamassima.*
1888	Italy. "The Aspern Papers."
1889–90	*The Tragic Muse.* Begins writing for theater.

1891 *The American* has brief theatrical run.

1892 Death of Alice James (sister).

1895 Failure of *Guy Domville*. Abandons theater, but determines to adopt "scenic method" for fiction.

1896–98 *The Spoils of Poynton, What Maisie Knew,* "The Turn of the Screw." Settles in Lamb House, Rye, Sussex.

1899 *The Awkward Age.*

1901 *The Sacred Fount.*

1902–04 *The Wings of the Dove, The Ambassadors, The Golden Bowl.*

1904–05 Travels in United States.

1907–09 *The American Scene.* New York Edition of novels and tales.

1910 Death of William James (brother).

1913–14 *A Small Boy and Others, Notes of a Son and Brother.*

1915 Becomes British subject in response to WWI.

1916 Dies (28 February).

Notes on the Contributors

Jean-Christophe Agnew is Professor of American Studies and History at Yale University. The author of *Worlds Apart: The Market and the Theater in Anglo-American Thought, 1550–1750* (1986), he is currently at work on a study of the conceptualization and practice of cultural history.

Peter Brooks is Tripp Professor of the Humanities and Chair of the Department of Comparative Literature at Yale University, where he also served as the first Director of the Whitney Humanities Center. Among his publications are *The Novel of Worldliness* (1969), *The Melodramatic Imagination: Balzac, Henry James, Melodrama, and the Mode of Excess* (1976), and *Reading for the Plot: Design and Intention in Narrative* (1984).

Jonathan Freedman is Associate Professor of English at the University of Michigan in Ann Arbor. He is the author of *Professions of Taste: Henry James, British Aestheticism, and Commodity Culture* (1990).

Carolyn Porter is Professor of English at the University of California, Berkeley. She is the author of *Seeing and Being: The Plight of the Participant Observer in Emerson, James, Adams, and Faulkner* (1981).

Julie Rivkin is Associate Professor of English at Connecticut College. The essay in this collection is part of her forthcoming book, *False Positions: The Representational Logic of Henry James's Late Fiction*.

Eve Kosofsky Sedgwick is Newman Ivey White Professor of English at Duke University. Her books include *Between Men: English Literature and Male Homosocial Desire* (1985) and *Epistemology of the Closet* (1990).

Mark Seltzer is Professor of English at Cornell University. He is the author of *Henry James and the Art of Power* (1984) and *Bodies and Machines* (1992).

Lionel Trilling (d. 1975) was University Professor at Columbia University. Among his most influential works are *The Liberal Imagination: Essays on Literature and Society* (1950), *The Opposing Self: Nine Essays in Criticism* (1955), and *Sincerity and Authenticity* (1972).

Ian Watt is Jackson Eli Reynolds Professor of Humanities, Emeritus, at Stanford University and a former director of the Stanford Humanities Center. He is the author of *The Rise of the Novel: Studies in Defoe, Richardson and Fielding* (1957) and *Conrad in the Nineteenth Century* (1979).

Ruth Bernard Yeazell is Professor of English at Yale University and the author of books on Henry James (1976) and Alice James (1981). Her most recent book is *Fictions of Modesty: Women and Courtship in the English Novel* (1991).

Bibliography

There is no single, standard edition of all James's fiction. The New York Edition of his novels and tales, issued in twenty-four volumes by Charles Scribner's Sons in 1907–1909 (rpt. New York: Augustus M. Kelley, 1971), incorporates the author's substantial revisions, especially of the earlier fiction; it also omits a number of works entirely—most notably, *The Europeans* (1878) and *The Bostonians* (1886). Critics continue to debate the comparative merits of the original and revised texts. James's Prefaces to the New York Edition were separately collected as *The Art of the Novel*, ed. R. P. Blackmur (New York: Charles Scribner's Sons, 1934). The complete literary criticism, including the Prefaces and works not previously published in book form, can be found in two volumes issued by the Library of America, *Henry James: Literary Criticism*, ed. Leon Edel and Mark Wilson (New York, 1984). In *The Art of Criticism: Henry James on the Theory and the Practice of Fiction* (Chicago: University of Chicago Press, 1986), William Veeder and Susan M. Griffin accompany their selection from the criticism (including a number of the Prefaces) with exceptionally helpful commentary and notes. The first book versions of the tales appear in *The Complete Tales of Henry James*, 12 vols., ed. Leon Edel (Philadelphia: J. B. Lippincott Company, 1962–64); the earliest published versions are being reprinted by Maqbool Aziz in *The Tales of Henry James* (Oxford: Clarendon Press, 1973–). Edel has also collected *The Complete Plays* (Philadelphia: J. B. Lippincott Company, 1949). *The Complete Notebooks of Henry James*, ed. Leon Edel and Lyall H. Powers (New York: Oxford University Press, 1987), includes some material not available in the earlier edition by F. O. Matthiessen and Kenneth B. Murdock (New York: Oxford University Press, 1947), but lacks Matthiessen and Murdock's excellent commentary on the entries. There is no complete edition of the letters. The most extensive selection to date, *The Letters of Henry James*, 4 vols., ed. Leon Edel (Cambridge: Harvard University Press, 1974–84), reflects the emphases of Edel's biography, and omits some letters published in earlier collections, such as the two volumes edited by Percy Lubbock (New York: Charles Scribner's Sons, 1920). F. W. Dupee's edition of the novelist's *Autobiography* (New York: Criterion Books, 1956) incorporates *A Small Boy and Others* (1913), *Notes of a Son and Brother* (1914), and *The Middle Years* (1917) in one volume. For other works by James, including art criticism, travel literature and novels omitted from the New York Edition, readers should consult *A Bibliography of Henry James*, ed. Leon Edel and Dan H. Laurence, revised with the assistance of James Rambeau, 3rd ed. (Oxford:

Clarendon Press, 1982). The fullest account of the novelist's life can be found in Leon Edel, *Henry James*, 5 vols. (Philadelphia: J. B. Lippincott Company, 1953–1972); its documentation of sources is not, however, very adequate. F. 0. Matthiessen, *The James Family* (New York: Alfred A. Knopf, 1947), includes selections from the writings of the novelist, his father, brother, and sister, together with biographical commentary. Selections from nineteenth- and early twentieth-century criticism can be found in *Henry James: The Critical Heritage*, ed. Roger Gard (New York: Barnes and Noble Inc., 1968). Guides to twentieth-century criticism can be found in Kristin Pruitt McColgan, *Henry James, 1917–1959: A Reference Guide* and Dorothy McInnis Scura, *Henry James, 1960–1974: A Reference Guide*, both published by G. K. Hall and Co. (Boston: 1979), and Judith E. Funston, *Henry James: A Reference Guide*, also published by G. K. Hall and Co. (Boston: 1991). There follows a selected list of twentieth-century James criticism. Articles included in the present volume and books excerpted for it have not been listed below.

I wish to thank Thomas J. Otten for his help in reviewing James criticism for this collection.

Anesko, Michael. *"Friction with the Market": Henry James and the Profession of Authorship*. New York: Oxford University Press, 1986.

Armstrong, Paul B. *The Phenomenology of Henry James*. Chapel Hill, N.C.: University of North Carolina Press, 1983.

Banta, Martha. *Henry James and the Occult: The Great Extension*. Bloomington: Indiana University Press, 1972.

Bayley, John. "Love and Knowledge: *The Golden Bowl*." In *The Characters of Love: A Study in the Literature of Personality*, 203–62. London: Constable and Company Ltd., 1960.

Bell, Millicent. *Meaning in Henry James*. Cambridge: Harvard University Press, 1991.

Bersani, Leo. "The Jamesian Lie." In *A Future for Astyanax: Character and Desire in Literature*, 128–155. Boston: Little, Brown and Company, 1976.

Blackmur, R. P. *Studies in Henry James*, ed. Veronica A. Makowsky. New York: New Directions, 1983.

Brodhead, Richard H. *The School of Hawthorne*, 121–200. New York: Oxford University Press, 1986.

Cameron, Sharon. *Thinking in Henry James*. Chicago: University of Chicago Press, 1989.

Cargill, Oscar. *The Novels of Henry James*. New York: The Macmillan Company, 1961.

Castle, Terry. "Haunted by Olive Chancellor." In *The Apparitional Lesbian: Female Homosexuality and Modern Culture*. New York: Columbia University Press, forthcoming.

Crews, Frederick C. *The Tragedy of Manners: Moral Drama in the Later Novels of Henry James*. New Haven: Yale University Press, 1957.

Feidelson, Charles. "The Moment of *The Portrait of a Lady*," *Ventures*, 8, no. 2 (1968), 47–55.

Fetterley, Judith. "*The Bostonians*: Henry James's Eternal Triangle." In *The Resisting Reader: A Feminist Approach to American Fiction*, 101–53. Bloomington: Indiana University Press, 1978.

Holland, Laurence B. *The Expense of Vision: Essays on the Craft of Henry James*. Princeton: Princeton University Press, 1964.

Horne, Philip. *Henry James and Revision: The New York Edition*. Oxford: Clarendon Press, 1990.

Howe, Irving. "Henry James: The Political Vocation." In *Politics and the Novel*, 139–56. New York: The Horizon Press, 1957.

Krook, Dorothea. *The Ordeal of Consciousness in Henry James*. Cambridge: Cambridge University Press, 1962.

Leavis, F. R. *The Great Tradition: George Eliot, Henry James, Joseph Conrad*. London: Chatto and Windus, 1948.

Matthiessen, F. O. *Henry James: The Major Phase*. New York: Oxford University Press, 1944.

Nussbaum, Martha Craven. "Flawed Crystals: James's *The Golden Bowl* and Literature as Moral Philosophy," *New Literary History*, 15 (1983), 25–50.

Poirier, Richard. *The Comic Sense of Henry James: A Study of the Early Novels*. New York: Oxford University Press, 1960.

Posnock, Ross. *The Trial of Curiosity: Henry James, William James, and the Challenge of Modernity*. New York: Oxford Press, 1991.

Poulet, Georges. *The Metamorphoses of the Circle* (1961), trans. Carley Dawson and Elliott Coleman, 307–20. Baltimore: The Johns Hopkins Press, 1966.

Sears Sallie. *The Negative Imagination: Form and Perspective in the Novels of Henry James*. Ithaca, N.Y.: Cornell University Press, 1968.

Tanner, Tony. *The Reign of Wonder: Naivety and Reality in American Literature*, 261–335. Cambridge: Cambridge University Press, 1965.

Van Ghent, Dorothy. "On *The Portrait of a Lady*." In *The English Novel: Form and Function*, 211–28. New York: Holt and Company, 1953.

Veeder, William. *Henry James—the Lessons of the Master: Popular Fiction and Personal Style in the Nineteenth Century*. Chicago: University of Chicago Press, 1975.

Wegelin, Christof. *The Image of Europe in Henry James*. Dallas: Southern Methodist University Press, 1958.

Weinstein, Philip M. *Henry James and the Requirements of the Imagination*. Cambridge: Harvard University Press, 1971.

Welsh, Alexander. "Breaking the Golden Bowl." In *Strong Representations: Narrative and Circumstantial Evidence in England*, 236–56. Baltimore: The Johns Hopkins University Press, 1992.

White, Allon. *The Uses of Obscurity: The Fiction of Early Modernism*. London: Routledge and Kegan Paul, 1981.

Wilson, Edmund. "The Ambiguity of Henry James." In *The Triple Thinkers: Ten Essays on Literature*, 122–64. New York: Harcourt, Brace and Company, 1938.

Wilt, Judith. "Desperately Seeking Verena: A Resistant Reading of *The Bostonians*," *Feminist Studies*, 13 (1987), 293–316.

Winner, Viola Hopkins. *Henry James and the Visual Arts*. Charlottesville: The University Press of Virginia, 1970.